REGNUM STUDIES IN MISSION

Urban Ministry and Social Networks

Series Preface

Regnum Studies in Mission are born from the lived experience of Christians and Christian communities in mission, especially but not solely in the fast growing churches among the people of the developing world. These churches have more to tell than stories of growth. They are making significant impacts on their cultures in the cause of Christ They are producing 'cultural products' which express the reality of Christian faith, hope and love in their societies.

Regnum Studies in Mission are the fruit often of rigorous research to the highest international standards and always of authentic Christian engagement in the transformation of people and societies. These are for the world. The formation of Christian theology, missiology and practice in the twenty-first century will depend to a great extent on the active participation of growing churches contributing biblical and culturally appropriate expressions of Christian practice to inform World Christianity.

Urban Ministry and Social Networks
Reconnecting the Disconnected

Enoch Jinsik Kim

First published 2024 by Regnum Books International

Regnum is an imprint of the Oxford Centre for Mission Studies
St. Philip and St. James Church
Woodstock Road
Oxford OX2 6HR, UK
www.regnumbooks.net

British Library Cataloguing in Publication Data
A catalogue record for this book is available from the British Library

ISBN: 979-8-8898-3881-4
eBook ISBN: 979-8-8898-3882-1

Cover image by JC Gellidon, www.unsplash.com

Typeset by Words by Design

Distributed by Fortress Press in the US, Canada, India, and Brazil

Dedication

Dedicated to Christian leaders and students
who are thirsting for the next chapter of urban ministry.

Foreword

With his rich experiences of working in China for sixteen years as a missionary, involvement in various mission organisations, and teaching communication and mission studies to doctoral students at Fuller Theological Seminary for many years, Dr Enoch Kim identifies the key engagement in urban ministry as social networking, and provides critical insights on important theories and practices for urban churches and individuals. He calls for urban churches to be equipped with socio-anthropological awareness and biblical perspectives for sustainable and effective ministry. This book is organised around the four key aspects of urban ministry: urban individuals, urban groups, urban space and time, and urban flows and transformation. Furthermore, Dr Kim provides readers with various illustrations, diagrams, tables, and statistics, and then suggests some concrete and robust steps to implement theories into practical life in urban contexts. This book is a must-read for those who are engaging in urban ministry, offering a fresh understanding and informed socio-anthropological insights. It also provides critical pointers for mission scholars, theological students and the general congregation for the furtherance of missiology. Therefore, I strongly recommend this timely and important book.

Sebastian Kim
Robert Wiley Professor of Renewal in Public Life
Fuller Theological Seminary

Acknowledgements

I praise God for loving the city so much that he gave his only Son. I am grateful for the encouragement of Dr Sebastian Kim, Robert Wiley Professor of Renewal in Public Life and Academic Dean for the Korean Studies Center at Fuller Theological Seminary, who set the right model as a scholar and leader for me. I am also grateful to Dr Amos Yong, Dean of the School of Missions and Theology during the writing period. Dean Amos first suggested Regnum Publishing to publish this book, and today, as a result, my writing comes from a publishing house used by God.

I would like to thank Dr Harvie M. Conn, Dr Manuel Ortiz, Dr Ray Bakke, and Dr Roger S. Greenway, all of whom have influenced my scholarship and spirituality as Christian urban scholars. I would also like to thank urban anthropologists John Gulick, Edwin Eames, and Claude S. Fischer, and urban sociologists William G. Flanagan and Mark Gottdiener. These scholars provided for me in their writing knowledge that was not available in traditional Christian academia.

I am grateful to the many leaders of the Global Missionary Fellowship with whom I have worked for over 30 years. Among them are Young Chan Joo and his office staff at the Helping Overseas Professional Employment mission, Dr Hyun Chul Hong at the Korea Research Institute for Mission, and missionary Kyungwoo Nam and his staff at Global Missionary Training Center. I would like to express my gratitude and love to the first president of the Institute of Asian Mission, Dr Timothy Kiho Park, and the current board members, as well as the Chinese board members of Grace International US, for making my life rich and meaningful. The spiritual support of Rev. Kim Taehyung and Rev. Amos Park of ANC Onnuri Church, where I have been a partner since 2000, is unforgettable. I am grateful to CEO Kim Jae-Sung, and Young-Wook, and the board members of 3C Community Clinic, who dedicate their lives to medical ministry for the transformation of the city. Working with them provided the spiritual energy for this book.

I would like to thank Charley and Mary Shin, CEO of Charleys Philly Steaks, for providing me with a two-week research location for my writing. Many thanks to Sunny Chang, Sooki Kim, and Brenda Oh for their prayers and support. I would also like to thank Dr Park Sung-Heum, a missionary in Argentina, and Dr Kyo-Hoon Son and Elder Ott in Germany, for providing good case studies for this book. I am also grateful to Missionary Lee Chow Yuan from China for sending me photos for the book.

I would like to thank my sons, Tim Heeseng Kim and Josephine Kim, for their help with the manuscript's English over the past seven years. I would like to thank my parents, Wonsup Kim and Haenyu Shim, for loving and supporting me. I would like to express my love and gratitude to Sarah, Hyaeran Ko, who makes my life meaningful and always gives me hope.

I would also like to thank Paul Bendor-Samuel and his staff at Regnum for allowing me to publish this book in English. I am especially grateful to Dr Grace Dyrness, Vice-Chair of OCMS, for her generosity in reviewing this book and for her willingness to meet with me in person during the pandemic. Her comments helped me to update the manuscript and even the title of the book.

I look forward to seeing what the God of missions will do through this book as he continues to work tirelessly to reach those in the city who do not know the difference between their right and left hand, as well as many animals.

Enoch Kim in Pasadena
Fuller Theological Seminary

Contents

Preface

I have written this book to help the urban churches discover the vein of gold gifted by God. Just as good parents do not send their children to school on their first day without preparation, God also does not give to city churches the task of urban mission for an urbanised world, unprecedented in human history as it is, without providing any help. God is the master of mission from start to finish, and the church's mission is the *Missio Dei.* As Comforter, Counsellor, and Advocator, the Holy Spirit is already aware of the needs of the churches in the city and guides accordingly. So then why is the urban church so frail today? Why do many churches seem powerless and struggle to merely sustain themselves amidst postmodernism, the online age, globalisation, and secularism? Although we talk about the burden the church has for the community around it, why is it that the distance between the church and the community seems to grow ever greater, and there seems to be little the church can do to engage with the corporate and professional world?

After sixteen years of ministering to the Muslim minorities in China and more than a decade participating in the Asian minority ministry in Los Angeles, I had one unanswered question: why do we so often conduct ministry as if we are driving in a place without roads? From the perspective of communication, evangelism can be described as a car carrying the Gospel that runs on the road of communication.[1] If this car is only to drive on roads where there are people to meet, interacting with them would be natural. Likewise, urban ministry can avoid unnecessary efforts and misunderstandings if done naturally.

Of course, there are times in ministry when the car must drive on roadless terrain. For example, when ministering to unreached people groups, we rely on God to establish new roads in the wilderness, deserts, and rivers (Is. 43:19-20). But would it not be absurd if one drives off the road when there is a paved road? Unfortunately, this is a common phenomenon in urban ministry. The following three experiences demonstrate why I compare urban ministry to off-road driving.

First, through encounters with my students, I realised a vast difference between a Christian worker in the city and a Christian urban worker. When I ask my students whether they believe they conduct urban ministry, usually over 90% answer yes. However, they found it difficult to explain how they did urban ministry beyond the fact that their churches were located in the city. Not all

---

1 Charles H. Kraft, *Communication Theory for Christian Witness* (Maryknoll, NY: Orbis, 1997): 117–19.

ministry that takes place in the city is urban ministry. An urban worker is a person who knows the people of the city and practices urban ministry. Without a socio-anthropological awareness and a biblical perspective on the city, one may become a worker in the city but cannot be considered an urban worker.

Urban workers with a limited understanding of the city tend to have a stereotypical view in their ministry rather than having God's heart for the city. Furthermore, rather than following God's guidance shown from the objective data and natural phenomena, they often copy and paste the same programmes, messages, and leadership styles from their former churches to their newly planted churches without appropriate critique. Stereotypical attitudes reinforce a self-centred view in ministry, resulting in a ministry that rarely affects its surrounding communities. These stereotypes come from many places, such as individual church education, church culture, biases learned from teachers and society, and narrow ecclesiological views. As a result, the Gospel-carrying car ends up driving on a deserted road.

Second, no matter how modern urban society is, the Gospel still flows through people and relationship networks, and it will continue to do so. One time at a gathering of about 200 believers in China, I asked, "Raise your hand if the person who introduced you to the Gospel was someone you already knew." Surprisingly, most of them raised their hands, demonstrating that most people decide to commit their lives to Christ upon hearing the Gospel from someone they know. Such a phenomenon is not unique only to societies with high group tendencies, such as China or Japan.[2] In any society, important news spreads through people whom we know and trust.

A city is a society in which urban characteristics connect the people. However, urban networks are changing rapidly, forming different characteristics from traditional society. Failure to recognise this change would result in an alienated minister who works on the outskirts of these networks. As a result, the car carrying the Gospel ends up driving off the road.

Third, the modern urban environment, where shepherds and sheep live in very different worlds, drives our car off the road as well. The twenty-year span of a pastor – graduating from seminary, serving as an assistant pastor, then a head pastor of a church – leaves very little in common with the world of non-believers. A bigger problem is that shepherds empathise with their sheep less as well. Shepherds interact with their sheep mainly on weekends when everyone is dressed up and well-behaved. But for the sheep, real-life happens between Monday morning and the following weekend, in an environment that shepherds cannot experience or fully understand.

Is there hope for the urban church? Can our churches conduct urban ministry? Before simply blaming secularism or postmodernism for how urban ministry is not what it used to be, we must first ask the following questions, "How do

---

2 David R. Bell and Mary Douglas, "Natural Symbols: Explorations in Cosmology," *The Philosophical Quarterly* 22(88), (1972): 35.

modern ministers become leaders?" and "How can we minister from the perspective of the sheep?"

I wrote this book hoping that urban Christian leaders have a receptor-oriented attitude. When a situation changes, what is natural becomes awkward and fruitful ministries become ineffective. Therefore, the urban environment challenges churches to rethink their familiar ways of ministry. If they neglect the change, the church slowly becomes a car driving in no man's land. Through this book, I pray for the following changes in urban ministry.

First is expanding the focus of urban ministry from congregation to urban lives and needs (Chapters 1 and 2). Second is participating in the emergence of new urban Christian leaders who will lead contextualised ministries in urban environments with increasingly stratified and neo-unreached groups (Chapters 3 and 4). Third is to acknowledge God's sovereignty in all urban spaces and participate in ministry that connects people who are separated by group and class in reconciliation and forgiveness (Chapters 5 and 6). Fourth is to serve as good Samaritans to urbanites victimised by competition and climbing the ranks (Chapters 7 and 8).

This book will understand the city as a multitude of networks. Understanding urban social networks helps us understand urban ministry and church transformation. Urbanites change because their worldview and social structures have changed, and their worldviews and social structures, in turn, change the information and resources they receive and distribute. We often look for urban characteristics in the physical environment, such as buildings or subways. However, these material structures are also a result of people's changing ideas and societies. Therefore, to understand urban change, we must first recognise the people and society. What is crucial is that the information and resources that change the way these people think flow primarily through social networks.

People create new social networks in the process of getting the information and resources they want. It is like villagers from the mountains coming down to the river to do their laundry. The villagers need the river as a resource for the laundry. However, at the river, people do not only do laundry – they socialise with others and share new information. Similarly, urbanites flock toward areas with urban flow (Chapter 7) – goods, networks, and ideas – and create new networks to work and compete with others who are looking for the same flows. This is the city. People come down from the mountain to the river that has the flow that they need, and, there, they interact and work with others, and even play tennis with them on the weekends. In other words, urbanites' social networks flourish where there are resources. So the church in the mountains may need to move near the river where the villagers gather, or schedule its worship service at night when they come back home.

Even if the church moves to the riverside, it is not guaranteed to flourish unless it understands the lifestyles and preferences of the people there, because the villagers from the mountain have now changed. The church must transform itself into a new wineskin to hold new wine. This book will share the essential information to become the new wineskin. A new wineskin means more than simply modifying church programmes or contextualising sermon topics. It involves new leadership, new believer identity, and new church structures.

This book is not concerned with evaluating the existing church or the overpowering presence of the city. Instead, this book will draw the reader's attention to the many possibilities and stepping stones that God has already placed around us. By opening our eyes to how hopeful and human urbanites are, how many urbanites have multiple identities, God's missional plan to reach the growing number of urban unreached groups, and how many people fall on their way to success, God encourages the urban church to conduct an unprecedentedly diverse, hands-on, and inspiring ministry. The new wineskin for the urban church is an effort of those who seek, recognise and rejoice at what God has already done and prepared, and work alongside Him.

This book is written for the following groups: urban Christians who want to know what God is doing for their city; church leaders who want to break stereotypes and acquire a new contextual model for the city; lay Christian leaders who dwell in marketplaces and social groups; and students who study urban ministry in an advanced degree programme.

Introduction

This book has eight chapters addressing four major themes: urban individuals and lives; urban groups; urban space and time; and urban flows and transformation. Each theme is addressed by a pair of chapters. Through the first chapters of each pair, readers will gain a sociological lens for interpreting the city and will expose themselves to the constituent aspects of a complex city environment by learning the key concepts and dynamics of urban units. As a result, readers will develop deeper missiological reflections as to the meaning of "urban identities" for Christian individuals and churches. In the latter chapter of each pair, using a social network approach, the readers will learn the key factors and dynamics of urban changes to approach the issues dealt with in the preceding chapters. The chapters will address the Christians' roles for the change and reflect on the missional opportunities God has given to today's city as an unexpected gift.

Theme 1 is about urban individuals and lives. Its purpose is to understand the individual urbanite more objectively. Understanding individuals not only helps readers comprehend the most fundamental aspects when understanding the city and city ministry but will also provide insight for the urban church, which is, of course, a group of urban individuals. Chapter 1 brings up our stereotypical understanding versus the reality of urban individuals' behaviours and emotions. The city is still their familiar place despite being surrounded by strangers, consumerism, impersonality, deviation, high stress, crowds, isolation, and powerlessness. They also have kindness, moral orders, friends and "our" groups, privacy, and passions. Readers will be invited to live as urban saints and as lighthouses in their networks. Chapter 2 introduces how urban individuals with dual-layered cultural settings connect to diverse networks, give limited degrees of contributions, and can extend their networks beyond original boundaries. To have these abilities, they live as multiple membership holders. Finally, in the missiological reflection section, the readers and churches will discover the incredible missional potentials in urban individuals.

Theme 2 deals with urban groups. People form and live within groups, where they become friends and neighbours. Chapter 3 highlights that "who I am" refers to the groups that one has belonged to or belongs in. The many groups that we have belonged to in our lifetimes have shaped the people that we are today. Therefore, it could be said that the people we are today are because of such groups, and because of the providence of God. Chapter 3 will explore the key concepts and types of urban groups. Because of their nature and human arrogance, groups often disconnect themselves from the outside. Chapter 4 introduces the changing patterns and social dynamics of urban secondary groups. Readers will understand the I-centred group packet and the synthesised freedom that ironically mingles with loneliness. With the introduction of newly emerging neo-urban unreached groups, the chapter discloses the church's lack of readiness for the new and emergent needs in the city. To address such needs, we will reflect on new wineskins of churches with the spirit of an ambassador.

Theme 3 introduces urban space and time and their meanings. Time and place by themselves do not have meaning; the people who are associated with them give them their meaning. As a result, place is narrative and social, and contains the meaning and value that has been given to it by people. In addition, time and space influence the identity of the people involved, according to their given meaning. Chapter 5 deals with key concepts and terms of space and time necessary to understand society and humans. Every urban space and time is socio-spatial and socio-temporal because they have narratives of people and society within them. Competition between groups and cultural differences make urban space constantly demarcated. However, God is the owner of all spaces, and he desires us to treat these spaces with holiness, not division. Chapter 6 deals with the space and time that humans have divided. The division of space also determines the values of the people who live in and use it, creating boundaries, classification, and segregation. As Jesus broke down the barriers of the dividing wall, this chapter will challenge Christians and churches to cross the border for reconciliation.

Theme 4 will explain the urban flows that drive the shifts in class, residence, ethnic hierarchy and identity, culture, and media trends. In Chapters 7 and 8, the readers will see that the people have the spirit of "move or lose"." Such a desire for competition, opportunity, and insecurity becomes a crucial motivation to move upward, and the urban flux enables them to move. This social environment pushes everybody to run. Using the contemporary metaphor of the Good Samaritan in Wall Street, Chapter 8 introduces the places of today's good neighbours within ideas of urban flow and common ground. The secondary social network is where urban Christians can naturally encounter these robbed neighbours. To avoid losing such opportunities, Chapter 8 proposes future leadership, the saint with a T-shirt, and a structure and leadership model to maintain and grow them.

Upon reading these eight chapters, readers will discover that the city is a gift from the missional God. A proper understanding of these four themes would allow us to move away from becoming the church in the city and instead become an urban church as a member of the people's natural networks, like a car that travels on interconnected roads.

THEME 1: URBAN LIFE

CONNECTING AND DISCONNECTING WITH STRANGERS

1. Connecting with Strangers

Box 1[1] – Ailen in Buenos Aires

Ailen Pena's family lives in rural Telsen, in Argentina. Populated by approximately 1000 residents, Telsen is a traditional Catholic village. Ailen's parents, Jose and Maria, do not have specific jobs but instead make a living by watching over their neighbours' sheep or by helping out in their fields or shops. They mostly receive news of the outside world from other villagers as they work in the village grocery stores or butcher shops. During the cold winters, they chat all day long in the village hall with other villagers. In the summer, the villagers take part in numerous festivals and parties. On the Day of the Shepherd, all villagers gather to celebrate.

Figure 1: Festa of Dog in Telsen Village
(Telsen, Argentina, 2020, Photo © Carlos Seongheum Park)

After graduating from high school, Ailen relocated alone to La Plata, the capital of Buenos Aires State. A few years later, she started working for a trading company that exports wool to Japan. Alone and surrounded by people she did

---

1 Ailen is a family member of Dr Carlos Sungheum Park's local co-worker. Dr Park is a missionary in Argentina.

not know, she initially struggled with loneliness and helplessness in a crime-ridden urban city. However, once Silvia, another woman in her neighbourhood, joined the company, Ailen's life changed dramatically. Silvia was a city woman who had spent her entire life in La Plata, and, through her, Ailen was able to meet good friends and engage in various hobbies. With these changes, Ailen's lonely and harsh life was now vibrant and new.

Although Ailen must take a crowded bus to and from work, she is able immerse herself in her own space as she listens to Japanese lessons and classical music through her earphones. The atmosphere of her company is excellent, but with a few exceptions, she knows nothing about her coworkers' families, religions, or weekend lives outside of work. In a single week, Ailen connects with multiple groups including the Japanese workers she meets every Monday at the import and export management office, her Uruguayan friends at her basketball club on Tuesdays, fellow believers at church on Sundays, and her knitting club with Silvia's friends. When going to these gatherings, Ailen shakes off her rural appearance, invests in her attire and hairstyle, and tries to change her dialect.

To excel in her company, Ailen also participates in an online Japanese language club. Ailen was surprised to learn that the friends she made in this club were, contrary to what she had heard back in Telsen, very conservative yet creative and adventurous enough to plan to study abroad in Japan. Life in the city has changed many things for Ailen. In the countryside, her door was always open, but due to the city's high theft rates, she has now installed several locks on her apartment door. Ailen has also grown indifferent to strangers' gazes on the streets. The pressure to maintain her hard-earned job and succeed for her family simultaneously acts as a driver and a cause for loneliness that she must overcome. Interestingly, despite these hurdles, after visiting her parents for the holidays, Ailen longs to return to the city.

The more Ailen embraces her city life, the more she drifts away from who she was back in Telsen. The way she dresses, her lifestyle, the people she meets, the information she receives, and even her aspirations are now different from those of her people back home. Wanting to become a city woman who hangs out with friends her age and receives praise from her boss, she imitates the other city women around her. Who are these city dwellers whom Ailen so desperately wants to become? In other words, which characteristics is she trying to acquire?

Cities are home to countless kinds of people. Some live in suburbs and commute to and from the city's centre by car, while others are forced to move from the city centre to poorer neighbourhoods of colour due to urban redevelopment. Some take the subway to work, grab a takeout coffee from a café after lunch, and work the afternoon shift. Others take the bus to work among strangers who speak different languages and toil in silence on construction sites all day. The housewife who drops her elementary school-aged son off at school in the morning and buys packaged food for the week on weekends is also an urbanite.

As such, numerous urbanites belong to thousands of classes and groups and live with different cultures and life patterns. However, the reason why all these different people can be called urbanites is because they all have something in common. In other words, the city is an environment that gives its inhabitants the characteristics that they should have as urbanites. As a result, urbanites develop common characteristics in their behaviours, emotions, work, values, and relationships.

The God who leads the city desires that all people within it be saved, their dignity be restored, and God's righteousness and authority be restored. Because a city is a place with countless "persons who do not know the difference between their right and left hand, as well as many animals", God cannot help but care for them (Jonah 4:11). For Christians to truly do ministry that aligns with God's heart, it is crucial to understand the urbanites just as God commanded Jonah to pour his heart out to the people of Nineveh.

To do urban ministry right, churches must first examine how much they know about the urbanites and whether their ministry is appropriate for them. It is naïve to identify with urban ministry simply because the church is located in the city. Critiquing ministries that are urban only by name, Paul G. Hiebert and Eloise Hiebert Meneses state "[…] but too often they start peasant-style churches and, therefore, are unable to reach city folks."[2]

In this chapter, we will take the first step to understanding urbanites, by focusing on the urban individual's tendencies, actions, and emotions. To do this, we will take an urban anthropological and urban sociological approach. To explore the tendencies and psychological states that affect the urban individual's life, this chapter will begin by asking the following questions:

- What are the urbanites' trends and behaviours, and what are some common misconceptions?
- What are some characteristics of the urbanite's emotional states, and what are some common misconceptions?

By the end of this chapter, readers may be astounded by how strongly urbanites desire connection. We will recognise that they are strong to rise amidst loneliness and ambitious to maintain hope and passion during difficult times. We will learn that, although they must arduously coexist with strangers, urbanites possess a relatively sustainable emotional state as they mingle among those whom they claim as "us". After observing the urban lives in a constant cycle of connection and disconnection, at the end of this chapter, we will discover God's missionary plan for urbanites and the need to renew our perspective on urban mission on this basis.

---

2 Paul G. Hiebert and Eloise Hiebert Meneses, *Incarnational Ministry: Planting Churches in Band, Tribal, Peasant, and Urban Societies* (Grand Rapids, MI: Baker, 1995): 325.

Urban Trends and Behaviours: Connecting Pieces to Create the New Identity

The city's customs and population distributions are changing. In the United States, the proportion of 65-year-olds in urban populations has increased from 11% to 16% over 16 years since 2000. In addition, the overall US urban proportion of white residents has decreased drastically from 51% to 44%.[3] Communication styles have also changed. The surge in social media usage, especially on mobile devices, is a new custom seen in almost all urban societies worldwide (Figure 2). In all the advanced economies surveyed, "large majorities under the age of 35 own a smartphone."[4]

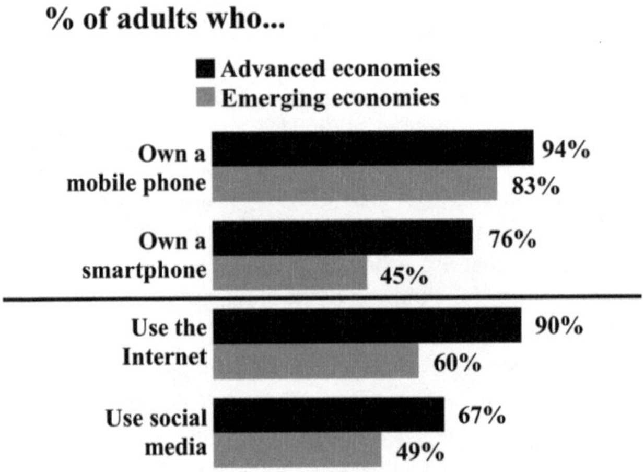

Figure 2: Mobile Technology, Internet, and Social Media Use More Common in Advanced Economies[5]

Such ever-changing trends of the city naturally prompt us to ask, "What exactly is urban life?" The life of urbanites is too diverse and complicated to explain with one or two simple perspectives. Therefore, instead of oversimplifying it, urbanists have attempted to define urban life by organising its cultural characteristics.

---

3 Kim Parker, Juliana Menasce Horowitz, Anno Brown, Richard Fry, D'Vera Cohn and Ruth Igielnik, "What Unites and Divides Urban, Suburban and Rural Communities," *Pew Research Center*, 22nd May 2018, [Available at: https://www.pewsocialtrends.org/2018/05/22/demographic-and-economic-trends-in-urban-suburban-and-rural-communities/], [Last accessed: 5th August 2023].
4 Laura Silver, "Smartphone Ownership Is Growing Rapidly Around the World, but Not Always Equally," *Pew Research Center,* 5th February 2019, [Available at: https://www.pewresearch.org/global/2019/02/05/smartphone-ownership-is-growing-rapidly-around-the-world-but-not-always-equally/], [Last accessed: 5th August 2023].
5 Silver, "Smartphone Ownership".

For more specialised understanding, we will now use an urban anthropological lens to analyse their worldview, and the consumption patterns of urbanites that traditional anthropology can hardly explain. As a result, we will learn that people live far more creatively and thrive more vibrantly than expected in an urban environment we often can view as simply negative.

Early urban anthropologists had pessimistic views towards urbanisation. They maintained deterministic views and saw that the city produced social disorganisation and personality disorders.[6] This determinism also explained that the city was relatively lacking in intimate personal acquaintanceship and that human relations are segmentalised, superficial, and transitory.[7] Such a deterministic view has supported this pessimistic view for a while, and Christians have too often fallen into it.[8] However, the four sub-sections from here will argue and show that human society did not just remain in such disorder. Despite the harsh environments, urbanites have re-created new connectedness to maintain their vitality within interactions, creativity, development and dignity as human beings. Such a connectedness demands new social networks and technologies to expand their relationships and power for success.

They Connect Fragmented Worldviews into One

Each society has its own worldview that its members recognise as their own. This worldview causes individual life and society to function in an integrated and systematic state, affecting lifestyles, families, economic activities, religious life, and political activities.[9] Even within the same country or nation, new

---

6 Eric O. Jacobsen, *Sidewalks in the Kingdom: New Urbanism and the Christian Faith*, The Christian Practice of Everyday Life (Grand Rapids, MI: Brazos Press, 2003): 36.

7 The major contributors to the development of Determinism were the Chicago Schools scholars, including George Simmel, Robert Ezra Par and Louis Wirth, who researched the psychological state of city dwellers rather than the city itself, in urban studies. Richard Sennett, *Classic Essays on the Culture of Cities* (New York: Appleton-Century-Crofts, 1969); Robert Ezra Park and E.W. Burgess, *Introduction to the Science of Sociology Including the Original Index to Basic Sociological Concepts* (Chicago, IL: University of Chicago Press, 1969); Georg Simmel, "The Metropolis and Mental Life," in Richard Sennett (ed), *Classic Essays of the Culture of Cities* (New York: Appleton-Century-Crofts, 1965): 47–60; Louis Wirth, "Urbanism as a Way of Life," *American Journal of Sociology* 44(1), (1938): 1–24.

8 Typically, the terminology Determinism is used to define a phenomenon in which individual freedom and character are reduced or restricted due to a particular social structure. In urban sociology, determinism is used when several small groups within a city lose their character and stability due to the larger overlying structure of the city. Nicholas Abercrombie, Stephen Hill, and S. Bryan Turner, "Dictionary of Sociology," in *Dictionary of Sociology* (London: Penguin Reference, 2006): 105; Enoch Jinsik Kim, *Mission Strategy in the City: Cultivation of Inter-Ethnic Common Grounds* (Eugene, OR: Pickwick, 2017): 67.

9 Paul G. Hiebert, *Anthropological Insights for Missionaries* (Grand Rapids, MI: Baker, 1985): 43, 45.

worldviews, in accordance with members' unique characteristics, are bound to develop if societal environments and atmospheres differ.

Worldviews shape the characteristics of the people who hold them. When urbanites demonstrate different characteristics from those of rural migrants, it is because urbanites carry an urban worldview. In other words, urbanites display urban behaviours not necessarily owing to their tall buildings, huge subways, or fancy shopping malls, but rather, it is their urban thoughts and worldviews that encourage them to build such facilities. Similarly, urban environments strengthen urban worldviews. As such, environments and worldviews become each other's cause and effect like two ping pong players. And as a result, the corresponding people end up with similar patterns of life and thought.

Worldview is an integrated system that contains few contradictory functions. [10] Therefore, people with common worldviews often share a homogenous way of thinking, and their lives and relationships are considerably predictable. In contrast, the worldviews of people in multicultural environments are not unified homogenous systems, but are combinations of various segmented worldviews. Bibby Reginald argues that modern people collect and combine bits and pieces of multiple worldviews and then traverse them as if they were in a maze. According to Reginald, such a multicultural lifestyle is like travelling between mazeways and fragmented worldviews.[11] Prior to Reginald, Anthony F.C. Wallace also referred to the fragmented maze to describe the logic of multiculturalists, and he explains that the mazeway is "the brain's organised and codified archive of cognitive residues of perception bearing on the characteristics of the extrabodily environment, the body itself, techniques, and values."[12] The fragmented mazeway is not a worldview that can be found in traditional society where the whole acts as a homogenous system, but it is a model that aligns with the thoughts and worldviews of urbanites who are familiar with various cultures.

People with multiple worldviews can adjust to different situations and live integrated lives. For example, Mr Carlos grew up in San Salvador, the capital of the Republic of El Salvador, and moved to the US for his studies. Later, he went on to make a family with a woman also from San Salvador and settled in the US. During the week, he works for an American company that imports coffee and sugar from El Salvador. When he returns from work, he leads his family in a Salvadorean fashion. On weekends, he spends time with his Asian neighbours at a local badminton club. All three groups co-exist in Carlos's worldview, but they seldom contradict each other. At work, he abides by American work culture; at home, he is a typical Salvadorian breadwinner; and at his badminton club, he reveres his seniors. Like Carlos, as urbanites live in various environments, they absorb a multitude of worldviews and integrate them into their own. As a result,

---

10 Hiebert, *Anthropological Insights*, 77–79.

11 Bibby Reginald, *Fragmented Gods* (Toronto: Irwin, 1987).

12 Anthony F.C. Wallace, *Revitalizations and Mazeway: Essays on Culture Change*, edited by Robert S. Grumet (Lincoln, NE: University of Nebraska Press, 2003): 170.

at work, Carlos can hide his Salvadorean masculinity and Asian-style respect for seniority to function as an effective American-style worker.

Having various integrated worldviews allows people to access numerous types of networks, naturally allowing them to belong to various other groups. During this process, they create a self made up of many different pieces. As seen in the previous example, Ailen also started from her village Telsen, then moved to La Plata where she absorbed the worldviews around her (of her colleagues in her trading company, knitting club, church, Uruguayan basketball team, and her online Japanese club) to form her own unique worldview. We can thus say that the worldviews of urbanites are a packet of systematic, unique and integrated worldviews.

They Find Belonging Through Consumption

A city is a place of consumption. Traditionally, consumption is an act of production and consumption. However, as resources became more abundant and relevant to people's societies, people have begun to add meaning to consumer behaviour and the objects that they consume.[13] In other words, consumption is beyond simply a movement of goods or personal preference, but is a social, cultural, economic, and political act that fulfil s people's economic and emotional values. People secure a sense of belonging, relationships, identity, and social status through consumption. Therefore, to urbanites, consumption has become a worldview, an act of survival, and a comprehensive act of cultural activity.[14]

Consumption in the city is an important means of forging connections between people. This is because the consumerism of urbanites is an act of expressing cultural needs and abilities.[15] The knowledge, skills and opportunities that they consume and create function as cultural capital. By eating certain foods, partaking in special cultural activities, and accessing members-exclusive goods and spaces, people develop a sense of status and belonging.[16] For example, people's cars, houses, and neighbourhoods, or even usage of coupons for free food demonstrate their social status and power. As such, consumption culture

---

13 Appadurai Arjun, "Disjuncture and Difference in the Global Cultural Economy," *Theory, Culture and Economy* 7(2), (1986): 295–310.

14 Wallace, *Revitalizations and Mazeway*.

15 Pierre Bourdieu, "Distinction: A Social Critique of the Judgment of Taste," in *Handbook of Theory and Research for the Sociology of Education*, trans. Richard Nice (New York: Greenwood, 1986): 243.

16 Edwin Eames and Judith Goode, *Anthropology of the City: An Introduction to Urban Anthropology*, Prentice-Hall Series in Anthropology (Englewood Cliffs, NJ: Prentice-Hall, 1977): 198; E.E. LeMasters, *Blue Collar Aristocrats: Life-Styles at a Working-Class at a Tavern* (Madison, WI: University of Wisconsin Press, 1976).

creates "a sense of belonging and identity, as well as community that is often quite distinct from or even in oppression to the urban mainstream."[17]

Consumption is part of cultural capital that helps people enter or maintain a specific social class.[18] In the story of Ailen, her investment in clothes and hair demonstrates her desire to look good and embrace and socially blend into her identity as a youthful urban businessperson. In addition, her efforts to also alter her accent and etiquette can be interpreted as a yearning to acculturate into the subculture.

Urban consumerism also develops leisure culture. As consumption becomes a culture in cities, it naturally creates a leisure culture that promotes luxuries like housing, cars, or coffee, which, once again, stimulates consumerism. [19] Furthermore, leisure culture naturally changes the city's structure. For example, cities eliminate old residential areas and establish new shopping malls and department stores. People line up in front of movie theatres and enjoy parks and restaurants with their families on weekends. They leisurely sit and drink coffee inside a trendy café which has chains worldwide.

The city's leisure culture continuously creates popular culture. This includes not only pop music, but also sneakers, smartphones, chain stores, studying at coffee shops in the evening, and more. Leisure trends allow people to create a kind of subculture.[20] Thus, leisure cultures do more than entertain; they serve as a channel for people to create and express their cultural identity and are a comprehensive activity that establishes economic superiority and power games among individuals and statuses.[21]

Urban consumerism creates a city's lifestyle, scenes, and popular culture.[22] Today's urban atmosphere and lifestyles are generally manifested through the mechanism of consumption. This is because consumption culture changes people's lifestyles and shapes their streets. As a result, people do place-making based on the image assigned to these spaces.[23] For example, if a street contains multiple pharmacies, it becomes "the pharmacy street" in the minds of the people.

As such, a city's consumption is more than just a commercial activity, it is a cultural act that expresses people's lifestyles, fashion, and values. Through this medium of consumption, people identify and experience a sense of belonging with certain groups and create connections with others who are socially like them.

---

17 Rivke Jaffe and Anouk de Koning, *Introducing Urban Anthropology* (London: Routledge, 2015): 99–100.
18 Jaffe and Koning, *Introducing Urban Anthropology*, 88–90.
19 Jaffe and Koning, *Introducing Urban Anthropology*, 91.
20 Andy Bennett and Richard A. Peterson (eds), *Music Scenes: Local, Translocal and Virtual* (Nashville, TN: Vanderbilt University Press, 2004).
21 Jaffe and Koning, *Introducing Urban Anthropology*, 95.
22 Jaffe and Koning, *Introducing Urban Anthropology*, 95.
23 Jaffe and Koning, *Introducing Urban Anthropology*, 23, 25.

They Are Kind in the Midst of Urgency

Urbanites are commonly believed to be colder and more indifferent toward others compared to rural or traditional inhabitants.[24] This indifference is present in people's eyes as they wait for the traffic light to turn green. Urbanites neglect the people next to them on the bus, and they often do not feel the need to demonstrate or even expect politeness. In a single day, urbanites live among countless strangers, from the crossroads to the shopping malls to the parking lots. They know very little about the people in other departments at work although they greet each other cheerfully every day. Such indifferent experiences with strangers combined with a romanticised view of traditional society convinces people that the city is a harsh society.

But are people from traditional and rural societies actually more sympathetic and amiable than their urban counterparts? We often assume that people living in the countryside are full of affection, friendly and kind, and sparing with their time. However, if a stranger was to appear in the country, would locals be any kinder than urbanites? Rural and traditional societies consist of a small number of people who encounter each other frequently. Therefore, internally, locals interact holistically through various dimensions, but such strong networks in turn make them warier toward outsiders. Furthermore, although the countryside's lower crime rates and generous leisure time may help create a friendly atmosphere for inhabitants, this can lead to a sense of indifference and distance toward strangers in public spaces.

There certainly are elements in the city that force people to treat each other with indifference. Urbanites are not naturally unfriendly or wary of strangers, but they struggle to consider others due to certain aspects of the atmosphere of the city. First, high crime rates impede compassion and hospitality.[25] News of crime unsettles people, causing them to fear strangers, look the other way, raise walls, and distrust. Second, the urban atmosphere's push for individual-based activities and achievements provokes apathy toward others.[26] Urbanites live anonymously in many places and enjoy private lives. In addition, success in the city relies relatively less on ethnicity or inherited status and can thus be achieved with individual effort and ability. This sense of freedom, possibility, and individualism encourages urbanites to focus on their own advancement and status. Time-oriented lifestyles and a competitive atmosphere also cause impersonality and indifference, inducing urbanites to view colleagues as competitors. The competitive atmosphere is pervasive in cities and societies where people are desperate to survive, advance, and succeed. This naturally

---

24 Impersonality is defined as "absence of human character, reduction of concern for individual needs, lack of emotional involvement", in Collins Dictionary. [Available at: https://www.collinsdictionary.com/dictionary/english/impersonality], [Last accessed: 5th August 2023].

25 J.P. Gibbs, "Suicide," in R.K. Merton and R. Nisbet (eds), *Contemporary Social Problems* (New York: Harcourt Brace Jovanovich, 1971): 271–312; L. Dublin, *Suicide* (New York: Roland, 1963): 188.

26 Hiebert and Meneses, *Incarnational Ministry*, 316.

forms a society that revolves around time, which is a resource. Time is so precious that urbanites now labour during their holidays or non-working hours.[27] Lastly, the development of technology has further made urbanites apathetic toward one another. From store transactions to communication between employees, opportunities to forge relationships are now standardised and automated, making it possible to function with minimal contact. High crime rates, individualism, a time-centred lifestyle, possibilities and opportunities, and technological advancements have made urbanites overly concerned with themselves, naturally resulting in a harsh urban society.

But are urbanites merely impersonal and indifferent? To varying degrees, urbanites also share friendships and compassionately help others. They are just as kind and friendly to friends, members of the same church group, and parents of their children's friends. In other words, urbanites can be the most hospitable people with those with whom they have a relationship. Just as Ailen, in the story box 1, could maintain a good relationship with her coworkers despite not knowing much about their private lives, urbanites tend to demonstrate civility and etiquette in smaller units like a company.

Urbanites are relatively more likely to help strangers. Interestingly, although urbanites may feel indifferent toward the strangers they come across on the street, they express as much interest as those in traditional societies for orphans and marginalised people who live across the globe that they see on TV.[28] In contrast to a traditional society whose strong communal bonds raise thick walls toward others, urbanites feel less distant from others as they encounter strangers daily. Moreover, urbanites subscribe to daily global news, receive public education from a young age, and are also trained to work and co-exist with strangers, which helps them understand the need to collaborate and help. Recognising these characteristics, Fischer states, "[…] according to available evidence, people in cities do not seem to be any more indifferent or callous than people elsewhere."[29]

Urbanites are more likely to help one another in smaller communities.[30] They actively aid those of the same ethnicity, company, school, or similar because they recognise a connection. Furthermore, urbanites turn extremely proactive when the community is so small that their inactions can lead to a catastrophe.[31] For example, it is difficult to pass by someone in pain while walking alone down the street. The severity of the situation also plays a role in the urbanite's willingness to help. People help more actively when they hear screams nearby, see someone

27 Hiebert and Meneses, *Incarnational Ministry*, 320.

28 R.R. Alford, "Critical Evaluation of the Principles of City Classification," in Brian J.L. Berry (ed), *City Classification Handbook: Methods and Applications*, ed. (New York: John Wiley, 1972): 349.

29 Claude S. Fischer, *The Urban Experience*, 2nd ed. (San Diego, CA: Harcourt Brace Jovanovich, 1984): 212.

30 Fischer, *The Urban Experience*, 207.

31 B. Latane and J.M. Darley, "Bystander 'apathy'," *American Scientist* 58 (1969): 244–68.

passed out from hunger, or are put in a situation where even the slightest bit of help can make a significant impact. On the other hand, if the community is too big, people are more reluctant to help others. When surrounded by multiple people in a large plaza or when around others who are more skilled, urbanites are less likely to step up.

Interest in others also affects cultural and networking characteristics. Altruism comes out more naturally in a collective society than in an individualistic one. However, people in collective societies are much more cautious toward strangers than those in individualistic societies.[32]

Another factor that affects people's willingness to help is the presence of social safety policies. With well-established welfare, police, and hospital emergency facilities, many are convinced that making a phone call is enough to help someone. Conversely, if there are no such facilities, many more would be willing to become Good Samaritans.[33]

In short, rather than being innately so, urbanites often act in an unfriendly and indifferent way because their structured environments establish disconnected encounters in public spaces, causing them to overlook the value of hospitality. Urban public spaces are large communities with strangers, intense competition, and high crime rates, and people thus hesitate to step up until certain criteria are met. In such harsh public spaces, people are vulnerable to unpleasant encounters, which again reaffirms their notion of the cold-hearted city.

The extremely polarized view of the city and the countryside served to exaggerate the harshness of the city.[34] Furthermore, the deterministic view has overestimated the city's ruinous capacity, comparing it to a flaming furnace that consumes humanity and melts down individuality.[35]

As we have seen, when provided the environment, urbanites help others and maintain affectionate relationships, just as in traditional societies. They are also highly attentive to those who are less privileged and socially disadvantaged across the globe. They too rely on basic emotional exchange and networking. Even today, the city is a place bustling with people who maintain their humanity as they meet with friends and serve the poor.

---

32 Joel Wallach and Gale Metcalf, *Working with Americans: A Practical Guide to Business Success for Asian Managers* (New York: McGraw-Hill, 1995): 165–71.
33 Fischer, *The Urban Experience*, 211.
34 This bi-polaristic view was developed by the determinists of the Chicago School, and it maintained an opposing view to that of the later compositionists. Richard Sennett, *Classic Essays on the Culture of Cities* (New York: Appleton-Century-Crofts, 1969); Robert Ezra Park and E.W. Burgess, *Introduction to the Science of Sociology Including the Original Index to Basic Sociological Concepts* (Chicago, IL: University of Chicago Press, 1969); Georg Simmel, "The Metropolis and Mental Life," in Richard Sennett (ed), *Classic Essays of the Culture of Cities* (New York: Appleton-Century-Crofts, 1965): 47–60; Fischer, *The Urban Experience*, 25.
35 The term, melting pot, was first coined as Israel Zangwill's 1908 Broadway drama title with a love story between a Russian Jewish and Cossack.

They Deviate, but Strive to Uphold Morals and Order

Every city has an overlying umbrella culture that every inhabitant must learn and follow. Determinists believed that this massive culture thrusts people into standardised education and competition, wiping out unique characteristics of class, region, culture, and ethnicity, rather than celebrating individuality and character. As a result, determinists hypothesised that urbanites would gradually lose their closest and most reliable connected relationships and be left with only co-workers and contracted partners.[36] People would be disconnected in this stranger-filled life where dignity and honour hold no value. As a result, the gigantism of the city would cause individuals to deviate rather than uphold and pursue individual interests over honour or morality. Such a phenomenon would then spawn high crime rates and hostility. In other words, the vastness of the city breaks down the moral order that was once maintained in smaller societies.

However, the city's unfamiliarity actually stimulates creativity instead of a breakdown in moral order. This social atmosphere delivers less social pressure and empowers urbanites to break away from what is considered conventional and acquire the freedom to try new activities. This unconventional mood becomes the foundation of new fashion, order of life, and other various creative activities. As urban populations consist of relatively younger, highly educated, and single people, urban unconventionality becomes the backdrop of infinite creativity and births new products and trends.[37] In this way, a disconnected environment can amplify inhumanity and sponsor creativity.

Contrary to the deterministic prediction that small groups will disappear, the city is full of groups that rely on maintaining moral order. For example, religious entities, businesses, communities, hobbies, the upper class, unions, kinship groups, and more follow the order set by their group and properly cultivate relationships. Unlike in larger settings, urbanites showcase a collective life that is much more civil and sympathetic in their smaller societies. In other words, the moral order is well-maintained. Similar to locals in smaller traditional communities, urbanites also fear being judged by others and undergo social pressure to act appropriately in their subgroups.[38]

Every community has its own identity, ethos, and behavioural expectations for its members.[39] These are called social norms – the formal and informal understandings that members must recognise and follow for their community to

---

36 The determinism was developed mainly by Chicago School. They stated that cities develop people intellectually and technically but due to individualism and yearning for freedom, cities may also increase solitude and disconnect the relationships in peoples' mentalities and lives. Sennett, *Classic Essays on the Culture of Cities*.

37 Parker *et al.*, "What Unites and Divides".

38 Fischer, *The Urban Experience*, 218–19.

39 Alan Smart and Filippo M. Zerilli, "Extralegality," in Donald Macon Nonini (ed), *A Companion to Urban Anthropology* (Chichester, West Sussex: Wiley-Blackwell, 2014): 236–38.

operate and multiply.[40] If a member is to ignore these rules, other members will protect their society through various means such as gossip, punishment, or lawsuits.[41] For example, Ailen from the story box 1 was surprised to learn that her city friends from her Japanese club were more conservative than what she had known back in Telsen. Regardless of how free-spirited the city was, they, too, were raised under strict parents and were taught morals from their schools and social lives since childhood. As such, urbanites adequately utilise their disconnectedness and connectedness to forge their lives and dreams.

Urbanites easily deviate from traditional order not because they themselves are necessarily different but because the immense size of urban society allows them to pursue their desires without as many social repercussions. Such an environment raises crime rates but also spurs new trends and creativity. Nonetheless, urbanites can still consider others and maintain traditional social values and altruism because they belong to multiple subgroups. Therefore, small societies serve as a bedrock that preserves and upholds the urbanite's humanity and dignity.

Urban Emotions: Overcoming the Distress to Succeed

Urban environments and societies have influenced the urbanite's psychological state. For example, early urbanologists such as M.B. Clinard believed that urban development would destroy social norms, creating normless societies. Clinard also thought that the city's anonymity, loneliness, impersonality, unconventionality, and crowdedness would cause various psychological disorders and diseases.[42] However, we all know that there are more than just negative emotions in the urbanite's heart. If the city was so horrible, why would people seek it and spend their entire lives in it? Are there not pull factors other than the economic reasons that attract migrants? Are there not unique elements that make urban life happy and enjoyable, despite being different from traditional society?

Perhaps our view of happiness is overly traditional, and perhaps our observations are too partial to notice the happiness among urbanites. It is essential to objectively seek out urbanites' psychological and emotional states.

---

40 Cristina Bicchieri, *Norms in the Wild: How to Diagnose, Measure, and Change Social Norms* (New York: Oxford University Press, 2017); Rachel T.A. Capra, Mary L. Rigdon, and Tanya S. Rosenblat (eds), "Game-Theoretic Accounts of Social Norms," in *Handbook of Experimental Game Theory* (Cheltenham: Edward Elgar, 2020).

41 Daniel R. Shaw, *Transculturation: The Cultural Factor in Translation and Other Communication Tasks* (Pasadena, CA: William Carey Library, 1988): Chapter 7; Gary P. Ferraro, *Cultural Anthropology: An Applied Perspective* (Minneapolis/St. Paul, MN: West, 1995): 250–59.

42 M.B. Clinard, "Deviation Behavior: Urban-Rural Contrasts," in C.E. Elias, J. Gillies and S. Reimer (eds), *Metropolis: Values in Conflict* (Belmont, CA: Wadsworth, 1964): 237–44.

To do this, let us examine how urbanites maintain themselves and pursue happy lives among strangers, despite the stress, frustration, and helplessness.

Creating "Us" Amidst Strangers

Urbanites spend much of their time in a state of disconnect. They walk among unfamiliar crowds and collaborate with strangers. Even their next-door neighbours are often strangers. As a result, almost everyone in the community is a stranger. Figure 3 compares how well urban and rural people know their neighbours. According to Kim *et al.*, rural adults are acquainted with 4 out of 10 of their neighbours while urban adults report 2.4.[43] Without question, urbanites live among strangers, even in their neighbourhoods.

Figure 3: Four in Ten Rural Residents Know All or Most of Their Neighbours (% saying they know all or most of their neighbours) [44]

Urbanites mingle with strangers in elevators, local markets, or bus stations. In fact, most people in the workplace are familiar strangers, despite working together for years. Other than a handful of people, co-workers are unaware of each other's religious affiliation or family composition. As a result, to urbanites, strangers are less like outsiders and more like those who they do not know personally, those who appear unusual, and those who seem unfamiliar and odd.[45]

Then, do urbanites just work every day, lonely and disconnected? The truth is that urbanites forge many more networks with various people than they would in traditional society. Like Ailen, urbanites constantly develop intimate relationships with people in church, sports clubs, online communities, and doing other hobbies. In these groups, some bonds are as strong as those between childhood friends. This is because urban networks have developed in a way that

43 Parker *et al.*, "What Unites and Divides".
44 Parker *et al.*, "What Unites and Divides".
45 Fischer, *The Urban Experience*, 95.

facilitates relations that are built through frequent interactions, despite the distance and unfamiliarity.

As such, through small communities, cities still provide familiar people who urbanites can trust and share information and emotions with. Urbanites may live amongst strangers in larger communities, but they maintain intimate connected groups in smaller communities such as families, church, class reunions, or clubs. Ailen initially walked alone in stranger-filled streets and felt powerless against the high crime rates. Nevertheless, in her small communities, she could develop intimate friendships and a sense of belonging, just as she had back in Telsen.

A Stressful and Chaotic Yet Bearable Life

Relative to traditional societies, cities do have high crime rates. From 1995 to 2003, the US reported higher rates of burglary, car theft, and all other aspects of crime in cities than in the countryside (Figure 4). Theft rates have decreased everywhere in urban, suburban, and rural areas, but other crime rates have remained similar over time.

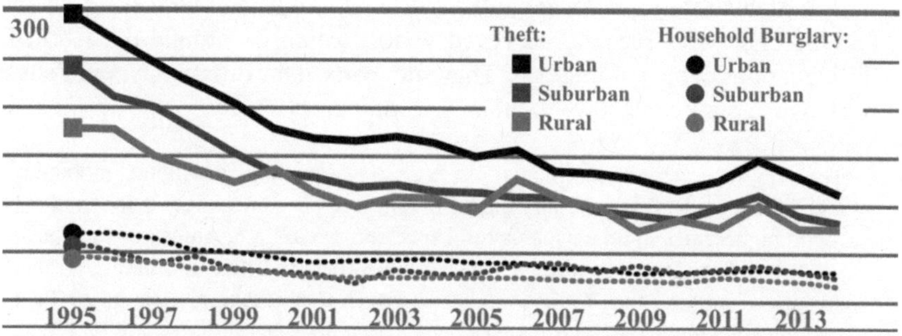

Figure 4: Household Victimization in Urban, Suburban, and Rural communities (rate per 1,000 households) Bureau of Justice Statistics[46]

According to The Bureau of Justice Statistics' National Crime Victimization Survey, it is likely that the contrast between urban and rural crime rates is not necessarily due to differences in population size but rather due to certain societal factors.[47]

Deterministic scholars hypothesised that the city's normlessness was the cause of its high crime rates. Normlessness refers to a state in which moral or social norms have collapsed, and as a result, people are unsure of what rules to

46 "Urban and Rural Victimization," *2017 National Crime Victims' Rights Week Resource Guide: Crime and Victimization Fact Sheets* (Washington DC: Office for Victims of Crime, the Office of Justice Programs, US Department of Justice, 2017): 1, [Available at: https://www.ncjrs.gov/ovc_archives/ncvrw/2017/index.html], [Last accessed: 5th August 2023].

47 "Urban and Rural Victimization," 1.

follow.[48] In a normless society, the ends justify the means, and people act or behave in whatever way they desire, satisfying themselves. According to determinists, in normless societies, higher crime rates result from increased stress levels and disorders among people. In fact, up until the 19th century, cities reported higher suicide and alcohol addiction rates.[49] High crime rates and tense atmospheres also create an unhealthy environment for relationships among urbanites. As a result, urbanites are forced to doubt and bypass their affections toward others to protect themselves and avoid being taken advantage of.[50] However, since the emergence of the subcultural theory, it has been revealed that the city's high crime rates correlate more with its population, societal scales, and networks than with the sheer number of evil people.[51] For example, the anonymous factor of the city increases crime rates. Crime spikes when people are unidentifiable, inconsiderate, self-interested, and unmonitored. Additionally, crime rates are lower in rural areas not because the people are purer or kinder but because they know each other and are identifiable through multiple angles. In these areas, criminals are easily exposed and are met with enormous social pressure on themselves and their families.

The high-stress levels of the city contribute to disease outbreaks. Gruebner and his colleagues recently surveyed various countries around the world for different rates of mental illnesses. They summarised the different types of stress-related diseases people have in urban and rural areas.

> The risk for some major mental illnesses (e.g., anxiety, psychotic, mood, or addictive disorders) is generally higher in cities. Studies on anxiety disorders [...] found higher rates in urban versus rural areas in several Latin American and Asian countries. The same was true for psychotic disorders in China and in large urban areas in Germany. In a Danish study, the risk for schizophrenia was more than twofold for individuals who had spent their first 15 years in a major city versus those who had grown up in rural areas [...][52]

Simply put, he claims cities have more stress-induced diseases and are thus normless.

It is important to note, however, that inaccurate and incomplete reports and records of stress and disease in cities often tend to exaggerate the infection rates and crime rates. The lack of social facilities and awareness in rural areas can lead

---

48 R.K. Merton, "Social Structure and Anomie," in *Social Theory and Social Structure* (New York: Free Press, 1980): 185–214; Clinard, "Deviation Behavior".

49 Gibbs, "Suicide," 188.

50 James S. House and Sharon Wolf, "Effects of Urban Residence on Interpersonal Trust and Helping Behavior," *Journal of Personality and Social Psychology* 36(9), (1978): 1029–43.

51 Eames and Goode, *Anthropology of the City*; John Gulick, *The Humanity of Cities: An Introduction to Urban Societies* (Granby, MA: Bergin & Garvey, 1989); Fischer, *The Urban Experience*.

52 Oliver Gruebner *et al.*, "Cities and Mental Health," *Deutsches Arzteblatt International* 114(8), (2017): 121–27.

to underreported infection and crime rates. For example, a police department with insufficient resources could inadequately handle a crime outbreak. It is also common for rural patients to visit urban hospitals, adding to the urban rate. As such, city disconnections cause people to become impersonal and normless, raising stress levels.

Despite this normlessness, the city can cleanse itself of stress and chaos. The city's powerful social standards strongly allow people to break free from lawlessness and instead pursue productive and orderly lives. For instance, a college student who used to sleep in every day may well be able to wake up early and dress neatly for work as soon as they get a job. There is intense pressure for people to abide by these social rules to become a member of society, no matter how freely they behave at home. In addition, the city's immense public power and social obligations maintain the city's social standards and quell crimes in advance.

Above all, the city's numerous small societies keep it orderly. Each urban subculture has its social norms. People must adhere to the respective orders to participate in church communities, schools, and even public parks have their rules and expectations. These smaller groups promote intimacy and develop an "us" mentality. Strong peer pressure exists in these small "us" communities, motivating people to act respectfully and maintain order. As such, the city's disconnection may cause crimes and various stress-induced side effects, but citizens continue to create a habitable environment by putting the broken pieces back together.

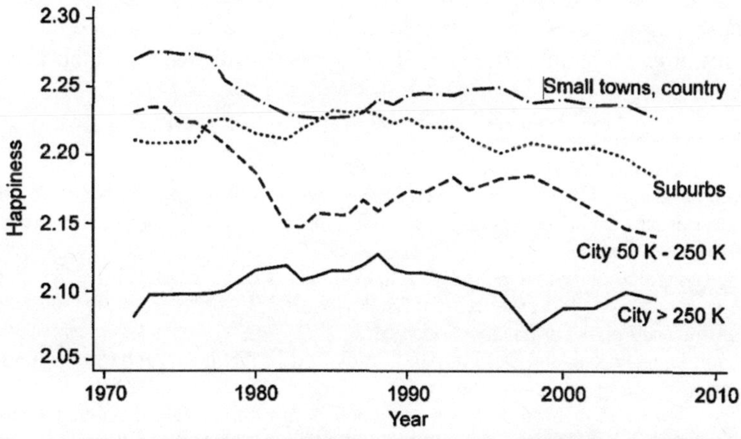

Figure 5: Urban-Rural Happiness Gradient[53]

53 Brian J.L. Berry and Adam Okulicz-Kozaryn, "An Urban-Rural Happiness Gradient," *Urban Geography* 32(6), (2011): 875.

How happy are urbanites? According to general notions and field surveys, cities were less happy than rural areas. The city's high stress, crime rates, and normlessness are the main culprits of these levels. Recent studies reveal that there is a clear urban-rural happiness gradient. For example, Canada's happiness researchers reported that people living in small towns and rural areas are happier than those in the city.[54] In the US, the happiness survey conducted from 1970 to 2010 also supports this finding (Figure 5). Clearly, people in large cities are less happy than those in rural areas. However, since 2000, happiness has decreased in rural areas and small and medium-sized cities, while it has increased in large cities with populations of 250 000 or more. This trend continued until 2018, when all four regions finally converged to roughly the same level of happiness.[55]

Despite high-stress levels, the city still offers happy and tolerable components. After all, 50% of the world's population today resides in the city and has been doing so for their entire lives. People continue to flock to cities bearing their hopes and dreams. But if financial and educational opportunities were the only reasons to live in the city, successful people would have already left the so-called painstaking city. Creating happiness entails subjective feelings, material abundance, convenience, comparison with others, the surrounding environment, trustworthy friends and people, and conditions for self-actualisation. For this reason, those who value the opportunities, possibilities, and convenience the city offers are happier. For example, unlike in Canada or the US, urbanites in less-economically developed countries displayed relatively high happiness levels. Migrants from these countries were also very satisfied with city life,[56] despite their everyday struggles to rebuild their lives from the ground up, accustom themselves to new environments, solve family issues, re-establish marital roles,[57] and provide childcare.[58] As such, despite stress and changes, urban migrants are reported to be greatly satisfied with their new city

54 John F. Helliwell *et al.*, *How Happy Are Your Neighbours? Variation in Life Satisfaction among 1200 Canadian Neighbourhoods and Communities*, NBER Working Paper Series; No. 24592 (Cambridge, MA: National Bureau of Economic Research, 2018).

55 The General Social Survey, NORC at the University of Chicago website [Available at: http://gss.norc.org/], [Last accessed: 5th August 2023].

56 Cantril, *The Pattern of Human Concerns.*

57 Thanh-Dam Truong and Des Gasper, "Trans-Local Livelihoods and Connections," *Gender, Technology and Development* 12(3), (2008): 285–302; Nana Oishi, *Women in Motion: Globalization, State Policies, and Labor Migration in Asia*, 1 online resource (Stanford, CA: Stanford University Press, 2005); Sarah J. Mahler and Patricia R. Pessar, "Gender Matters: Ethnographers Bring Gender from the Periphery toward the Core of Migration Studies," *IMRE International Migration Review* 40(1), (2006): 27–63; Nicola Piper and Mina Roces, *Wife or Worker?: Asian Women and Migration* (Lanham, MD: Rowman & Littlefield, 2003).

58 Michael P. Todaro, "Urbanization in Developing Nations: Trends, Prospects, and Policies," in Pradip K. Ghosh (ed), *Urban Development in the Third World* (Westport, CT: Greenwood, 1979): 7–26.

lives.[59] For example, only 3% of Chinese migrants prefer to live in the countryside.[60]

La Plata from the story box 1 is a typical city with high crime rates, crowded buses, and countless strangers, but it is an environment sufficient to make Ailen smile, make friendships, and self-motivate her to work hard. Friends, church, success, hobbies and convenience keep her in the city. Although she loves to revisit her family home for holidays, she enjoys returning to the city even more.

Although happiness levels may be lower in the city due to higher stress and crime rates, urbanites nonetheless share friendships, bonds, trust, and joy with their small communities, or connected relationships, just like those in traditional society. These small communities and identity-building workplaces, the city's convenience and equality, and the opportunities and resources of the city keep many urbanites overcoming hardships and living dynamically.

Enjoying Personal Lives Even amid Crowdedness

Cities are often portrayed with bustling crowds and lonely individuals walking amongst strangers. Therefore, it often seems that the city's disarray and unfamiliarity are tiring and overloading.

Such perspectives led scholars like Daniel Stokols and S.D. Cohen to produce the crowding theory, claiming that a complex and congested society intensifies competition due to interference between people and a lack of resources.[61] Resources are not limited to materials, but they also include privileges such as securing a favourable place or opportunities for status promotion. As urbanites pour their energy into securing these scarce resources, they naturally undergo mental stress and physical exhaustion. Crowding theory compared such environments to rat cages where people develop psychological and societal problems as they are cramped yet must co-exist.[62] As a result, people would lose personal space, leisure, rest, and constructive thinking. The crowding theory, however, has lost credibility due to the following three facts.

First, cities have developed congestion-reducing facilities. Although rural areas are generally characterised by spacious fields, mountains, and rivers, in the residential areas, dozens to hundreds of generations tend to inhabit a single side

---

59 Joan M. Nelson, *Access to Power: Politics and the Urban Poor in Developing Nations* (Princeton, NJ: Princeton University Press, 2017).

60 John Knight and Ramani Gunatilaka, "Rural-Urban Migration and Happiness in China," in Richard Lavard, John F. Helliwell, and Jeffrey Sachs (eds), *World Happiness Report 2018* (New York: Sustainable Development Solutions Network, 2018): Chapter 4.

61 Daniel Stokols, "The Experience of Crowding in Primary and Secondary Environments," *Environment and Behaviour* 8(1), (1976): 49–86; S.D. Cohen, "Environmental Load and the Allocation of Attention," in Andrew. Baum and Jerome E. Singer (eds), *Advances in Environmental Psychology.* Volume 1, The Urban Environment, 3rd ed. (Hillsdale, NJ: Erlbaum, 1978): Chapter 2.

62 John B. Calhoun, "Population Density and Social Pathology," *Scientific American* 206(2), (1962): 139–49.

of a field. In addition, the scarcity of modern goods and opportunities in the countryside can result in intense competition and conflict. Cities, however, effectively appropriate their limited land spaces by constructing skyscrapers, large apartments, or offices. Despite crowdedness, cities efficiently implement mass transportation systems. Furthermore, private automobiles are spaces where individuals can create their own world. Compared to rural areas in less-economically developed countries where people must squeeze into village buses that appear once or twice a day, cities often offer buses running every ten minutes and thus provide a relatively comfortable commute, except during rush hours.

Second, the city has developed independent mindsets and environments. In addition to physical spaces, the guarantee of privacy also depends on networks and culture. Urbanites can decide how much they reveal of themselves and leave the rest within their private spaces. Meanwhile, personal space is limited and less privacy is guaranteed in group-oriented or traditional societies. Members eat, work, and mingle with the same people and thus know each other very well.[63] And because they are culturally a group society, people are accustomed to submitting to the will of the leader or collective group rather than their own. As a result, such traditional lifestyles may be more physically and socially crowded than commonly perceived.

Third, discordance within our notion of urban crowdedness corresponds to the amount of time urbanites spend in crowded settings. This is because people tend to feel crowdedness not necessarily due to the city's density but rather from the tiring and complicated encounters they experience in their own micro-environments. For example, E. Sundstorm said, "it is not high density per se that brings negative aftereffects but the aversive events that sometimes accompany high density."[64] In fact, urbanites spend more time focused at work with their ten colleagues than inside congested buses or on the street. After work or on weekends, they enjoy their lives with those they love. Like Ailen from the story box 1, no matter how populated the neighbourhood may be, if urbanites can live in cozy apartments, plug in their earphones and create their own space on the bus to work, quietly focus on their work, and have time to enjoy leisure activities on the weekends, they would not consider their lives as being overwhelmingly crowded. This is because regardless of the city's high population density, the environments urbanites live and function in are low-density areas.

As such, crowdedness can be described as the inconvenience felt when disconnected people get too close to each other. Connected people, on the other hand, desire intimacy. Therefore, people tend to feel crowded not because they live in a crowded society, but because they have personal encounters that emphasise the crowdedness. Urbanites live complicated lives not because of the

---

63 Ronald Frankenberg, *Communities in Britain: Social Life in Town and Country*, Modern Revivals in Sociology (Aldershot: Gregg Revivals, 1994): 244.

64 E. Sundstorm, "Crowding as a Sequential Process: Review of Research on the Effects of Population Density on Humans," in A. Baum and Y.M. Epstein (eds), *Human Responses to Crowding* (Hillsdale, NJ: Lawrence Erlbaum, 1978): 61.

city's objective population density, but because they develop the feeling of crowdedness from experiences like rush hours or ethnic conflict. However, urbanites spend a considerable amount of time by themselves, on their work, on their pursuit of dreams and aspirations, and on their privacy. As such, the city is a place where people can live their own lives amidst crowdedness.

Undying Passion Even amid Feelings of Helplessness and Solitude

The city's enormous size and complex transportation systems, congestion, complex laws and policies, accelerating competition and professionalism and constantly curb people's ability to relax. Every day, the media portrays the extremely wealthy, beautiful, powerful, and talented to the masses, making viewers feel insignificant.[65] As a result, regular people feel inadequate, helpless, and thus disconnected from hope as they compare themselves to the city's enormity, strangers, and competent others. This feeling of helplessness occurs when the comparison is so large and distant that it causes disconnect from hope.

On the other hand, the city's enormity also motivates urbanites to live earnestly. In fact, cities constantly stimulate people to climb the social ladder and strive for success. Accordingly, the city's social facilities, welfare systems, and educational opportunities provide the basis for achieving such a desire.

Additionally, the city evokes tremendous enthusiasm in migrants, who undergo much higher levels of stress and chaos to survive than mainstream urbanites. Nonetheless, because the city offers them a means to break away from their former social status and customs and start anew, they work tirelessly to grasp such opportunities. For instance, Ailen's (from the story box 1) friends from her Japanese study group seek to study abroad in Japan. Back in Telsen, her hometown, people would not fathom studying in another country, but the environment and atmosphere of the city produces such creative and adventurous people.

Contrary to what determinists claim, helplessness is more prominent in traditional societies than in cities. Traditional societies may provide more emotional companionship and security in their homogenous environments, but with their ties with fatalism, traditional religions intertwine human relationships. For example, the inherited social statuses and social customs make it more difficult for individuals to alter their fate or status ambitiously. Individuals face helplessness as their limits and status are predetermined by others, in addition to the scarcity of social opportunities and facilities. Banfield (1958) analysed the

---

65 Research shows that the more time people spend on Facebook and Instagram, the more they compare themselves socially. This comparison is linked to higher social anxiety and lower self-esteem. Kathi Diel, Sonja Grelle, and Wilhelm Hofmann, "A Motivational Framework of Social Comparison," *Journal of Personality and Social Psychology* 120 (2021): 1415–30, [Available at: https://psycnet.apa.org/doiLanding?doi=10.1037%2Fpspa0000204.

differences between mainland Italians and Italian immigrants in the US and reported that people in rural areas carried a much more fatalistic mindset.[66]

As such, the life of an urbanite balances between a degree of helplessness and a passion for success. It is true that many feel overwhelmed by the urban atmosphere, small compared to the heroes exhibited on media, and devastated due to cultural and linguistic differences. As mentioned, urbanites are exposed and vulnerable to mental illnesses, crime, solitude, and crowdedness. Yet, they continue to sprint fervently towards success, utilising the city's abundant resources, networks, and competition. Ailen from the story box 1, who toils to succeed in her trading company while also learning Japanese in her personal time, is an example of this.

In addition to helplessness, urbanites also suffer from loneliness. The loneliness is caused by feelings of isolation, which peak when people are disconnected from their surroundings. With increased social security, facilities and the development of communication systems, urbanites spend more time alone than ever. After being assigned a task at work, they often work in solitude until they leave, barely interacting with anyone on their way home. Even after dinner with their families, they may fulfil their individual hobbies and emotional lives alone. With advanced social security systems, people can be hospitalised without the help of relatives and no longer feel the need to live with their children in old age. Urbanites are thus perceived to be isolated from their surroundings, as we compare their customs to those of Asian countryside villages where locals gather to share snacks and watch TV.

A close examination of urban life shows that the city offers abundant connection nets and facilities which help people build relationships, although still less than the Asian countryside villages. People can easily forge connections with cell phones and reconnect with relatives and acquaintances through mobile apps, in ways impossible in the past.[67] Modern transportation allows people to visit friends living on the other side of the city. In fact, through hobbies and religious and social activities, urbanites constantly connect with others and maintain robust relationships as strong as those in traditional societies.

If traditional societies are less isolated, then they should demonstrate lower levels of loneliness. To study this, ethnographers researched levels of trust between people, which is one indicator of isolation. Surprisingly, results displayed little difference between the trust levels of the countryside and city. Some results showed that people in rural areas were less trusting of their fellow villagers.[68] Figure 6 is a chart comparing the loneliness levels experienced by

---

66 Fischer, *The Urban Experience*, 192.

67 Barry Wellman, *Networks in the Global Village: Life in Contemporary Communities* (Boulder, CO: Westview, 1999): 355.

68 Laurence Wylie, *Village in the Vaucluse,* 2nd ed. (Cambridge, MA: Harvard University Press, 1964): 204–205.

urban and rural residents of Manitobans, Canada.[69] Cities generally harboured milder types of loneliness, while rural areas exhibited more intense types. This reveals that urbanites generally bear some degrees of loneliness, but it is, in fact, the people in rural villages who experience more intense forms of loneliness that affect their livelihoods.

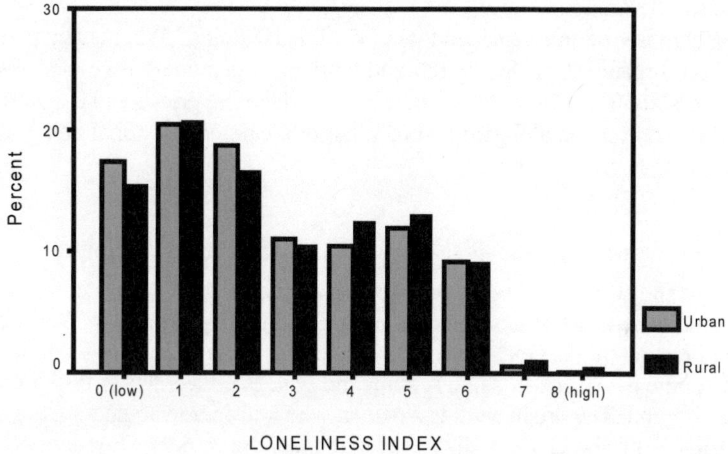

Figure 6: Loneliness Ruralites and Urbanites[70]

People generally feel lonelier and more isolated in larger, less intimate groups, often after watching an extravagant performance, cheering with a crowd, or finishing a romantic soap opera. On the other hand, people build trust and overcome their loneliness in smaller, long-lasting relationships. These smaller groups thus vitalise urbanites to persevere and fight on. Although they may remain distant from relatives or immediate neighbours, urbanites connect and maintain a different form of friendship and neighbourhood.

As such, urbanites suffer from helplessness due to the isolation between disconnected people. However, through close, connected relationships, they can convert their insecurity and helplessness into passion.

Missiological Reflection: Back to Our Identity

Even in disconnected environments, urbanites never cease to create various connectivities. This is possible because they are able to assemble and integrate multiple shards of worldviews into one. Consumption behaviours are more than simply purchasing habits; they act as identification that displays one's social

69 Betty Havens *et al.*, "Social Isolation and Loneliness: Differences between Older Rural and Urban Manitobans," *Canadian Journal on Aging* 23(2), (Summer 2004): 129–40.
70 Havens *et al.*, "Social Isolation and Loneliness", 134.

class. Competition for success and a stranger-filled environment thrust urbanites into a life of relational disconnection. In addition, the disappearance of communities that positively monitored each other through multiple dimensions has made the city a harsh place ridden with crime. These factors cause urbanites to fixate on their success and neglect their honour and reputation. Yet, despite feeling alone amongst public crowds, they continue to form diverse connections with smaller groups.

Where is God in all this, and what work is He doing? What is His perception of these urbanites? If the church and Christians genuinely love God, we must immediately join Him at the place where He labours, grieve and experience His burden, and rejoice alongside Him. What biblical and missional being must we become to bear God's heart?

Urban Believers' Identity: Living as an Urban Saint

To read the city as God sees it and to be a partner in what God is doing, we must first have the heart of God. Such a person is the urban saint, a person who puts God first and thinks God-centredly, even in the midst of an ever-changing urban environment. An urban saint is someone who is concerned with the eyes and heart of God. The urban saint is a person who knows how to be a part of the city and live with the city just like everyone else, but seeks to live biblically as a forgiven sinner rather than compromising with the urban trend. Now that we've seen the characteristics of urbanites, how can we live like saints in the city?

First, urban saints must learn how to reject secularism and success-ism and be grateful for their surroundings. Like everyone else, if we take for granted the well-being and opportunities that cities provide, and compare ourselves only to those who are better off or higher up, we too will be miserable in our relative poverty. However, godliness actually is a means of great gain when accompanied by contentment (Tim. 6:6). Christians must be grateful for themselves, their families, neighbours, colleagues, the environment of the city, and their leaders. A grateful and content mindset secures the energy to get back up and serve, despite the city's anxiety and chronically low happiness levels.

Furthermore, the city saint must be able to read the emptiness and anxiety of those enslaved to success. In the end, their futility reveals once again that what all urbanites really need is Jesus. Only He can satisfy their thirst. Many urbanites are already exhausted from the vanity of success. They await the urban saints to demonstrate, rather than explain, what true success looks like.

Second, urban saints must overcome reductionism and read their city through the principles of creation. Reductionism attempts to interpret the objects using a single perspective or forcibly apply narrow principles to the whole.[71] In the context of the city, these reductionists implement the local phenomena in the entire city. For example, Jacques Ellul describes the city as a predominantly evil

---

71 Hans Rytger Kricheldorf, *Getting It Right in Science and Medicine: Can Science Progress through Errors? Fallacies and Facts* (Cham, Switzerland: Springer, 2016): 63.

place. By citing mankind's first cities: the city started by Cain, rebellious Babel, Sodom, Gomorrah, and Babylon, Ellul argues that the city is a symbolic place which illustrates the sinful natures of the people living there.[72] Eric O. Jacobsen also highlights the negative aspects of the modern American city, characterising individualism, independence, freedom, and other urban American values as false gods.[73] On the other hand, Harvey Cox explores the city as a place of great hope and freedom. By comparing the city's elements of freedom and anonymity to traditional society's restrictiveness and obstinate social status quo, Cox claims that the city animates God's creation principles and people's individual dignity.[74] Edward Glaeser, who praised "The Triumph of the City", also described it as the victor of the long-standing competition against traditional society and as a place that generates creativity, abundance, opportunities, and restoration of humanity.[75] However, reducing the city's natures into purely positive or negative virtues helps explain only a fraction of the city's complex social phenomena. Furthermore, doing so neglects critical components that we must recognise and study.

On the contrary, unlike reductionism, the principle of creation expands our perspectives and sees cities as creations of God more comprehensively and objectively. As God is the creator of all things, He is also the creator of the city. The city comprises of the "God saw that it was good" (Gen. 1) handiworks of God. In addition, the city is a product of humans created in His image and wisdom. This approach also paints the city as a network of people made in the image of God, presenting urbanites as people who are called to grow, prosper and cultivate the land with freedom, passion, co-operation, and creativity. Not only this but it also helps people overcome the notion that city is a tentative place where we temporarily reside before moving to heaven. Simultaneously, the creationistic view brings us to view the city as a place torn down by human sin and corruption and a place to be managed and nurtured to fulfil God's principles of life.[76]

---

72 Jacques Ellul, *The Meaning of the City* (Grand Rapids, MI: Eerdmans, 1970).
73 Jacobsen, *Sidewalks in the Kingdom*, 21–28.
74 Harvey Gallagher Cox, *The Secular City: Secularization and Urbanization in Theological Perspective* (Princeton, NJ: Princeton University Press, 2013).
75 Edward Glaeser, *Triumph of the City: How Our Greatest Invention Makes Us Richer, Smarter, Greener, Healthier, and Happier*, Reprint edition (New York: Penguin, 2012).
76 Creationistic principles, as urban ecology claims, involve and indicate the effort to create a sustainable and remedial society. Tim Ingold, "Toward an Ecology of Materials," *Annual Review of Anthropology* 41 (2012): 427–42, [Available at: https://www.annualreviews.org/doi/abs/10.1146/annurev-anthro-081309-145920], [Last accessed: 6th December 2023]; Peter Newman, *Cities as Sustainable Ecosystems: Principles and Practices* (Washington DC: Island, 2008); D. Torsello, *The New Environmentalism? Civil Society and Corruption in the Enlarged EU* (Farnham: Ashgate, 2012); Cressida Jervis Read, "Urban Pollution: Cultural Meanings, Social Practices – Edited by Eveline Dürr and Rivke Jaffe," *Journal of the Royal Anthropological Institute* 18(2), (2012).

Third, urban saints must view themselves as connectors. The creationistic perspective directs Christians' attention to missional reconnecting. God desires the reconnection of disconnected people, and for knowledge about Him to be spread. Even those who have been divided or indifferent for long periods of time have no choice but to mingle with each other when they arrive in the city. People from vastly different cultures gather every day in school or the office, and both the rich and poor root for the same football team. Cities can transfer hate and bias which have developed from differences and indifferences into mutual understanding and synergy, allowing people to uncover the principles of creation and knowledge of God, which are hidden in the nooks and crannies of cities. God's principles thus allow cities to become a place full of art, creation, knowledge, abundance, justice, moderation, and virtue.

God longed to embrace the rebellious city of Jerusalem, like a hen who gathers her chicks under her wings (Mt. 23:37). As such, God desires to bring us, who are divided by hate and prejudice, together in the city to hold us in His arms. Urban saints are thus God's ambassadors, as they connect diverse groups who have been divided by hate and prejudice, reuniting them so that they may be embraced by God. Hence, the duty and ministry of urban churches are more than providing church programmes. Although it may not be a direct programme of the church, are they not serving and vitalising our neighbours and connecting the communities in accordance with missions and creationistic efforts?

Urban Church's Identity

The worldview, behaviours, emotions, and values of urbanites highlight the need for urban churches to develop a relevant identity and ministry for the city. If a church replicates the ministry and message of previous churches, rather than getting to know the urban person and their context, then the church is, at the very least, not an urban church. In order to minister to urban people, the church must first be transformed into a church for urban people and minister with the heart of God.

Church for Urbanites

In order for the church to be appropriate for the people in the city, they must fulfil their basic commission as churches. The church is a place where congregations form a community and perform regular worship and sacraments under the guidance of the Holy Spirit, with Christ as the cornerstone. The church should function like a family who accepts, a hospital which heals, a school which teaches about Christ, and an army which triumphs against the enemy. The church should nurture the saints to follow Christ by making them whole and dedicate itself to local and outside missions and communities. These are basic identities that any church in any place or situation must harbour.

Second, the church must be contextualised to the circumstances of its ministry. Contextualisation requires consideration of a church's surroundings and its members, which implies that no two churches are the same. A church's contextualisation indicates its readiness to serve its neighbours and become their pillar. Such contextualised churches act as lighthouses to their surroundings. Although lighthouses may not play significant roles in day-to-day life, they are life-saving benefactors for ships during storms. Similarly, the urban church must become a primary refuge for those in need, regardless of its usual popularity or noticeability. As mentioned earlier, urbanites carry heavy burdens in their lives. As urban determinists describe, constant competition and stress force them to live among urban dysfunction and disorder.[77] Just as ships seek out lighthouses during a crisis, there will come a time when urbanites seek help.

Migrants, in particular, need such lighthouses because they could easily "become socially alienated by the sheer size of the urban centres."[78] For Ailen, it was when she first arrived in La Plata that she needed a lighthouse, as she struggled with feelings of loneliness and helplessness living in a crowded and crime-ridden environment. To become lighthouses, urban churches must regularly build trust within their local contexts and become places where people can expect to find the solutions to their problems.

Third, churches should strive to restore urban sacredness. This is different from the religious life that isolates us from the outside.[79] It is like the growth of a beautiful flower in a murky pond. Even as the roots live amongst dirty waters, the flower sustains its beauty.[80] Such a flower then becomes the pride of the pond, not only because it is beautiful but because such beauty was created in dirty waters. This is what urban churches look like when they protect the city's sacredness.

Having the Heart of God

Having God's heart is the first step of participating in his ministry to the city. To do so, churches should first see the big picture of the city. Seeing the big picture requires more than opening a map and locating things or merely examining state-published statistics reports of the city. The big picture is attributed to reading the city with the heart of God. For this, we must know who God is and what is currently happening in the city. Specifically, the phenomena occurring throughout the city, objective numerical data and records, and major headline events expose God's sorrow, expectations, ministry, and plans for the city. Therefore, the church should spare no effort in first securing these objectives and big pictures instead of continuing what has been done in the past. Afterward, the

---

77 Sennett, *Classic Essays on the Culture of Cities*; Park and Burgess, *Introduction to the Science of Sociology, Including the Original Index to Basic Sociological Concepts*; Simmel, "The Metropolis and Mental Life."

78 Bob Hitching, *McDonalds, Minarets and Modernity: The Anatomy of the Emerging Secular Muslim World* (Sevenoaks, Kent: Spear, 1996): 14.

79 Hitching, *McDonalds, Minarets and Modernity*, 68–76.

80 The lotus becomes a symbol of the beautiful flower in the murky pond in many Asian societies.

church should pinpoint specific ministries in accordance with individual gifts and circumstances and seek the necessary people for those roles. The following are resources that can help us understand the big picture of the city.

First, the past and present of a city identify its meaning and people. What we see in the city today is merely its outermost layer. Throughout thousands of years of history, cities have acquired countless layers. God remembers the city's history of conflict, war, and hunger to comfort and heal the people, and wishes to celebrate and commemorate their prosperity, achievements, and glorious cultures.[81] Recent social phenomena and trends are also important clues to understanding today's urbanites. Changes in thoughts and fashions, new regimes, economic transitions, ethnic and social conflicts, pollution, and crime rates are all data that describe the social situation of the city.

The city's environment and structure also address its current state.[82] The natural environment and the city's architectural styles are signs of the previous generations' interests and worldviews. The city's design of roads or facilities tell us whether the city is authoritative or egalitarian, efficiency-orientated or people-oriented, and favourable only to the able or accessible to all.

The city's places and its various signs and symbols express the city's personality. By observing a city's abundance of bars, factories, or farm equipment stores, one can imagine what it would be like to live there. The city is full of cultural heritage, characteristics, values, and the beliefs of its residents.[83] For example, the city's forest of skyscrapers, streets aligned with surfing stores, downtowns experiencing urban blight, elephant mascots on Bangkok souvenirs, and marketplaces with Muslim and non-Muslim restaurants aligned on the same street are symbols that portray the complexity and values of its residents.

What people consider important reflects their values. In individualistic culture, personal spaces are developed and both individuality and personal time are respected. In cultures where time is valued like money, social commitments and structures develop to be as efficient as possible.[84] As such, money, power, scarce resources like art, or anything else that is considered valuable can be used to understand people's values and dedication. The city's ideals, pride, beauty, and virtues pursued are all signs of what the city is like. Beauty standards, artworks, heroes, and role models depict people's aspirations. And creativity, freedom, generosity, justice, and civic consciousness allow the church to understand the innermost parts of the city.

---

81 See the 'Urban Times: Made of Sociotemporal Narratives' in chapter 5 of this volume for deeper theories and cases.

82 Donald K. Smith, *Creating Understanding: A Handbook for Christian Communication Across Cultural Landscapes* (Grand Rapids, MI: Zondervan, 1992): 234–67.

83 See the 'Built Environment as Extensions of People' in chapter 5 of this volume for deeper theories and cases.

84 Hiebert and Meneses, *Incarnational Ministry*, 317–320.

This chapter depicts urbanites as strangers in familiar places. The art of people's connection has shown remarkable results in transforming an urban environment filled with loneliness and heartlessness into a liveable place. This calls for urban churches to shed the subjective ministry philosophy and look beyond the local church-centred view to read the city with God's eyes. In the next chapter, we will examine the work that the missional God has already done in the midst of the urbanites. We will not only see God's passion to make good things flow to every corner of the city, but also confirm that God's mission (*Missio Dei*) is still underway.

2. They Are Well Connected: Bridge or Egoist?

The city changes a person. We see change when we welcome our kids home after university or through old school friends as they move away and live their own lives. As mentioned in the previous chapter, Ailen changed significantly after moving to the city of La Plata. Ailen lives a very different life than her parents in terms of their ways of thinking, spending, her relationships, and how they acquire information. How do cities have the power to change people so much? The power of this change lies in people's networks of relationships and informational channels. Through these connections, people exchange values, abilities, relationships, and knowledge, and as a result, the people change. Thus, understanding these networks and pathways is critical to identifying the causes of change in people.

The Gospel is good news. Because this good news is likewise a piece of information, the Gospel has a message-like quality. Information can only flow if individuals are connected in some way. In other words, the Gospel is designed to spread through the human network – which is made up of channels built between people [1] – and the trusted relationships that are formed between individuals can become an excellent lubricant for them to accept this Gospel. As a result, comprehending a city's human network and information channels is significant to urban ministry and for evangelising urbanites. To this objective, this chapter will begin with the following questions:

- Compared to traditional societies, what are some characteristics of urban social networks?
- How does the urban cultural system affect the formation of networks between urbanites?
- What role does the urbanite's diverse and growing network have in spreading the Gospel?
- Who has multiple identities, and what are their missional values?

At the end of this chapter, we will understand God's will in gifting urban Christians with multiple identities and reflect the missional opportunities and responsibilities He gives through them.

---

1 Smith, *Creating Understanding*, 144–80.

The Urbanites Are Well-Connected

Understanding the urbanite's network reveals their social relationships, values, information, financial resources, power relationships, and more. This is because a network is like a highway where people trade information, resources, and emotions.[2] The nature of the people's networks reveals how their society looks. Therefore, naturally, urbanites' social networks differ from those living in traditional societies.

Their Connections Are Dispersed and Controllable

It is uncommon for urbanites to cross paths again in another group with individuals they encounter in one group. In other words, the urbanite's network does not tend to overlap often. People in cities engage in a wide range of activities and interact with a diverse selection of people groups. However, the group members' understanding of each other is severely limited.[3] On the other hand, people's networks in traditional societies often overlap. This means that it is common to run into the same individual in different organisations and participate in activities with them. This is because each person holds multiple positions within the same society.

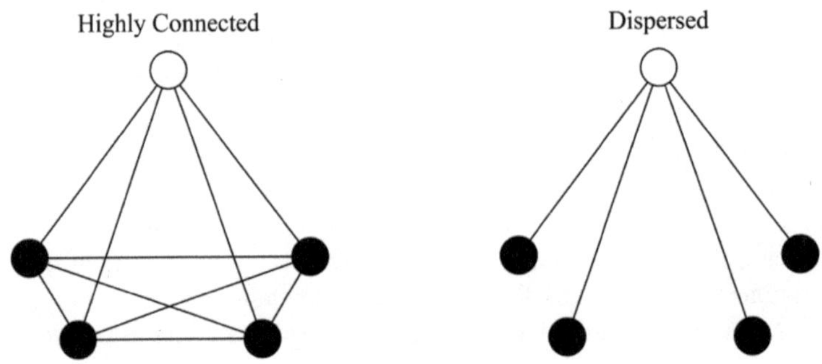

Figure 7: Comparison of Rural and Urban Network Structure.[4]

Due to the lack of knowledge about their colleagues and peers, urbanites can have a different face for each of their networks. Flangan introduced the diagram

2 Travis J. Grosser, Virginie Lopez-Kidwell, and Giuseppe Labianca, "A Social Network Analysis of Positive and Negative Gossip in Organizational Life," *Group & Organization Management* 35(2), (2010): 177–212; Jeremy Boissevain, *Friends of Friends; Networks, Manipulators and Coalitions*, Pavilion Series Social Anthropology (Oxford: Blackwell, 1974): 47.
3 Ulf Hannerz, *Exploring the City: Inquiries toward an Urban Anthropology* (New York: Columbia University Press, 1980): 232.
4 William G. Flanagan, *Urban Sociology: Images and Structure*, 5th ed. (Lanham, MD: Rowman & Littlefield, 2010): 111.

below that compares the types of networks that we have discussed so far between urban people and people in traditional societies (Figure 7).

The figure on the left shows the network of a traditional society. In a traditional society's network setting, information about a person is heard through multiple channels. That is, in a traditional society, one person makes contact multiple times and is exposed in multiple dimensions to the same subjects. The figure on the left depicts how one person can have multiple roles (including neighbours, co-workers, fellow club members). Because the people connected below also have various roles (egos), they exchange information with the ego above in various settings.

As a result, the ego mentioned here exposes various aspects of themself to different groups of people, and the people around them connect and exchange information about the ego. As a result, the ego on the left feels a burden as if all eyes are on them. At the same time, they can have a deep and strong relationship with everyone because they are connected to all people in multiple ways. A good example is Ailen's parents in the story box. In the rural city of Telsen, they acquire information from tending other people's flocks, helping with their shops and fields, and from town halls and festivals. Her mother receives her information from her network of other women. In rural areas with no division of labour or specialisation, everyone is involved in more than one task, just like Ailen's parents. Because of this, while they may take on various tasks, in reality, they meet and work with the same people. For this reason, Ailen's parents can understand their neighbours' circumstances in multiple dimensions. It is like viewing information collected from multiple antennas on a single 3D monitor. Such networks allow the surrounding people to learn more about that one person (ego), including private issues. In addition, the villagers understand a person's situation three-dimensionally because they have seen and know the person's childhood well and stories of their parents and grandparents. To borrow a Korean expression, this can be described as a relationship of "knowing even the number of spoons that family possesses." This three-dimensional understanding of one person can be seen not only in the countryside but also in urban slums or urban ethnic villages. Because they lack social resources compared to the city at large, they do most of their activities with the same people. As a result, their activities and networks also tend to appear similar to those of the traditional society.

The diagram on the right depicts the network of urbanites. Urbanites are specialised in their roles, and they prefer to play different roles with different people. Also, they cannot exchange information because the people around them are not connected, as shown in the lower part of the diagram. In addition, when the people at the lower part interact with the person above, they act based on the one component of the person linked to them, not the total aspect of that person. Here, the person at the top interacts with each of the people in the lower using only a portion of themselves.

Compared to traditional societies, urbanites are connected to a wider variety of networks. In particular, urbanites have many opportunities to connect with diverse economies, hobbies, politics, and various organisations. However, these connected networks rarely overlap with each other. Consequently, the surrounding people only understand the part of the individual that relates to themselves. They do not know the other egos that the individual has created in other networks. Ulf Hannerz also points out this aspect: "Under urban conditions, [...] audiences are different each time. We may say that under such circumstances, the difference between what is made known about the self in a particular situation and what could be known involves the parts which the individual plays in all other situations."[5] Ailen from the story box 1 is an excellent example of this concept. She is active in many groups, but the members of each organisation do not overlap with each other. The people she meets during the day, night, and at private gatherings throughout the week rarely know each other. As a result, if she so desires, Ailen can participate in various settings as a completely different character for each setting. Because members of one group have no other connected route, their knowledge of Ailen is confined to what she decides to show them.

As such, urbanites understand how to use and regulate their networks as they see fit. For them, the fragmented network is not something that is confusing and overwhelming, but an opportunity to grow and choose what they want.

Actively Connecting with Various Groups

The city offers people exceptional social mobility. The city's diverse groups, urbanites' social desires, and the opportunities the city provides form the fundamental environments that enable the city's networks to have social mobility. This social mobility includes characteristics such as diversity, scalability, and initiative.

For starters, the urban social network is far more diversified than that of traditional communities. This is not just due to the city's immense scope and size but also because they have opposing viewpoints. They do not believe that they should exclusively associate with acquaintances from their hometowns or people of similar backgrounds in social situations.[6] They are quite comfortable working with persons from various backgrounds so long as their relationships are mutually beneficial and they have a shared purpose. They may even welcome new information from an outside source and treat it as a source of pride within their community. Furthermore, modern urbanites have found it easier to meet people due to globalisation, enhanced social capacity of individuals, and increased communication channels between classes and ethnic groups.

Second, the urbanites' networks are highly scalable. The city's connectivity makes urbanites connect in various social arenas. On top of this, the development

---

5 Hannerz, *Exploring the City*, 232.

6 Xiaowei Zang, Jonathan N. Lipman, and Matthew McKeever, "Ethnicity and Urban Life in China: A Comparative Study of Hui Muslims and Han Chinese," *The China Journal* 60 (2008): 205.

of transportation and communication networks help them easily expand their network of relationships. As a result, urbanites can travel long distances to carry out activities despite the physical distance and communication strain. For example, one may travel far for religious activities, to meet a co-worker who lives on the other side of the city every day, and work outside the office more.

Third, cities provide an environment where people can be more proactive in networking. Public education, various chances to improve one's status, medical benefits, and welfare facilities convince people that they can be released from their ascribed status and background and encourage them to shape their futures through their own work and choices. Such possibilities and hopes become the driving force that makes people actively regulate their own lives.

As such, the city's diversity, scalability, and social mobility powered by urbanites' individual initiatives allow them to establish an urban network.[7] Likewise, this social mobility of the city's networks was also the reason why Ailen was able to get to know many people in the city and be active in various groups through Silvia.

Figure 8 is a conceptual diagram depicting the secondary network of those living in traditional societies and the city.[8] The figure on the left is an individual's network in a traditional society. Such individuals usually socialise within their villages or ethnic groups. They mainly trust and participate in social activities with their family and people from similar backgrounds. Therefore, their secondary network consists of people of similar backgrounds, thus remaining within their ethnic group or culture. Additionally, the network is primarily very strong and formed in proximity. These networks are thicker and shorter in diameter because, as previously mentioned, people in traditional societies interact with one another in a multi-layered manner, and one person is repeatedly exposed to limited people. Such a network system makes people feel that they can solve daily problems within not outwith their ethnic groups. Like urban societies, traditional networks are connected in all directions, meaning that one is connected to all the networks one needs. Ailen's parents, Jose and Maria, in Telsen are excellent examples for the diagram on the left. They have spent most of their lives with people of the same ethnicity. Because the same individuals repeatedly do various jobs, the community becomes homogenous within and, although the network's density is high due to the overlapping network as a whole, it can be described as strong and short in range.

---

7 Spradley and McCurdy said, "Social mobility refers to the process of gaining rank in a system of social stratification." James P. Spradley and David W. McCurdy, *Anthropology, the Cultural Perspective* (New York: Wiley, 1980), 160.

8 Jeremy Boissevain, *Friends of Friends: Networks, Manipulators and Coalitions*, Pavilion Series Social Anthropology (Oxford: Blackwell, 1974): 24; William G. Flanagan, *Urban Sociology: Images and Structure*, 2nd ed (Boston: Allyn and Bacon, 2002): 22; Edwin Eames and Judith Goode, *Anthropology of the City: An Introduction to Urban Anthropology*, Prentice-Hall Series in Anthropology (Englewood Cliffs, NJ: Prentice-Hall, 1977): 157.

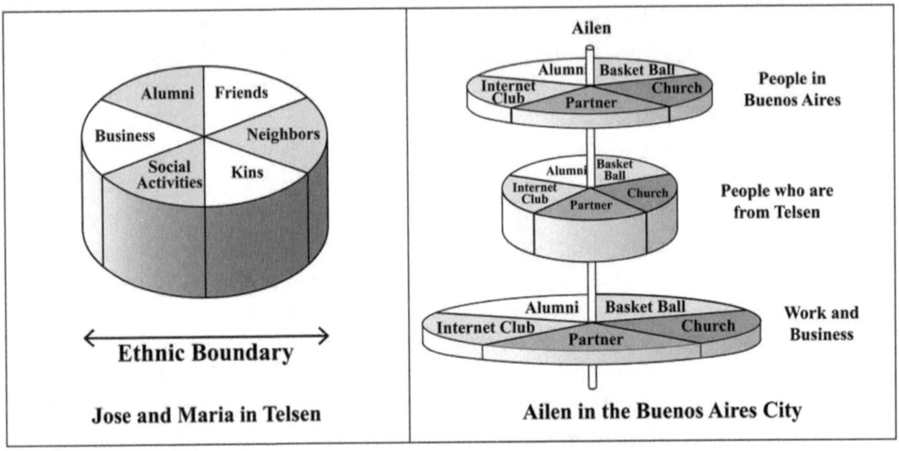

Figure 8: The Secondary Network Comparison

The figure on the right is the conceptual diagram of a single urbanite's secondary network. Ailen, who has resided in La Plata for a long time, falls under this category. The network of a single person can be divided into many disks depending on the cultures and subclasses with which they interact. Each network (disk) has distinct characteristics and does not know much about each other. In the case of Ailen, her main network consists of not one but three disks – the networks formed by neighbours and social life such as hobbies, networks with people who share the same background, and corporate and business relationships – because each of them is an entirely different world. The diameter and thickness of these disks are also significant. A large diameter means that the network extends to people of various distances, and a thin one implies that the relationship is shallow. For example, Ailen's thick and narrow middle disk (a network of people from Telsen) suggests that she only engages in repetitive and strong bonds with people not professionally connected but rather with whom she communicates well emotionally.

The same groups of people can be found in different disks. Ailen usually visits a hairdresser (second disk) from Telsen who lives in the same neighbourhood, but before an important event, she finds a more professional hairdresser (first disk). As such, there are various social relationships in each disk, so how closely, with whom, and which disc one chooses to interact with depends on each individual's preference and situation. As a result, when seeking a job, attending a reunion, or visiting an internet club, Ailen does not have to look for someone who is also from Telsen or of the same status.

As such, rather than bonds based on their ascribed backgrounds, urbanites' secondary networks are mediated by economic values and shared interests, resulting in networks with diversity, scalability, and activity that can transcend existing social boundaries.

Dual Layered Cultural Setting

What characteristics does the urban individual's cultural setting have? Modern urbanites are continually exposed to change. They grow among social groupings of different cultures, move to new places, and live in multicultural communities. As people grow up and socialise, they basically have two cultural systems: original and social.

Those who live in a monocultural environment with little social change have little difference in their social settings. On the other hand, if oversimplified, people who live in global cities are forced to live in at least two cultural contexts – traditional and social – and hence must have multiple social identities.[9]

This dual-layered cultural structure is especially evident in the lives of migrants. The enormous cultural differences that they must deal with in their new environment cause many changes and confusion not only in themselves, but also in their homes, jobs, and preferences. As a result, they must design a new social framework on top of their original (homogeneous) cultural systems. From this, they attain a cultural setting made up of two layers.

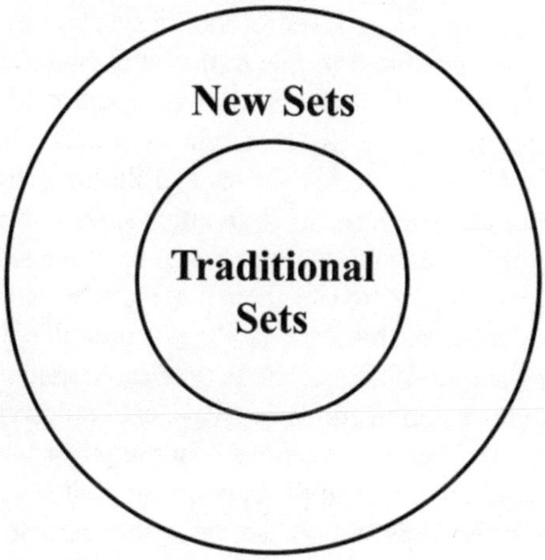

Figure 9: Dual Layered Cultural Setting[10]

Figure 9 is a conceptual diagram depicting these two cultural settings. The inner layer represents the individual's original cultural elements, while the outer layer comprises elements acquired from their new setting.

---

9 Through the field research of Muslim migrants in China, Enoch Kim found this dual layered cultural pattern. Enoch Jinsik Kim, *Receptor-Oriented Communication for Hui Muslims in China: With Special Reference to Church Planting* 34, American Society of Missiology Monograph Series (Eugene, OR: Pickwick, 2018).

10 Kim, "Ministry to Hui Muslims in China" in *Margins of Islam*, 97.

The outer layer of the picture allows people to live their lives in accordance with the common order and values of an urban society. Furthermore, this outer layer allows one to empathise and improve work performance when interacting with others from various backgrounds. Even if someone comes from a different culture, they may work together and enjoy each other's company because they share characteristics in their exterior layers. These commonalities make it possible for them to communicate with each other.[11] The fact that Ailen in the story box 1 can work with Japanese businesspeople, play basketball with people from Uruguay, and pursue other hobbies with other urbanites is due to the similarities and communication channels she has secured with them.[12] While this expanded contact point allows an urbanite to communicate with people they did not know before, it also creates conflicts that had not previously existed. Conflicts or commonalities are all made possible because each individual's cultural outer layer serves as a bridge through which they can communicate with each other. With this outer layer, urbanites can not only connect with a wide variety of people but also reconnect relationships that they have traditionally been indifferent or hostile toward.

Even for those who have grown accustomed to city life, the inner circle often exerts a powerful force. This inner layer refers to a system formed in a traditional setting. For those who have lived in one culture for their whole lives (such as Ailen's parents), those who are migrants from the countryside to the city, or are first-generation immigrants, the inner circle occupies almost one's entire process. However, their inner circles shrink and the outer rings grow as time passes. Therefore, people who have lived in cities since ancestral times or have been less influenced by traditional culture naturally have smaller inner circles and a wider outer circle compared to their inner circle. No matter how much social influence they receive, the inner circle is rooted deeply within urbanites and remains in every corner of their lives. People can notice that their emotional roots revive when they celebrate ethnic festivals, eat homestyle food, or listen to ethnic music. Despite their ethnic identities becoming less present in their lives, they can become rekindled while simply supporting their soccer teams or if their ethnic religion encounters persecution. So, no matter how long Ailen has lived in the city, hearing someone belittle her hometown of Telsen would not sit well with her.

For migrants, saying that the generational gap comes from changing this dual-layered cultural structure is not an exaggeration. The first generation of migrants often live almost exclusively in their internal culture, meaning that they must learn basic social skills to survive, but otherwise maintain a thicker layer of the original culture. However, as the migrants reach beyond the 2nd generation, their culture of origin gradually decreases. This does not mean that they become the

11 Smith, *Creating Understanding*, 23–40.

12 Enoch J. Kim, "A New Entrance Gate in Urban Minorities: Chinese Muslim Minority, the Hui People Case," *Missiology: An International Review* 39(3), (2011): 363–65.

same as the native people, because the inner circle, no matter how small, can be revitalised under certain circumstances. Singapore is a good example of this, as the communisation and revitalisation of China in the 1950s restored Chinese pride and self-respect, which led to a resurgence of Chinese pride and culture in Singapore.

The dual-layered cultural pattern is not a unique phenomenon to migrants, but applies to everyone who socialises in a culturally different circumstance from the one in which they grew up. Therefore, most people are bound to have a dual-layered cultural structure. Especially as societies become more complex, globalisation becomes more influential, and an individual's decision become important, their outer layers are bound to become much thicker. Even for those who have been living in the mainstream society of cities since birth, this two-layer structure has become a universal phenomenon that everyone must have to survive, because society and information are constantly changing and people are constantly recreating themselves with new skills and values.

This dual-layered cultural structure gives people both a sense of security and insecurity. Having two systems provides a sense of social security because they are able to deal with, and benefit from, both. On the other hand, the dual-layered cultural structure is also a settling structure because it is hard to belong fully to either side, since the habits and desires of one side are alive even when on the other.

The Multiple Identities Have Missional Potentials

In any society, each individual (ego) lives with several roles and positions. For example, a pharmacy clerk is a mother at home and a pianist at her church. All societies fall under this structure, but the complex social structure of a city makes urbanites take on even more diverse roles and positions. Urbanites must constantly encounter other groups and obtain resources to achieve success and self-realisation. To deal with such diverse groups, they have no choice but to have multiple identities instead of just one. This is like having multiple membership cards in one's wallet, utilising a different card for each unique situation and acting according to the group to which it belongs.

The idea of one person having multiple identities is an area that has already been studied in various academic circles. In some academic settings, the term "multiple identities" has been used to characterise multiple-personality disorder. However, while multiple-personality disorder describes a person who has multiple owners and has difficulty controlling them, multiple identity describes a person who has a single personality that is under strict control and shows aspects that are appropriate for each situation. For example, psychologist Kenneth J. Gergen explained people who possess multiple identities as being when the same person appears with a different mask for each situation. He argued that such multiple identities do not confuse the person, but rather, if used appropriately, it is an action that makes the person more socially and emotionally stable.[13]

Scholars of cultural acculturation have also studied people with multiple identities. They focused on urbanites and immigrants who had to give up their old identities and embrace a new one.

Everyone has several identities to some extent, but immigrants, people from foreign cultures, and people living in multicultural communities require considerably more multiple identities to survive. Becoming acculturated in a new society involves numerous stages. As they pass through these stages, the cultural momentum shifts. As such, every stage is ruled by different multiple ascriptive identities, and none of them is ruled by a single element.[14] For example, even after 25 years of immigration, a study group of Lithuanian immigrants had retained both their native and American identities.[15] They continue to live their native culture in parallel, no matter how engaged they are in mainstream American society.[16]

Possessing multiple identities may seem as though it could confuse the individual, but instead, these people efficiently utilise their various identities. Several features can be seen in their use of multiple identities.[17]

First, instead of becoming "alienated from white society or lack of identity [...] they have chances to express multiple identity, a good proportion of members of each ethnic group."[18] Despite not fully identifying with a particular society, they distribute their identities in such ways that help manage themselves in a multicultural environment rather than living a life lacking connection. In regard to such people moving back and forth between different cultures without fully belonging to one, Wallman states, "not because he lacks a single identity focus and is [therefore] 'in crisis', but because multiple identity is itself a healthy

---

13 Kenneth Gergen, "Multiple Identity: The Healthy, Happy Human Being Wears Many Masks," *Psychology Today* 12 (May 1972): 31–35.

14 Donald L. Horowitz, "Ethnic Identity," in Nathan Glazer and Daniel Moynihan (eds), *Ethnicity* (Cambridge, MA: Harvard University Press, 1975): 118.

15 Liucija Baskauskas, "Multiple Identities: Adjusted Lithuanian Refugees in Los Angeles," *Urban Anthropology* 6(2), (1977): 141–54.

16 Multiple fields, including sociologists and historians, showed interest in studies on people with multiple identities, and each field created and introduced its vocabulary according to its own characteristics. Among them are transnational subjectivities, translocational positionalities doing belonging, instrumental ethnicity, and so on. Anna Rastas, "Ethnic Identities and Transnational Subjectivities," in Paul Spickard (ed), *Multiple Identities: Migrants, Ethnicity, and Membership* (Bloomington, IN: Indiana University Press, 2013): 45–49; Serine Gunnarsson, "Doing Belonging: Young Women of Middle Eastern Backgrounds in Sweden," in Spickard, *Multiple Identities*, 88–110; Enzo Colombo and Paola Rebughini, "The Children of Immigrants in Italy: A New Generation of Italians?," in Spickard, *Multiple Identities*, 209.

17 S. Wallman, "Identity Options," in C. Fried (ed), *Minorities: Community and Identity* (Berlin, Heidelberg, New York, Tokyo: Springer-Verlag: Dahlem Konferenzen, 1983): 69–78.

18 Wallman, "Identity Options," 74.

choice."[19] As such, they use their multiple identities to make decisions based on the situation and context at the time, rather than committing to a single identity or association.

As the society gets reframed and becomes multiethnic and multicultural, the issue of having multiple identities becomes a matter not only to immigrants but also to ordinary urbanites.[20] As a result, urbanites take on different roles and positions at work and home, on weekends and during the week, and in online communities.

Multiple identities are like a person's abilities gained from exposure to different cultures and communities. Having numerous cultural frames while being integrated, they can interact and react appropriately within multicultural environments. Although their networks span across a wide range of social classes and cultures, these individuals have a great deal of control over their network. In addition, due to their dual-layered cultural setting, they can act as a bridge between their original culture and the secondary network groups with which they have connected.

Multiple identity holders function as bridges and this has immense missionary potential. Their bridging function can connect many groups who have been isolated and separated for an extended period. This is because these bridges may act as infrastructure allowing knowledge, values, trends, and materials that have previously remained on one side to be shared and diffused. Traditionally, good information and privileges have been restricted to specific groups and classes. However, the bridging function of the city's multiple identity holders allows such good things to flow smoothly to other classes, cultures, and groups previously overlooked. Among these good things that can flow across boundaries is the Gospel. God may have sent a new kind of people, the modern urbanites, to the church as a gift to let the good news flow through barriers. Then, it can be said that the complex and chaotic phenomenon of urbanisation contains an incredible opportunity for God's mission.

Missiological Reflection: Read Urban Individuals through God's Eye

Previously, we examined the unique characteristics of the secondary network of urbanites. Their network is diverse and scalable because the urban environment makes people proactive. Urban society makes individuals live in a dual-layered pattern, and the diversified secondary network makes them owners of multiple identities. Owners of these multiple identities are able to reconnect groups whose relationships have long been distrustful and hostile. These connectors can be bridges that reconnect the broken parts of the city and allow the good things on one side to flow to the other. As a result, Christians in the city must be aware of

---

19 Wallman, "Identity Options," 74.

20 J. Useem and R. Useem, "The Interfaces of a Binational Third Culture: A Study of the American Community in India," *Journal of Social Issues* 23(1), (1967): 130–43.

their incredible missionary potential. They must also be able to read and feel excited about the magnificent plan of the missional God who manages the city environment. Let us now examine what the city's Christians and churches will do considering this expectation.

Urban Believer's Doing: Knowing the Missionary Potential in You

Depending on how they use their gifts, urban Christians' dual-layered cultural setting and capabilities from their various identities can either be used for their greed or as a bridge for God.

First, Christians must remember that the urban environment's secondary networks and multiple identities are not intended for individual enjoyment and selfishness. Productive metropolitan environments, superior technology, and numerous individual rights and freedoms may cause Christians to abuse their privileges. As a result, the city's freedoms and opportunities can easily accentuate people's sinful natures of greed and self-indulgence. They do not let others enter their personal space and the increased individuality encourages people to heighten their desires. As such, this maximised freedom of choice can lead us to dangerous places. We are, in such ways, sinners. Furthermore, due to the nature of the city network, where people can participate in one group with a completely different image from what they showed to another group, they can easily create an image of themselves and hide behind it. In other words, cities are locations where we, as sinners, can quickly become arrogant, indulgent, and selfish.

Urban Christians must be cautious that the urban environment does not further amplify their sinfulness. This is because the freedom given to us is not "an opportunity for the flesh," but rather an opportunity to "serve one another" through love (Gal. 5:13). This is why the Apostle Paul regarded whatever things he gained as rubbish so that he may gain Christ (Phil. 3:7-9) Today, when freedom grows explosively and "my rights" are more important than ever, the Apostle Paul is God's message to us. Paul's restraining his own freedom and pursuing Christ acts as a message given to today's urban Christians by God. The voluntary limiting of one's freedom is an essential posture for urban believers to have a missional identity. Today's Christians must not prioritise enjoying the convenience of the city and fulfilling selfish dreams. Instead, we are called to be bridges of reconciliation and forgiveness for those who are constantly divided and competing.

Second, urban Christians must fully understand their potential as bridges and carefully accept the missionary potential God has given them. Sharing the Gospel is like connecting people on one side to the resources they need on the other side. Therefore, to be a bridge person, it is necessary to understand both sides. The Bible shows many cases of those with multiple identities who became bridge persons between multiple cultures. These people naturally possessed a dual-layered setting because of their multicultural background. For example, in the Old Testament, Queen Esther and her uncle Mordecai were an unfortunate minority who were taken captive to Babylon, the most advanced and powerful nation at the time. Mordecai raised Esther thoroughly with both Babylonian and Jewish identities (Esther 1). Later, Esther, who became queen when the entire Jewish population was on the brink of slaughter, connected King Ahasuerus and the Israelites (Esther 2:10, 20). Her role as a bridge saved their people and played a major role in bringing the name of God to glory throughout Babylon.

Not only Esther, but various types of connectors and owners of multiple identities used by God appear in the Bible. Among them are Paul who grew up in a diaspora family from an early age; Timothy who was born in a multiethnic family; Joseph, Daniel, and Nehemiah who lived as ethnic minorities of an empire; and Phoebe, Prisca, and Aquila, who lived abroad. In addition, there are numerous multicultural diasporas in the book of Acts and Romans 16. As such, the Bible introduces many figures with multiple identities who were used at the forefront of missions. As cities now become a forefront of mission, such Biblical figures offer much insight for today's urban Christians.[21]

The potential of Christians with multiple identities to become bridge persons of the Gospel is enough to make us excited. Such excitement can become the power to overcome the temptation to become selfish and is a motivation to restrain one's freedom voluntarily and to obey Christ.

Urban Church's Doing: A New Perspective to the Ministry Fields

What does God's sending of urban believers who hold diverse and expanded networks to urban churches tell us about His expectations for the urban church? What plan makes God send such Christians with multiple identities to the urban church? How should the church equip them differently from in the past? What alternatives should the church come up with if the cultural nature and information flow of Christians and non-Christians are indeed changing?

To stick with their God-given calling, the church first needs to be closely connected with its ministry environment. Just as the field represents the heart of the people in Jesus' parable, the field in which the church must work is the people to whom it minsters (Mt. 13:11-30). This means that understanding the fields begins by understanding the sheep that God left to the shepherd.[22] Therefore, the kind of people the church is filled with is a basic signpost to determine God's direction to the church ministry.

Only when the church has a good understanding of its field can it develop its own missional identity and carry out appropriate activities. It needs to know where the church members pour their lives into, what kind of people they usually

---

21 Roger S. Greenway and Timothy M. Monsma, *Cities: Missions' New Frontier*, 2nd ed. (Grand Rapids, MI: Baker Books, 2000), 82–90.

22 The theological foundation that the church is composed of a congregation is well-expressed in the concept of *Ekklesia*. *Ekklesia* as the designation of the Christian community suggests that the New Testament believers viewed the church as neither an edifice nor an organisation. This term is used as church in Matthew 16:16; Ephesians 1:23; Rome 16:16.

spend time with, what field they do business in, and what values they work with because this all tells what kind of people make up the church.

To do this, churches should be able to do the following.

First, the church must remember that its primary role is to equip the saints, not nurture the church itself (Eph. 4:12). This entails more than simply raising members who are dedicated to church activities. Instead, the church must help and nurture its sheep so they may stick to the correct path.

Second, churches must train and encourage people with multiple identities to communicate contextual messages in their fields through word and deed. Cities are becoming increasingly populated with groups that traditional churches find difficult to reach. On the other hand, believers with multiple identities can get along with others from different backgrounds. They can unlock the good that has remained within an exclusive group known as the church to anyone. They are people who understand how to share the Gospel by translating it into a format that can be used by businesses, institutions, neighbourhoods, and other organisations to which they belong. That is, Christians in the urban church are sheep in the pen who are able to communicate with other sheep outside the pen (Jn 10:16).

The Gospel can only exert its dynamics when contextualised to its listeners.[23] God wants the Gospel to be equally dynamic to every group of the city.[24] In other words, in any group or situation, the power and results that the Gospel originally intended must be present. If the Gospel is regarded as foreign or far from one's field of life, the message is destined to lose its dynamism. The challenge is whether today's church will be able to connect with the various groups in the city that have been disconnected for an extended period. If a traditional church is to serve a specific group in the city, it would need to recruit missionaries, budget for and train them over several years, spend much money, and hold countless meetings.

In this respect, dual-layered believers are a group with great potential to reconnect what is separated in this society. Surprisingly, God already has well-

---

23 Dean S. Gilliland, *The World Among Us: Contextualizing Theology for Mission Today* (Dallas, TX: Word, 1989): 3; Stephen B. Bevans, *Models of Contextual Theology* (Maryknoll, NY: Orbis, 2000): 27; Paul G. Hiebert, "Cultural Differences and the Communication of the Gospel," in Ralph D. Winter and Steven C. Hawthorne (eds), *Perspectives on the World Christian Movement: A Reader* (Pasadena, CA: William Carey Library, 1999): 381–82; Harvie M. Conn, *Eternal Word and Changing Worlds: Theology, Anthropology, and Mission in Trialogue* (Phillipsburg, NJ: P&R, 1984): 232.

24 John Parratt, *A Guide to Doing Theology*, 35, SPCK International Study Guide (London: SPCK, 2000): 19; Dean S. Gilliland, *Pauline Theology & Mission Practice* (Jos Plateau State, Nigeria: Albishir, 1983): 212; Charles H. Kraft, *Christianity in Culture : A Study in Dynamic Biblical Theologizing in Cross-Cultural Perspective* (Maryknoll, NY: Orbis, 1979): 320–23; Hiebert and Meneses, *Incarnational Ministry*, 164.

trained and earnest Christians active in all parts of the city. They have various membership cards in their wallets, which means they have trusted relationships with people the church struggles to approach. As such, God wants to fulfil his unchanging mission in a constantly changing city by sending new types of Christians to the urban church.

In the next part, we will go beyond the city's individuals to understand its groups and God's providence and missional plan within them.

THEME 2: URBAN GROUPS

NEW FRIENDS AND NEIGHBOURS ARE COMING

3. Connected People Become Groups

Story Box 2[1] – An Immigrant in Los Angeles Now Has New Neighbours

Liu, who lives in LA, is an American born of Chinese and Korean descent. His parents divorced when he was a teenager, and after that, Liu lived with his mother until marriage. When his mother struggled financially after the divorce, her relatives kept close by, helped them financially, and helped his mother find a job.

As an adult, Liu tried several different jobs. He worked as an employee in a small clothing factory, managed a coffee shop, and now works in a real estate office. Later, Liu married a Korean woman and had children. He goes to a Korean-affiliated church with his wife. As their economic situation improves and they live a married life, the Liu couple hardly see their relatives anymore. They only call Liu's mother, who lives alone, about once a week, and they meet at church on Sundays to have lunch together.

Liu is very friendly, so he talks endlessly once he starts a conversation with the neighbours. Nevertheless, despite living in the United States for a long time, he always feels that he is an immigrant and cannot enter mainstream society. In the past, Liu has worked as the secretary of the local badminton club. There are many Asians in the badminton club, so he is much more comfortable with the members. He is also active in an online community that discusses Asian American history. However, he moved to a cycling team after he injured his wrist while exercising. Due to his fluent English and sociability, he is also passionate about activities for the rights and interests of Asians at ethnic events and government activities. In short, Liu is known as a good neighbour in many groups.

Still, Liu can't escape this strange feeling of loneliness. Although he is active in many groups, it is still difficult to find true friends in any of them. While he has many friends, but he does not seem to have a soul friend. For him, churches and online discussion clubs are not just places for religious life and discussion. They comfort his loneliness and build self-esteem, so Liu considers them his friends and hometown. But the closeness often hurts Liu because his expectations of people are too high; it is why Liu had to move churches due to a recent clash with members. This time is his third time moving churches.

1 Liu is a friend of mine who lives in Los Angeles.

People live and create their identities among people. They gather and form groups, and these groups teach people survival skills, knowledge, relationships, passions, values, and formalities. Therefore, who one is today is the result of the groups one has lived in. These groups not only create one's identity but are also channels that provide advantages and disadvantages in one's life, like an investor's portfolio. In other words, the types of groups one associates with affect how many benefits or disadvantages one will achieve in one's life.

God made people meet each other by connecting them in groups. Through groups, he gives us the opportunity to create valuable relationships, understand people and society, and build ourselves. Therefore, belonging to a group is not only a responsible choice but also God's providence.

Compared to traditional societies, cities have more diverse groups to choose from. Urbanites are also able to select from many groups. An urbanite becomes an urbanite because they become a member of an urban group, learn urban patterns and values, and live a city life. In other words, urbanites can be active as urbanites because they belong to urban groups. Therefore, urban groups can be said to be the domains that form people as urbanites.

Liu from the story box 2 is also an urbanite and belongs to several groups. He belongs to several ethnic groups and cultures by birth, is a member of the family and kin, and must be part of the appropriate groups to have relationships with friends and neighbours and to pursue various jobs, social activities, religions, and hobbies. While Liu's personal qualities may have contributed as well, the different groups he has belonged to have shaped his life to be the way it is today.

By belonging to various groups, urbanites enjoy a sense of belonging, economic activity, emotional stability, and social benefits. The influence of these groups is so great that people often sense they belong to their small groups, such as their company or church, rather than to a large city.[2] As such, cities are comprised of various groups which are made up of members, thus people.

Socio-anthropologists classified communities formed closely around one individual (ego) as the primary group, and communities formed widely as the secondary groups.[3] Primary groups generally refer to very strong relationships such as those from birth or blood relations.[4] On the other hand, secondary groups are relationships that have been obtained through social activities. These

---

2 Fischer, *The Urban Experience*, 113.

3 Boissevain, *Friends of Friends*, 24; William G. Flanagan, *Contemporary Urban Sociology* (Cambridge; New York: Cambridge University Press, 1993): 22; Eames and Goode, *Anthropology of the City*, 157.

4 Fischer defines the Primary group as those "[…] that help shape our personalities, influence our values and opinions, encourage or restrain our actions, and that give us the most grace and the most grief. Our individual experiences of the world are filtered through these primary groups and largely interpreted in ways they have taught us. Fischer, *The Urban Experience*, 143.

secondary groups are networks that one connects with on becoming active in society.[5]

Urban people also have more freedom and choice when choosing a group. In other words, in a traditional society, individuals are often chosen by their groups or predestined, whereas urban societies are environments in which individuals often choose their own groups. In such an environment, the group to which one belongs can be said to be a packet that can give a glimpse of the individual's values, abilities, preferences, and background.

Meanwhile, inescapable loneliness and anxiety are pains that can plague all urbanites. It is the reason why they need groups even more. Furthermore, with new needs and various options, urbanites keep changing groups to find a place to soothe their loneliness and make themselves feel safer. Like Liu, who changed churches three times, urbanites constantly change groups to progress, relieve their loneliness, and not damage their reputation. Not only that, but as their needs change, urbanites may even distance themselves from groups they have been close to for a long time. This can be seen in Liu as he distanced himself from the relatives with whom he had once given and received much help and limited his primary relationship to his family. In this way, although urbanites change their groups and search for the direction of their lives, the issues of loneliness, anxiety, aspiration for success, and reputation are still not resolved and can stay alive in their hearts.

This chapter will examine how individuals in a city are connected with their groups and by which cohesion factors. Understanding these cohesion factors will show us how urbanites maintain networks with people important to them. First, for primary groups, we will examine the characteristics of urban families and kin. Afterward, the secondary groups will be divided into residential groups, groups in ethnicity, and socioeconomic and political institutions, and we will examine what groups exist within them. In particular, we will explore the characteristics of groups in the online space, where the activities of modern urbanites have increased rapidly.

The following are the key questions for this chapter.

- How do urbanites connect with the primary groups?
- How do they connect with friends and neighbours as urban residential groups?
- How do they connect with their ethnic groups?
- How do they connect with socio-political groups?
- How do they connect with online groups in cities?

Lastly, we will reflect missiologically on the role of urban Christians and churches.

---

5 Fischer includes residential community, formal associations, class and occupational groups, special-interest groups, and neighbourhoods as secondary groups. Fischer, *The Urban Experience*, 114.

Primary Groups

The most fundamental groups of people are family and kin. These relatives and family groups related by blood are representative of predestined groups. The concept of family differs slightly from culture to culture. In some cultures, all relatives are considered family, while others only regard the nuclear family as such. The concept of a family also differs from generation to generation. For grandparents, family may mean from themselves to their grandchildren, but grandchildren may only consider their parents and siblings as family.

Urbanites' primary groups have several characteristics. Firstly, not only have the types of families become diversified, but society is also receptive to such various types. There is also a significant sense of disparity between individuals' attitude toward their immediate family and their relatives.

The Nest of Variety Types of Families

In general, many societies consider the nuclear family the standard and basic family unit.[6] The nuclear family is one in which the parents and their children live in the same house.[7] However, different types of families other than the nuclear family exist in any society. For example, most societies have single-parent families, extended families (or relatives), childless families, blended or stepfamilies, and grandparent families. However, since these types of families have been perceived as not so-called "normal", their presence is not as significant. On the other hand, in cities, these various types of families are treated as legitimate members of the urban society, and the society has the conditions to provide various supports. For example, the heads of single-parent families must make more efforts and sacrifices to maintain the family. Nevertheless, cities have many facilities and systems that reduce the burden on single-parent families, such as educational facilities, regular commuting hours, after-school academies, and city-level support.[8]

In cities, childless families also feel relatively weak social pressure. In the traditional society, childless families are often not recognised as normal families, and they are even treated as socially immature. On the other hand, in an urban society, there are many cases in which people have no children as they must put all their energy into their careers and advancements, and there is often much less unspoken pressure to have children. At least in terms of their social life and career management, childless families live almost the same as other people.

---

6 According to the United States Census Bureau, 70% of children in U.S. lived in a nuclear family unit as of 2010. U.S. Department of Commerce, "America's Families and Living Arrangements: 2010," *United States Census Bureau* (blog), 2010, https://www.census.gov/population/www/socdemo/hh-fam/cps2010.html.

7 Conrad Phillip Kottak, *Cultural Anthropology*, 13th edn (Boston, MA: McGraw-Hill, 2009): 248.

8 According to the United States Census Bureau, 12.1% of minors in the U.S. live with single-parents in 2020: https://www.census.gov/data/tables/2020/demo/families/cps-2020.html Family Groups, Table FG10.

The number of remarried families and grandparent families also increases in the city. A remarried family is a case in which previously different families are united into one. As individualism and life expectancy increase along with economic growth, the urban society's atmosphere also becomes more accepting and understanding toward remarriage. Additionally, a grandparent family refers to a family where grandparents and grandchildren live without parents. In 2010, it was found that about 7% of children in the United States live with grandparents without parents due to their death, parental addiction, discord, or neglect.[9]

Lastly, the number of one-person family units increases significantly in cities. A one-person family is a case in which a person lives alone like a single person but is a sufficient family unit by themselves. Unlike singles in their early 20s, these one-person families refer to people who do not plan or feel the need to get married in the future or who live alone even if they have a family. There are many different types of one-person households, such as those who never get married, divorcees, widows, or those whose children have become independent adults. In urban society, such one-person families are rapidly increasing. This is because the urban environment provides sufficient facilities and products for single families to live, and the social awareness that accepts them is gradually growing. The increase of these non-family units creates great changes in the overall society, such as the city's economy, products, and architecture. For example, more single-serve food markets and single-person homes are emerging, and social gatherings where people living alone can socialise are increasing.

Other than this, there are many more types of families – such as children families, elderly families, adopted families, and multicultural families – and their numbers will increase in the future. Of course, these diverse family types exist in traditional societies as well, but the reason they stand out more in urban society is that individualism is common in society, which leads to an increase in anonymity, resulting in more diversity. This eventually creates a social atmosphere that allows one to be free from the standard family type. In such cases, the social security system and urban infrastructure positively help parents survive and raise their children.

Intimated Family, Estranged Kins

What characteristics do the family and kin networks in cities have compared to those in traditional societies? Usually, in traditional societies, the cohesion factor that creates a sense of family is present not only within the family but also among the entire village and relatives.[10] In other words, since the family is surrounded

9 U.S. Department of Commerce, "America's Families and Living Arrangements."
10 D.H. Olson, "Circulplex Model of Marital and Family Systems: Assessing Family Functioning," in F. Walsh (ed), *Normal Family Processes* (New York: Guilford, 1993): 10 4–37; Rebecca Sapp, "Family Conflict and Family Cohesion: Their Relationship to Youths' Problem Behaviors" PhD thesis, University of Tennessee. (Knoxville, TN: University of Tennessee, 2003).

by the whole town rather than being independent, while an individual is a part of their nuclear family, they are also strongly regarded as a member of their kin. Urban people, on the other hand, have a stronger bond with their immediate family than with their kin network. In other words, the identity of individuals as members of the nuclear family predominates. This is because, first of all, the living environment of urbanites supports them in leading a family-centred life. In a city that operates based on a time-centred work life, the commute times for adults and children are relatively predictable and the border between public and private lives is clear. As a result, they spend more time with family than with relatives. Children also become more attached to their family and immediate parents than to their relatives. Young and Wilmott, for example, report that London's middle class is very family-oriented and tends to want to live close to their parents even after they marry.[11]

The attitudes of urbanites toward their family networks are very different before and after they reach adulthood. Moreover, when a person gets married, their relationship with their parents changes as they belong to a new nuclear family. Liu, introduced earlier, also had close relationships with his single mother and relatives before marriage. However, his relationship with them rapidly diminished after marriage, and instead, he focuses on his nuclear family. Although Liu still has good memories with his mother and relatives, urbanites' busy daily lives and the Western-style family concept make Liu focus on his immediate family.

This does not mean that the city has only negative elements in its kin relationships. Rather, the city's developed transportation, communication media, and social environment make networks with relatives active. With easy-to-connect phone calls, e-mails, social media, and quick access to transportation, relatives can gather whenever they want.[12] The urban environment, which enables religious activities, various hobbies, and volunteer activities, also activates relationships with relatives. Liu calls his mother about once a week. He does not live very far from his mother, but they usually think it is sufficient to say hello over the phone. Since his mother has been working until recently after the divorce and is still in good health, it is not that difficult for her to live alone. Additionally, meeting at church on Sundays and having lunch together gives them much emotional fulfilment. Unlike rural kin networks, where one must stay close to others, urbanites can afford to only be as close as they want.

Usually, urbanites with many social resources have weak relationships with kin. In other words, poor or socially vulnerable people tend to be close to kin, while on the contrary, socially advantaged and self-sufficient people tend to depend more on social resources than kin. Therefore, the role of the extended kin

11 Michael Dunlop Young and Peter Willmott, *Family and Kinship in East London*, Reports of the Institute of Community Studies, 1 (Glencoe, IL: Free Press, 1957).
12 Christina Rufenacht, "2000 Technology Strengthens Family Bonds," *Women in Business* 52(1), (2000): 46.

is still essential for the poor and working classes.[13] For those with weaker social resources, their extended kin can be able to help with survival and success. This is even more evident in the lives of migrants,[14] as their relatives might act as a nest providing help.[15] Liu also received much help from his relatives after his mother divorced. As Asian immigrants, the scarce social resources made them more trusting and dependent on their relatives.

As social resources increase and self-reliance becomes possible, urbanites' cohesion factors for their networks disperse to various places. The social security system provided by national festivals, ancestral rites, common ancestors and history, and kin, which were cohesion factors in traditional society, do not significantly affect urbanites. Rather than meeting kin in person, urbanites maintain relationships by phone or e-mail. This is due to the specialised city life requiring them to devote too much energy to survival and success. Likewise, after Liu later had a job, he moved into mainstream society rather than among relatives and replaced his source of income with that from work. Moreover, because the sense of safety and socio-economic benefits provided by kin society in the past are now given by urban social facilities and social security systems, the relationship with kin becomes more distant.

One interesting point is that urban affluence and social security facilities also play a positive role in helping urbanites improve their relationships with their elderly parents. For example, in a field study conducted in China, contrary to expectations, the relationship between adult children and elderly parents was found to be better in cities than in rural areas.[16] This is because while rural areas are poor and people struggle to live in a small space, elderly parents in the city are more financially relaxed, can afford to have their own space, and have social

---

13 Theodore Caplow *et al.*, *Middletown Families: Fifty Years of Change and Continuity* (New York: Bantam, 1982): 195–223; Harry K. Schwarzweller, James S. Brown, and J.J. Mangalam, *Mountain Families in Transition; a Case Study of Appalachian Migration* (University Park, PA: Pennsylvania State University Press, 1971); James Watson, "Restaurants and Remittances; Chinese Emigrant Workers in London," in G. Foster and R. Kemper (eds), *Anthropologist in Cities* (Boston, MA: Little Brown, 1974): 201–11; Eugene Litwak, "Occupational Mobility and Extended Family Cohesion," *American Sociological Review* 25 (1960): 9–21; Eugene Litwak and Ivan Szelenyi, "Primary Group Structures and Their Functions: Kin, Neighbors and Friends," *American Sociological Review* 34 (1969): 465–81.

14 For example, Edward M. Bruner reported that Indonesian Batak people had stronger kinship after moving to a large city like Medan than when they lived in their native mountain villages. Mangin, *Peasants in Cities*, 123–24.

15 William Mangin, "Sociological, Cultural, and Political Characteristics of Some Urban Migrants in Peru," in Aidan Southall (ed), *Urban Anthropology: Cross-Cultural Studies of Urbanization* (Oxford: Oxford University Press, 1973): 318.

16 Martin King Whyte, "Postscript: Filial Support and Family Change", in *China's Revolutions and Intergenerational Relations* (Ann Arbor, MI: Center for Chinese Studies, University of Michigan, 2003): 305.

security such as health insurance. As a result, the relationships with their children also tend to be more relaxed.[17]

On the other hand, cities provide a convenient environment for people to live as (nuclear) families.[18] A routine city life, where people go home after work every day, allows urbanites to focus on their families after work or on weekends and make family planning more stable. Due to this regularity, the family increasingly becomes the only home for urbanites. Various ethnographic research has found evidence that urbanites still value family.[19] They bond with each other through modern activities, including unique leisure opportunities and hobbies and various household chores on weekends together. Likewise, Liu's mother also lives close enough to attend the same church as her son. Liu's nuclear family and his mother are always available when one side needs help, and she can easily visit on holidays and birthdays to reunite with her grandchildren again.

As such, the city is not a place that unconditionally weakens or strengthens people's kin and family networks. Rather, urbanites' primary family and kin networks are strengthened or weakened depending on their relatives' circumstances and social status and their individual priorities, emotions, and social abilities. Nevertheless, urbanites generally have weaker networks with relatives and stronger immediate family networks than those of traditional societies.

Residential Groups: Connectivity Rather than Distance

People naturally make friends and neighbours where they live or engage in social activities. A group of people who meet naturally like this form a residential group, which reflects the area in which they are active. Several cohesion factors play a role in the formation of such regional groups.

First, local points such as a local club or activity centre work to gather people. People join and engage in various structures and facilities such as nearby religious facilities, clubs, gatherings for hobbies and interests, socio-political activities, economic facilities, and educational facilities.[20] These activities naturally bring friends and neighbours together, compensating for their lack of

---

17 Whyte, "Postscript", 307.

18 P. Crowe, "Social Networks in an Urban Context," in M.C. Romanos (ed), *Western European Cities in Crisis* (Lexington, MA: Lexington Press, 1979): 67–80; T. Koyama, "Rural-Urban Comparisons of Kinship Relations in Japan," in R. Hill and R. Konig (eds), *Families in East and West* (Paris: Mouton, 1970): 318–37; E.G. Youmans, "The Rural Aged," *Annals* 429 (1977): 81–90; Claude S. Fischer, *To Dwell Among Friends: Personal Networks in Town and City* (Chicago, IL: University of Chicago Press, 1982).

19 John Gulick, "Urban Anthropology," in J.J. Honigman (ed), *Handbook of Social and Cultural Anthropology* (Chicago, IL: Rand-McNally College, 1973): 979–1029; Young and Willmott, *Family and Kinship in East London.*

20 Mithum Jacqueline, "Cooperation and Solidarity as Survival Necessities in a Black Urban Community," *Urban Anthropology* 2 (1973): 25–34.

strong personal relationships.[21] Liu, introduced earlier, becomes good friends with those who live next door, people in the church, and people in his badminton and cycling clubs. These are all local friends and neighbours in residential areas where he is comfortable going.

Second, emotional empathy for each other is a cohesion factor. The same memories, ethnic feelings, and time spent together strengthen relationships. Groups with such emotional empathy can be easily found in lower social classes or ethnic enclaves.[22] Because the poor and marginalised lack social resources to rely on, they are highly dependent and sympathetic toward each other because of their many similarities.[23]

The third cohesion factor is external threats and internal interests. For example, if a project led by a large capital company, such as railway construction or waste reclamation, brings disadvantages to an entire village, or if there is competition and conflict with other villages, the people unite rapidly. Conversely, issues in which internal interests are at stake also unite groups. For example, in a large apartment village, when residents' safety is threatened after a reduction of security guards, or when they receive a notice that their electricity bill is raised, the residents unite and target the management office to make a plea.

Friends in the City

Urbanites meet their neighbours and friends through local gatherings. These friends and neighbours exist both within cities and traditional societies. However, urban friends and neighbours are quite different from those in traditional societies. Unlike primary groups, one can make friends through social activities and all stages of life.[24] People meet friends in their neighbourhoods, with relatives, on the street, at work, in the same hobbies, at church, and so on.[25] Also, the conditions and definitions of friends are cultural.[26] For example, in the case of Asian urbanites, friends may have priority over blood ties because of the bonds formed between colleagues in their reputation-based culture.[27]

In a traditional society, friends and kin often overlap because they become friends with those who live close to them, such as neighbours and kin.[28] Even

---

21 Fischer, *The Urban Experience*, 120.

22 William Mangin, "Squatter Settlements," *Scientific American* 217(4), (1967): 21–29.

23 Helen Safa, "The Social Isolation of the Urban Poor: Life in a Puerto Rican Shanty Town," in I. Deutscher and E. Thompson (eds), *Among the People: Encounters with the Poor* (New York: Basic Books, 1968).

24 G.A. Allan, *A Sociology of Friendship and Kinship* (London: Allen and Unwin, 1979).

25 N. Shulman, *Urban Social Networks* (Toronto: University of Toronto, 1972).

26 Sherwood Lingenfelter, *Transforming Culture: A Challenge for Christian Mission*, 2 (Grand Rapids MI: Baker, 1998).

27 Mary Douglas, "Cultural Bias: Royal Anthropological Institute Occasional Paper" (London: Royal Anthropological Institute, 1978).

28 Kim, *Mission Strategy in the City*, 151–52.

when they become adults and lead their own social lives, most of their friends are still from the same ethnicity and live in the same neighbourhood. This phenomenon is also common for the people in the ethnic enclaves in cities.[29]

On the other hand, since there are many different ethnic groups and classes in cities, people can make different kinds of friends.[30] In other words, there is no reason not to cross ethnic boundaries when making friends.[31]

Depending on the requirements met, friends can be divided into several types of degrees of relationship. The conditions for becoming close friends are very strict, whereas they may be distant friends if the connection is not as deep. The various networks of urbanites include soul friends who have deep spiritual fellowship, colleagues who only exchange information and functions, friends with emotional connection and no business, people whom one knows because of proximity, and "just friends" that one runs into here and there.[32] According to a field survey, among the urbanites' friends, the proportion of "just friends" was high, and the types of friends were more diverse.

Neighbours in the City

Along with friends, neighbours are representative of the residential group. Traditionally, neighbours referred to the people who live next door.[33] They are people who are both close in distance and have active interactions which each other.

So, do urbanites have such neighbours? Michaelson argued that for a neighbour relationship to be formed, they must at least have closeness, perception of homogeneity, and mutual needs.[34] Traditionally, neighbours are people who live in the same neighbourhood, engage in economic activities together, and have frequent exchanges due to similar languages and cultures.[35] Therefore, they are people who meet the three conditions of Michaelson's neighbourhood formation. On the other hand, since urbanites seldom even knock on their apartment neighbour's door, one might argue that there are almost none who meet Michaelson's criteria in the city. However, this does not mean that urbanites have no neighbours. Although they may not have neighbours who live in the same area and who they meet often, urbanites still live among neighbours.

---

29 Kim, *Mission Strategy in the City*, 151–52.

30 Zang, Lipman, and McKeever, "Ethnicity and Urban Life in China," 21.

31 Kim, *Mission Strategy in the City*, 153.

32 "Just friends" means that a friend who is familiar but maintains a superficial relationship. Fischer, *To Dwell Among Friends*, 108–23.

33 In order for such a traditional neighbour to be created, Fischer stated that the following three conditions must be satisfied: functional interdependence, prior relationships, and lack of alternatives. Fischer, *The Urban Experience*, 131–34.

34 William M. Michaelson, *Man and His Urban Environment: A Sociological Approach*, Revisions (Reading, MA: Addison-Wesley, 1976): 190.

35 Kim, *Mission Strategy in the City*, 119.

Neighbours do not disappear in the city, but rather live scattered in various places instead of directly next door.[36]

Similar to the "just friend", Claude Fischer called people who live close simply in distance as "just neighbours."[37] In a traditional society, people living in the same neighbourhood were considered neighbours. In other words, those just neighbours in those societies are neighbours. However, neighbours in urban society have quite different characteristics. So, what are the characteristics of the city's neighbours?

First, neighbours in urban society do not becomc neighbours just because they live nearby. In other words, just neighbours in a city does not always mean being neighbours. Because of the city's large social environment, advanced transportation, and media, people's range of activities expands while their meetings with hyperlocal people decrease. As a result, they tend to often meet people at work, religious activities, or clubs while being separated from people who live closer by. In other words, the urbanite's neighbours are the distant neighbours who live far away. For this reason, the city's neighbours are scattered according to the route and time of one's frequent activities.

Second, the city's neighbour networks are relatively heterogeneous, and people do not know each other well. In traditional societies, the neighbour networks are often overlapped with other kinds of networks. For example, people living in a neighbourhood (residential network) may have the same ethnicity (ethnic network), and they mainly derive income from similar businesses (occupational network).[38] That is, even when doing other work, the neighbours reappear and work together. Contrastingly, the urban neighbours' networks are dispersed and do not overlap with other networks. Therefore, neighbourhood networks tend to be very heterogeneous because, except for the fact that they are neighbours, members live in almost different worlds.

Third, urbanites also meet their neighbours through activities in proximity groups. A proximity group is a group that meets the various interests and needs of urbanites, such as religious life, hobbies, education, interests, politics, and civic activities.[39] People share ideas and information in these groups, achieve fellowship by sharing activities and time, pursue individual and common interests, and realise their ideals.

As such, urban neighbours also meet the conditions for being neighbours – closeness, a sense of identity, perception of homogeneity, and mutual needs –

36 William M. Michaelson defined the neighbourhood as follows: "[…] crucial factors in active neighbourhood interactions are (1) actors' perceptions of homogeneity with those who live close to them and (2) an awareness of mutual needs that can be met in terms of propinquity." Michaelson, *Man and His Urban Environment*, 190.

37 Fischer, *The Urban Experience*, 131.

38 Kim, *Mission Strategy in the City*, 126–29; Eames and Goode, *Anthropology of the City*, 160–215.

39 Greenway and Monsma, *Cities*, 124.

despite not living in the same location as traditional neighbours.[40] Urbanites likely spend much more time with their co-workers than the person next door.

So far, we have discussed how the concept of friends and neighbours for urbanites' residential groups differs from that of the past. We have seen that these neighbours and friends also include translocal people that urbanites often meet, no matter if they live far away or close by. In this way, a residential group in the city is not tied to a time and place as in the past but is instead a gathering of people who often meet and do activities together at an agreed time and place.

Groups in Ethnicities: Naturally Connected but Changing

The city's large size can acknowledge diversity more and provide more opportunities for ethnicities to mix.[41] The ethnic groups of these cities constantly go back and forth between cultural assimilation and cultural continuation to establish their own identity. Cities make it impossible for any ethnic group to avoid its influence. In particular, as the generations pass, the people of a city increasingly assimilate to the city's culture. At the same time, they try to maintain their own culture. Urban ethnic groups work together, speak the same language, and work in groups to create a powerful force that preserves their original culture. For this cultural continuation to be possible, urban ethnic groups must have various cohesion factors within them.

Among the cohesion factors, a sufficient number must be secured for the continuous development of the group. When a new ethnic group first migrates to a city, their number is very small and their presence is insignificant. Especially when they move to an area that is more well off, migrants naturally have weak pride in their culture and language because their influence and ability to survive are weak. Therefore, they may not reveal their original identity and they try to assimilate into mainstream society. However, as the number of migrants increases, they gradually form their own society. When the number of migrants exceeds a certain number, or critical mass, the migrants' ability to survive is stabilised, they develop cultural pride, and even create their own new culture.

Second, spaces where the same ethnic group can continuously gather also allow them to achieve cultural continuation. These are the ethnic enclaves or locations run by ethnic groups. For example, Little Bangladesh and Chinatown have various events and facilities including stores, restaurants, convenience facilities, religious places, grievance centres, hospitals, social welfare facilities, broadcasting stations, ethnic schools, and ethnic soccer teams.

Third, economic institutions and socio-political networks such as stores, businesses, social projects, and political activities run by the same ethnic group also provide appropriate environments for cultural maintenance. For example, Liu (introduced earlier) used his English skills, the relationships he formed with Asian Americans, and the knowledge he had accumulated at Asian American

40 Michaelson, *Man and His Urban Environment*, 190.
41 Fischer, *The Urban Experience*, 80–82.

history discussion groups to engage in socio-political activities representing their rights and interests.

Fourth, conflicts, persecution, or competition also unite ethnic groups. Efforts to protect the interests and self-esteem of one's own ethnic group in a multi-ethnic society create the power to unite groups. For example, in the 1880s, Italian immigrants were subjected to harsh criticism and persecution from the mainstream American public. However, such public opinion actually united them and they eventually developed Italian-American pride and identity.[42]

Finally, the revival of migrants' original hometowns enables ethnic groups to revive. The image of the migrant's home country has a significant influence on their social status and perception. Minority groups who have migrated to more developed countries usually want their children to adopt the language and culture of the new place. On the other hand, when the status of their home country rises, their self-esteem increases and they try to recover their language and culture again.

Despite this cohesion, the ethnic groups in the city continue to change. The reason why groups in the city change is because the group and its members change.[43] Countless factors bring change among groups within ethnicities, including departure from the traditional religion, intermarriage, public education, culture in mainstream society, and mass media such as TV. As a result, they become members of another society and naturally absorb its social identity and values. In this way, ethnic groups in cities set their own direction while repeatedly changing and continuing. Such groups affected by these two forces and the individuals within them come to have a dual identity.[44]

Socio-Econo-Political Groups are Flourishing

Urbanites naturally form diverse groups for economic, social, and political activities. The city's ability to actively engage in social activities was possible thanks to the creativity and technological support of the people and their desire to prosper and realise their ideals. These include economic activities such as work-life, social groups such as hobbies, club activities, religious activities, and political groups for the realisation of ideals and interests. With advanced transportation facilities and media, people can easily find the people and information they want, and as a result, groups that can realise these ideals are quickly born. The establishment of such voluntary organisations and institutions transforms the past system – in which representative organisations such as the

42 Luciano J. Iorizzo and Salvatore Mondello, *The Italian Americans*, revised (Boston, MA: Twayne, 1980): 236–38.

43 Stephen Cornell, "Discovered Identities and American Indian Supratribalism," in Paul Spickard and W. Jeffrey Burroughs (eds), *We Are a People: Narrative and Multiplicity in Constructing Ethnic Identity* (Philadelphia, PA: Temple University Press, 2000): 98.

44 Kim, *Receptor-Oriented Communication for Hui Muslims in China*, 2018, 34: 98–105.

government or religious institutions took leadership – into a multiple nuclei society where various social, political, and economic groups take leadership. Such a multinuclear society provides an environment where citizens can participate in various social driving forces rather than one, and as a result, citizens live with multiple diverse memberships.

The social, economic, and political groups to which urbanites belong can be broadly classified into proximity groups, economic groups, and other governmental and non-governmental groups.

First, regardless of their background, urbanites seek proximity groups of people with similar goals for their interests, self-actualisation, emotional needs, or hobbies. In this proximity group, the person's current interests and abilities are more important than the person's background. For example, in parental gatherings, the fact that the children attend the same school creates proximity between parents. In a place like this, it is more important to know each person's proximity factors rather than their ethnic background or social status.[45] As such, a sense of homogeneity is formed by the common hobby in a cycling club, the same denomination in a church, the spirit for service in a medical service group, and common values for a political party. In recent years, communities based on such similarities have formed and grown in online spaces as well. Cities mass-produce incredibly diverse proximity groups because the urban environment stimulates people to new desires and constant development. These needs are difficult to satisfy with only the information and resources provided by the primary, ethnic, or residential groups discussed above.

Second, urbanites gather in economic groups to engage in economic activities. Cities provide countless jobs and, for urbanites, these jobs play into their status.[46] In a traditional society, status determines occupation, whereas, in cities, occupation determines status.[47] For example, people think that the pilot of an aircraft is of a higher status than a taxi driver. It is not only because the pilot's salary is higher but also because they and their workplace have higher social awareness.

Since status and economic power are important and pressing issues that must be well-protected for social mobility, the upper classes need each other even more. Because status and income are so important to these people, they must consider whether their national consciousness, past friends, relationships with local people, leisure activities, friendships, donation activities, and social activities help maintain their status.[48] Conversely, the socially disadvantaged do

45 Roger Greenway introduced three channels through which information can flow within a city: the ethnic channel, the class channel, and the social group channel. Greenway and Monsma, *Cities*, 124.

46 Status is, of course, a broader concept than merely occupation. We will take a closer look at the social status in the city in a different section.

47 Paul G. Hiebert and Eloise Hiebert Meneses, *Incarnational Ministry: Planting Churches in Band, Tribal, Peasant, and Urban Societies* (Grand Rapids, MI: Baker Books, 1995): 287–89.

48 David Jacobson, *Itinerant Townsmen* (Menlo Park, CA: Cummings, 1973).

unskilled, short-term, low-income, and labour-intensive jobs. In particular, migrants who lack social resources tend to be driven into occupations in certain fields such as hospitality, factories, and so on, based on these ethnic-based niches.[49]

Third, urbanites engage in governmental and non-governmental groups for national policy and realisation. Usually, the state establishes different types of units of local governments such as various municipalities, towns, villages, cities, and counties in each region to govern and collect opinions from the people. Good examples are the DMV, SSN offices, district offices, police stations, fire stations, and so on. In addition, government-run institutions and companies such as public schools, state-owned enterprises, and railroad corporations are also important state institutions that support cities.

Non-profit organisations (NPOs) or Non-Governmental Organisations (NGOs) are organisations that are led by civilians regardless of government institutions. These are voluntary, non-state, and non-economic associations run by citizens for self-fulfilment and for the public good in what is known as civil society. These include religious groups, cultural groups, academic associations, independent public opinion media, sports and leisure associations, forums, citizen plazas, civic activist associations, political parties, labour unions, and so on.

Unlike NGOs, governance is an institution that works among the government, civic groups, and communities.[50] Governance is an institution that balances the government and the market and enables the state and private organisations to voluntarily participate, consolidate, communicate, and collaborate.[51] Governance builds collaborative networks to help states, citizens, and markets recognise and interdepend upon each other.[52] Because governance has

---

49 Harold Gould, "Lucknow Rickshawallas: The Social Organization of an Occupational Category," *International Journal of Comparative Sociology* 6 (1965): 27–47.

50 Leon Lindberg, "Economic Governance and the Analysis of Structural Change in the American Economy," in John L. Campbell, J.R. Hollingsworth, and L.N. Lindberg (eds), *Governance of American Economy: Structural Analysis in the Social Sciences* (Cambridge: Cambridge University Press, 1991): 3–34; Roger Hollingsworth and Robert Boyer, *Contemporary Capitalism: The Embeddedness of Institutions* (Cambridge: Cambridge University Press, 1997).

51 In the early days, governance was mainly state-led, supporting state-led policies or pursuing general interests from the government's point of view. After that, this governance gradually expanded into a globalised area or, conversely, developed into a local governance with expertise and specificity. Wolfgang Streeck and Philippe Schmitter, "Market, State, Community, and Association? The Prospective Contribution of Interest Governance to Social Order," in *Private Interest Government: Beyond Market and the State* (London: Sage, 1985).

52 Jon Pierre breaks down four types of city-local governance: managerial governance, organisational governance, growth governance, and welfare governance. J. Pierre, "Models of Urban Governance: The Institutional Dimension of Urban Politics," *Urban Affairs Review* 34(3), (1999): 372–96.

participation, empowerment, division of power, autonomy, and equality, the organisation is formed to be relatively participant-centred and network-based.[53]

Online Groups Are Another City Community

As traditional print media and wave media such as TV and radio lose prominence to digital media, it is not an exaggeration to say that almost all the numerous groups in cities already mentioned exist online as well. Primary network relationships such as family interact more online than in real life, and neighbours share necessary information about the neighbourhood with people of the same zip code using their smartphones. Social, economic, and political interest groups also abound such as digital community associations, stock investment, and citizen opinion forums. Among the online groups, the growth of the proximity group is prominent. Groups for high school friends, churches, dog lovers, political support, environmental protection, and countless other purposes are constantly being created and deleted.

Online groups have both similarities and differences from offline groups.[54] Because online group activities allow asynchronous interaction, accurate communications can be recorded whenever convenient compared to offline groups.[55] In addition, both on- and offline space can be utilised as needed.

Yi Jong Seo organised these online communities by type and purpose.[56] Community types were further divided into those of the church, theatre, and cafes. In the church-type, one leader leads the remaining members just like a pastor leads the sheep. For example, experts with extensive knowledge in the field lead historical discussion or cancer-fighting communities. A theatre-type community is a society of people who have interests, values and hobbies in a shared field, such as clubs for camera lovers, environmental protection, and vegetarians. Lastly, cafe-type communities are those whose purpose is to get to know new friends. For example, groups for high school alumni, people who like songs from the 70s, or people living in the same area consist of members with homogeneous qualifications and backgrounds.

Yi Jong Seo further divided the online community into five categories by purpose: hobby, discussion, locality, age group, community service, and daily

---

53 Sangpil Park, *NGO Hak* (Seoul: Arke, 2011): 316.
54 Robin Hamman, "Introduction to Virtual Communities," *Cybersociology: Magazine for Social-Scientific Researches of Cyberspace*, Issue 2, 20th November 1997, [Available at: http://www.cybersociology.com/files/2_1_hamman.html], [Last accessed: 24th December 2023]; Myungsoo Kang, *Dijitel Sidae Community Hualyong Junliak [Strategy for Community Building in the Digital Age]* (Kyung Gee, Korea: Korea Academic Information, 2006): 41–42.
55 A more detailed definition of virtual space and virtual community is explained in chapter 5.
56 Yijong Suh, *Internet Community Wa Hangook Sahue [Internet Community and Korean Society]* (Seoul, Korea: Hanwool, 2002): 106–22.

life.[57] A hobby community is a community where members' hobbies are the central topic to enjoy, share experiences, and discuss information together. A discussion club is a type of community that provides a space for in-depth discussions with experts on topics such as homosexuality, philosophy, history, and the environment. A locality community aims to exchange information and promote bonds between people from the same hometown or school or living in the same area. In an age group community, people of similar ages can socialise, discuss interests, and share benefits. Lastly, community service and daily life communities are gatherings who help people in need. For example, the Let's Overcome Cancer club is operated not only to exchange disease-related information but also to promote friendship and encouragement between cancer patients and their families.

As mentioned earlier, cities create far more groups compared to traditional societies. This phenomenon has accelerated even more as groups have moved online. As online technology develops and people become accustomed to the online environment, the boundary between online and offline gradually disappears, and people freely switch between the two. With its development in transportation and environmental conditions that allows individuals to realise their interests and hobbies, the urban environment promotes the use of the online space to its maximum. Changes in social perception, increase in individual needs, development of technology, and the advent of a multiple nuclei society have opened a new dimension in urbanites' secondary social network. As a result, new on- and offline groups in the city continue to form, maintain, and perish.

Missiological Reflection:
Us, Who Are Sent to the Groups as Good Neighbours

We meet neighbours and friends through groups. God uses the group and the people in it to shape the self. Who one is today is the result of the groups that one has been part of through God's providence. God puts us in our groups to allow us to come to know Him, to enrich our lives, to equip ourselves, and for self-fulfilment. Therefore, the questions "Who am I?" and "In what group have I grown up?" are inevitably very similar. This question is also an important topic to address to correctly shape one's future. Choosing a good group is an important and responsible act for deciding one's future self.

Not only that, but God sends us to groups to share good things with people (Gal. 6:10). In other words, we are sent with a missionary identity to the groups we belong to now. In this way, our existence is made up of the groups we meet in God's providence, the groups we choose responsibly, and the identities we have been sent to. So now, let us see what position the city's Christians and churches must have in the presence of its numerous groups.

---

57 Suh, *Internet Community*, 122–40.

Urban Christian Identity: Good Neighbours Connecting the Disconnected

God sends urban Christians to many groups. When we are with our neighbours and colleagues, we are not just spectators who leave after fulfilling our own goals. This is because those who are sent should be good neighbours who give hope and good news to those around them.

A person who is sent to be a good neighbour first tries to see the group they belong to as their ministry field (Mt. 5:13). In other words, the first step for a person who has been sent by God is to be a good neighbour to those with whom they spend much of their time. Therefore, the urban Christians should not confuse their ministry fields with the ministry in the church. Although the church is a spiritual home, a safe zone, and a community that offers much empathy, it is not the place we live. Usually, modern believers spend far more time with people outside the church than within. Therefore, it can be said that our sent field is outside the church (Mk 12:31).

A good neighbour is respected within the domain of the real needs of their peers in the group. All people have similar problems and needs as human beings. In other words, most of the problems that non-Christians face in their lives are problems that Christians also experience. Being a good neighbour means coming up with a more complete and correct answer to these problems than non-Christians. Such people, although not usually popular, rouse the respect of non-Christians. This trust that has been built on a daily basis makes people want to come to us first when they are in crisis, just as the robbed traveller desperately needed a good Samaritan.

Also, a good neighbour is a courageous meddler. In the group, people not only expose themselves to a very limited extent, but also try not to invade each other's privacy. In other words, it is polite to be indifferent. However, one who is sent by God does not merely be polite to others and watch from afar. This is because a fragrance is a fragrance only when it can stimulate the interest of others. To truly love, we must enter others' lives. Christians should be able to knock on other people's lives, although it is uncomfortable.

Jesus also expects Christians to be good and missionary neighbours in their primary networks, such as amongst family and relatives, and in their secondary networks such as neighbourhoods and social activities.

Identity of the Urban Church: Transformation for Urban People

What kind of identity should the church have to fully nurture members and serve as a lighthouse to the community in an urban society composed of various groups? What should change in the churches of today's cities so that the members can be sent to their group and serve as good neighbours? Can the urban church maintain the traditional view of neighbours and communities?

As Charles Van Engen said, the church is a place that gathers and scatters.[58] It is a community that gathers believers first and nurtures them with the Word of God. It is also the starting point for the members to be scattered into the world to act as light and salt. To be scattered into the world does not mean to go without direction, but to go to where they are sent. Urban Christians leave the church on Sundays and routinely disperse into their own groups. In other words, today's urban Christians are already living a life of back and forth between the church and their field. The church's job is to encourage and support these Christians to become urban bridges, connecting the disconnected among their neighbours, healing those who have encountered robbers, introducing Jesus, and becoming role models and people needed for the group. To become an encouraging and supportive church, the urban church should be able to make at least the following cognitive changes.

First, we must redefine the concept of neighbour. Traditionally, the churches have mixed the practice of faith with activities within the church and, as a result, zealous believers tended to devote much time and attention to the church. As a result, their attention is primarily focused on their neighbours inside the church, and churches naturally required more programmes and facilities to grow and sustain themselves. However, with urbanisation, believers increasingly spend more time with their neighbours outside of the church. Given that neighbours form through social networks, urban churches' neighbours are no longer just inside the church, but wherever their members are active.

Therefore, if the members participate excessively in church activities, or if they are taught that such activities are the only way to work for God, they would be confused about who their neighbours are. Furthermore, they would be confused about where they were sent. Therefore, the urban church must ensure that the members do not stay confined to activities within the church more than is necessary.

Of course, Christians must be sufficiently nurtured in the church and live as church community members. This nurturing refers to perfecting the members and helping them to grow to maturity. Living as mature Christians means remaining intact even in their fields or contexts and maintaining their identities as people sent by God. In other words, they should be taught how to be salt and light to their homes, relatives, neighbours, and friends in their work and social lives after they are scattered among various groups in the city.

This new paradigm requires much change in the church's identity, the content of its nurturing, its leadership, and the abilities of its leaders for it to become suitable for the urban setting. These changes indeed come as threats and burdens for church leaders who have been prepared and trained traditionally. However, such changes do not mean abandoning the fundamental identity and leadership of the church. Rather, we must see it as God's opportunity and challenge to make the church more contemporary and church-like. The fact that believers are

58 Charles Van Engen, *God's Missionary People: Rethinking the Purpose of the Local Church*, 6th edn (Grand Rapids, MI: Baker Books, 2001).

already active in various groups is God's amazing missionary opportunity for the scattered church. By allowing people of different religions, ethnic groups, classes, and occupations to naturally engage in activities in the same place or online space, God provides opportunities for missions unimaginable in traditional societies. Therefore, to become a truly dispersed church, it must train its members to be the object of admiration and praise by the nonbelievers around them and know what kind of good news is appropriate for them even in a completely different environment from the church.

In this way, God is providing today's urban churches with opportunities that were previously unimaginable. With this expectation, in the next chapter, we will study people's attitudes toward their groups and look at the new urban unreached groups that emerge despite strong Christian influence.

4. Is the Old Wineskin Enough to Change Urban Groups?

The city is like a living creature, constantly changing every day. On the surface, the city seems to change because its buildings and transportation facilities change; in reality, it is because the people inside it change. This is because constructing new buildings and transportation facilities first requires the minds of the people who build them. Conversely, change in the city also changes people. Accelerated transportation facilities, the development of media, and new parks are sure to make a difference in the lives of urbanites.

Furthermore, change in the city is driven by change in groups. Earlier, we looked at the many different groups living in the city. Because these groups are units made up of people, change in cities is therefore caused by change in the people and their communities, and thus in groups. Therefore, these cities, people, and groups can be said to be agents that cause change in one another.

With this in mind in this chapter, we will consider the changes that groups in the city undergo. Additionally, we will address new missional opportunities and challenges that newly emerging groups offer.

To this end, here are the key questions for the chapter:

- What are the characteristics of the changing groups?
- How do people in the city organise their groups?
- What are the missional opportunities and challenges given by the urban groups?
- How are neo-unreached groups created, and how should the church think of them?

Based on the objective facts learned through these questions, the Missiological Reflection section will point out the limitations of the church's geographical region-based and programme-driven traditions and the leadership of seminary trained pastors. As an alternative, the section will propose a new identity for urban Christians, an alternative nurturing system for the church, a new type of missions organisation, and urban leadership as a new wineskin.

City Groups Are Changing

Urban groups are full of life and ever-changing. This is because the urban environment gives the groups enough forces and conditions to cause such change. Groups are independent while also being connected and interacting diligently with other groups.[1] Such connection and change are due, above all, to the initiative of the group's members, that is, the urbanites and their rich individual capacities. Now, let us examine this in detail.

City Groups Are Interconnected

Groups in the city are associated with a much wider variety of groups than traditional societies. This kind of connection between groups is possible because its members are connected to various groups. Ulf Hannerz states that contrary to traditional society, in urban society "life takes place on a multiplicity of separate stages […] And audiences are different each time."[2] As such, urbanites are more diversely connected than we think. For example, as introduced at the beginning of the previous chapter, Liu has been associated with numerous groups through online clubs, real estate offices, badminton club, churches, and relatives. These people around him were what made Liu possess the values and knowledge he has today. At the same time, Liu redistributes the information and worldviews that he has received to his groups.

Unlike cities, inter-group interaction in traditional communities has many limitations for various reasons. Even within the same ethnic group, there are differences in economic power, status, family and background, and access to power and these limited exchanges practically with people from other classes or far away. Interaction with other ethnic groups was even more difficult due to regional, linguistic, and cultural distance and hostility. As a result, people had no choice but to have most of their exchanges with people of the same class in the same ethnic group, especially with those close by. Such an environment caused groups to create their subcultures and develop their own identities, organisations, traditions, and lifestyles. When multiple numbers of ethnicities co-exist, people become even more segregated. Language and cultural barriers, as well as frequent confrontations and prejudices between other ethnic groups, made them even more confined within their own social barriers.

In contrast, groups in the city are heavily interconnected. Interactions between groups in the city are inevitably active because they are connected like parts of a body. For example, although arms and legs move independently, they rely heavily on each other. Likewise, while urban groups are independent entities, they are interconnected and interdependent.

Meanwhile, urban groups function and interact within themselves and with each other because the different people within them play their appropriate roles. Intergroup interactions and members' interactions with the outside become cause and effect for each to accelerate such interactions. When a group interacts with another, their members interact with each other, which in turn creates further change within the group. Due to these dynamics, urban groups are bound to be interrelated.

---

1 Fischer, *The Urban Experience*, 37–38.
2 Hannerz, *Exploring the City*, 232.

The fact that groups are connected means that they have channels of information to interact through. This information flows on the group level and also on the individual level. Such interaction with the outside affects the group's original values and behaviour, eventually stimulating change within it. As such, the city's groups interact with each other tremendously, and large amounts of information and values flow through these channels.

City Groups Are Vibrant

Incredibly diverse groups come together and connect to create a city. Urban groups are not passive or static but rather very active and motivated. A city can be seen as an entity made up of such active groups. Scholars went through extensive debate and fieldwork before realising the obvious fact that cities being made up of groups was a major aspect of understanding a city.

Urban scholars started paying attention to urban groups after the development of research on urbanism. The Chicago Schools developed the study of urbanism in the United States from the beginning of the 20th century. Early Chicago Schools – later called determinists[3] – assumed that the city was a homogeneous object, tried to identify the characteristics of the city, and sought solutions to city problems through the unified view. This perspective of homogeneity later became the basis for the melting pot theory. The determinists theorised that any group, once it enters the melting pot of the city, gradually melts, absorbs, and gives up its distinctive features.[4] However, some urban scholars have drawn attention to groups that retain their original culture and habits even within the city. These scholars, later named compositionists, found that numerous types of groups, such as kinship, ethnicity, residence, occupation, lifestyle, and similar social attributes, maintained their characteristics over time rather than melting into the city.[5] Therefore, for these compositionists, a city was a collection of various groups that kept their identity.[6] Based on this, compositionists described

---

3 Forerunners of the Chicago School included Georg Simmel, Robert Ezra Par, and Louis Wirth. They were the first urbanologists to be interested in the psychological state of urbanites rather than the city itself in urban studies. Sennett, *Classic Essays on the Culture of Cities*; Park and Burgess, *Introduction to the Science of Sociology, Including the Original Index to Basic Sociological Concepts*; Simmel, "The Metropolis and Mental Life."

4 Andrew M. Greeley, *Ethnicity in the United States: A Preliminary Reconnaissance* (New York: Wiley, 1974): 305; T. Devos and M.R. Banaji, "American = White?" *Journal of Personality and Social Psychology* 88(3), (2005): 447–66.

5 The term "compositional theory" was established by Claude S. Fischer in his book "The Urban Experience." Fischer, *The Urban Experience*, 32.

6 Herbert Kotter, "Changes in Urban-Rural Relationship in Industrial Society," in Nels Anderson (ed), *Urbanism and Urbanization* (London: Brill, 1964): 22; Richard Dewey, "The Rural-Urban Continuum," in Albert N. Cousins and Hans Nagpaul (eds), *Urban Man and Society: A Reader in Urban Sociology* (New York: Alfred A. Knopf, 1970): 82.

the city as a mosaic of social worlds.[7] Compositionalism has considerable value and meaning – it compensates for the shortcomings of determinism, but it also tends to ignore the dynamics of change around the group.

In an attempt to overcome the limitations of determinism and compositionalism, the next generation of urban scholars, led by Claude S. Fischer, paid attention to the phenomenon in which urban groups influence each other. These scholars, later called subculturalists, found that, although cities were made up of groups, they did not stand still or change unconditionally but rather exchanged influence between their surrounding groups. People in different social worlds often do "touch" through a common code (functional language), just as youth groups, companies, senior citizens' associations, and Chinese groups in the same city influence each other, and help, conflict with, and complement each other through various interests. Above all, urban complexity is the most powerful force that makes the urban groups have more diverse and vibrant inter-subcultural relationships than their rural counterparts.[8]

Groups in a vibrantly changing city influence other groups around them, and this influence even goes beyond the surrounding groups to stimulate the entire city to be active. In this respect, it can be said that the constructivist view of the city simply being a mosaic of subcultural groups is lacking. Instead, it is more realistic to view a city as the integration of subcultural groups that are alive, vibrant, and functional.[9]

Urban groups affect and are affected by the larger worlds of which they are a part. In some cases, an event that started in a small group may spread throughout the city, and its influence may even last until hundreds of years later. For example, Xi'an in China is famous as a city that fuses the ancient Tang dynasty and ancient Chinese Buddhist culture. This fusion culture began in 654 AD, when the high Buddhist monk Xuanzang brought Buddhist scriptures from India to Xi'an. Afterwards, Buddhist architectural styles and images spread beyond Buddhist groups to the entire city of Xi'an. In this way, some groups spread their influence throughout the city. Conversely, the city also influences urban groups, meaning that such groups reflect the city's overall character to those who join them. As ancient Buddhism and Tang culture became Xi'an's main image, any unrelated groups were also influenced by the whole of Xi'an. For example, numerous small groups related to this cultural heritage, such as technology, business partners, arts and culture, schools and academic societies and trade

---

7 Duncan Timms, *The Urban Mosaic: Towards a Theory of Residential Differentiation* (Cambridge: Cambridge University Press, 1971): Chapter 1.

8 Fischer says, "According to subcultural theory, the signs of disorganisation appear, not because social worlds break down, and people break down with them, but quite the reverse – because social worlds are formed and nurtured." Fischer, *The Urban Experience*, 39.

9 The subcultural group theory revealed its limitations as the social network theory that appeared later. Social network theory showed that even those groups are not the smallest unit, but the individual is the smallest unit that makes up the city.

businesses, reflect the culture of Xi'an. Such vigorous activity of urban groups change themselves and those around them.

City Groups Become Proactive

Group change is the reaction of members and leaders after evaluating internal and external stimuli in the light of their identities and interests. Since there are constantly various stimuli inside and outside the group, it is rare for groups to remain the same. Especially in cities, since group members have diverse networks, external stimuli and challenges flow into the group more easily. Although the patterns of change for groups in the town are very complex and varied, they can be summarised into at least five types of change – intensification, extinction, conversion, continuation, and new birth.[10]

First, among the urban groups, some groups change toward further intensification of their existing identity and power. They change into a more rational and strengthened form while maintaining their identity and values. This is the case when a church or religious organisation implements technology not previously used, and the group's membership diversifies, bringing together different races and social classes. However, this intensifies the members' values and core identity.

Second, the influence of cities can also make a group become extinct. Groups no longer needed by people are bound to disappear. Usually, this process of extinction proceeds as members within a group move to another or are only formally affiliated. Factors that previously played important roles but are not desperately required by urban society, such as regular gatherings of relatives, family associations, or companies that do not adapt to the digital age, increasingly lose their need to exist.

Third, groups in the city are converted into new forms. As the theory of determinism explains, the city's powerful forces cause groups to change.[11] This change is also due to change within its members. The more conservative or long-established the group is, the more painful these changes are.[12] Nevertheless, the group has no choice but to face the movement of change, as members are already exposed to new ideas from other networks.

---

10 David Burnett identified four results after worldview change: demoralisation, submersion, conversion, and revitalisation. David Burnett, *Clash of Worlds* (Eastbourne: Monarch, 1990): 33; 122; 125–36.

11 Simmel, "The Metropolis and Mental Life"; Ernest W. Burgess, "The Growth of the City: An Introduction to a Research Project," in Robert Ezra Park, E.W. Burgess, and Roderick Duncan McKenzie (eds), *The City* (Chicago, IL: University of Chicago Press, 1925): 47–62; Roderick Duncan McKenzie, *The Metropolitan Community* (New York; London: McGraw-Hill, 1933); Charles Horton Cooley, *Human Nature and the Social Order* (New York: Charles Scribner, 1902).

12 Maris Boyd Gillette, *Between Mecca and Beijing: Modernization and Consumption among Urban Chinese Muslims* (Stanford, CA: Stanford University Press, 2000): 8–14; 53; 233.

Fourth, some groups continue their original appearance. These are the types advocated by compositionists, maintaining their identity instead of being absorbed into other groups.[13] Usually, these groups are made up of people who are not significantly affected by external stimuli. These people are very proud of their groups and do not have much exchange with the outside world, both structurally and emotionally. A group of people called insulationists within a Mexican community discovered by Shirley Achor in Dallas, Texas, apply to this category.[14] These people cut themselves from mainstream society and only interact with people from their own culture. Since they are proud of their ethnicities, they maintain the traditional religion of their people.

Finally, urban culture gives birth to new groups. For example, online ballpark clubs did not exist before but were newly born due to the activation of the Internet. Of course, ballpark clubs have been around for a long time, but online communities were only able to be created with the development of technology. As a result, baseball enthusiasts have conversations and discussions in online communities, and on weekends they can gather in person at the baseball stadium to watch the games. In addition to this, the city constantly creates new gatherings such as new companies, interest groups, and neighbourhood gatherings.

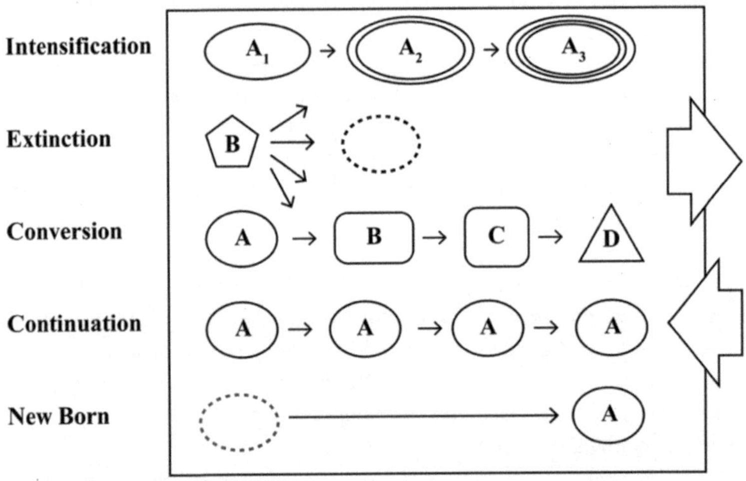

Figure 10: Five Types of Changes to the Hui Subculture

13 Oscar Lewis, "Urbanization Without Breakdown: A Case Study," *The Scientific Monthly* 75(1), (July 1952): 40–41; Nathan Glazer and Daniel P. Moynihan, *Beyond the Melting Pot: the Negroes, Puerto Ricans, Jews, Italians, and Irish of New York City* (Cambridge, MA: MIT Press, 1963); Herbert J. Gans, "Urbanism and Suburbanism as Ways of Life: A Re-Evaluation of Definitions," in Arnold Marshall Rose (ed), *Human Behavior and Social Processes: An Interactionist Approach* (Boston, MA: Houghton Mifflin, 1962): 644–45.

14 Shirley Achor, *Mexican Americans in a Dallas Barrio* (Tucson, AZ: University of Arizona Press, 1978): 116–28.

Figure 10[15] is a conceptual diagram illustrating these five groups. The whole diagram refers to a culture, such as ethnicity or country, inside of which the five subgroups respond to surrounding stimuli over time. Each group interacts with or is cut off from other groups within the culture, or a new group is born. The boundary line from the outside surrounds all five types, and all of them are subject to influence from the outside world.

As such, urban groups take the initiative to set their future and change. Just as living things are born, change, reproduce, and die, urban groups actively respond to external and internal stimuli.

I-Centred Groups Packet: That Creates the Freedom and Loneliness

Urbanites constantly select the groups they will join and proactively change them. Among them, work influences one's livelihood, and political party activities give belief and authority; people usually commit significantly toward such groups related to their livelihood or values. While people do not readily change these groups, they tend to join other social groups relatively easily and do not commit too long or too much. This is because people cannot focus on one place since they must connect to so many groups, and due to the quickly changing urban environment, urbanites do not need to maintain the same group for so long. As a result of these frequent and diverse group changes, it is difficult for urbanites to deepen their relationships with others. Pescosolido and Rubin also commented on modern people's changed degrees of commitment, saying that groups, "that is, individuals, free to move in and out of relationships that were once tightly connected but now are connected only ephemerally, experience the very tenuousness of social life to which postmodern theorists react."[16]

Figure 11 is a diagram conceptualising modern people's relationships with groups. The small dot in the centre represents an individual (ego), and the circles around it are the groups the person is related to. Pescosolido and Rubin called this relationship "the Spoke Structure," which has the self at the centre and several groups surrounding it.[17] This "Spoke Structure" refers to a structure in which, instead of having a few groups that are difficult to join or leave, or where they are forced to belong, the ego has several groups that they can lead and select themselves. It is like a kind of I-centred groups packet that one has chosen and formed around oneself.

---

15 Enoch J. Kim, "Receptor-Oriented Communication for Hui Muslims in China: With Special Reference to Church Planting" (Pasadena, CA: Fuller Theological Seminary, 2009): 71.

16 Bernice A. Pescosolido and Beth A. Rubin, "The Web of Group Affiliations Revisited: Social Life, Postmodernism, and Sociology," *American Sociological Review* 65(1), (February 2000): 63.

17 Pescosolido and Rubin named this shape "the Spoke Structure".

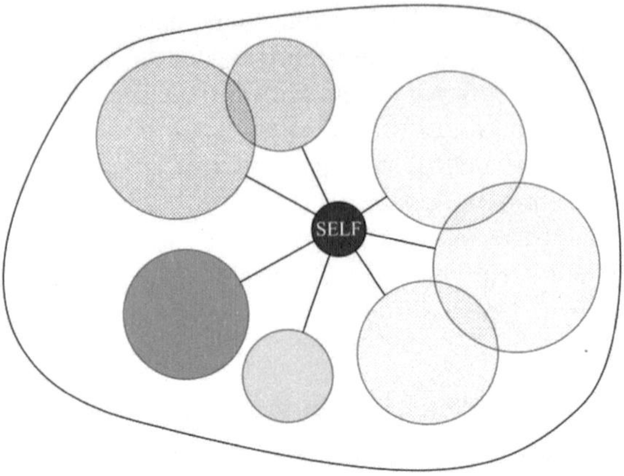

Figure 11: The Spoke Structure[18]

The I-centred packet both gives urbanites freedom and burdens them greatly. This is because a packet of groups – that can be organised only as far as the individual's ability allows – within an urban society, where everything must be done on one's own, makes urbanites free but also immersed in loneliness and anxiety. The tremendous competition created by the city, and the obsession that one can only survive through change, burden the self to think that they must connect with better groups.

In urban society, the packet of groups that one connects with becomes a symbol that represents their social class. This social status becomes the domain that determines the people one spends one's time with and the type of membership one obtains. Therefore, for urbanites, having a better education, job, and car are symbols that show how high their group and status are.

As such, the abundance and freedom of the city, a place where one can easily select and leave the group one belongs to, ironically fuels urbanites' loneliness and anxiety.[19] This is because it is difficult to meet friends to keep a close relationship inside a group that one can leave at any time. As such, individual freedom and empowerment make urbanites lonely once again, and this loneliness causes them to change their I-Centred group packets yet again. Previously, Liu changed jobs frequently, distanced himself from the relatives who had helped him after his marriage, and left the badminton club where he even worked as a secretary to join the cycling club. Moreover, he has already moved churches three times. These images show the thirst of urbanites for better lives, to overcome their anxiety, and to find better friends.

---

18 Pescosolido and Rubin, "The Web of Group Affiliations Revisited," 63.

19 Maryanski Alexandra, *The Social Cage: Human Nature and the Evolution of Society* (Stanford, CA: Stanford University Press, 1992).

For urbanites, the group's composition is a kind of self-creation, and the groups one belongs to become a kind of portfolio that builds one's abilities and status. This is because the groups one joins are the basis for explaining their experiences, the people they can connect with, their background, and even who they are today. Just as the food one eats makes up one's body, the groups one has met and been active with are what make one who they are. Furthermore, this I-centred group packeting method determines the scope of one's social identity, consumption preferences, ability to obtain information, authority, and responsibility, and ultimately creates one's social identity.

The Growing Neo-Unreached Groups

All groups in society have their social norms. This social norm refers to the emotions, history, common sense, values, abilities, leadership, relationships, and worldview that members of the same group consider normal and acceptable.[20] Therefore, social norms determine how members can operate in a group. Furthermore, this social norm is the operating system that moves the group, its method for control, and the informal understandings that one needs to survive.[21] Additionally, this social standard allows groups to create a filter that selects and interprets external information. Because of this filter, the group has adequate closure to the outside. This closure actively absorbs beneficial information while being very strict or resistant to their value or existence information.

Ironically, the highly specialised groups of the city sometimes cut off people from the outside because of their profession. Due to their expertise, they become too immersed in their field, face limitations in communicating with other groups and lose interest. In particular, groups with high professionalism and solid goals or groups with high self-esteem and exclusivity carefully select and accept external information through a powerful filter. For example, gatherings with specific standards, such as a highly specialised semiconductor company, or a group of religious leaders, often only live within their unique interests and culture. The filters created at the group level significantly influence the group members' communications with the outside world. In other words, the group's powerful filter causes the people inside it to neither know nor be interested in the world outside of the group. While ethnic boundaries and social status act as strong filters in traditional societies, these social norms, specialisation, and loyalty work as the filters in an urban society. As a result, urban residents have different cultural codes for each generation and a great sense of the disparity between professions.

---

20 Cristina Bicchieri, Ryan Muldoon, and Alessandro Sontuoso, "Social Norm," *Standard Encyclopedia of Philosophy*, 1st March 2011, [Available at: https://plato.stanford.edu/entries/social-norms/], [Last accessed: 24th December 2023]; Brennan Geoffrey *et al.*, *Explaining Norms* (New York: Oxford University Press, 2013).
21 M.K. Lapinski and R.N. Rimal, "An Explication of Social Norms," *Communication Theory* 15(2), (2005): 127–47; Michael Hechter and Karl-Dieter Opp, *Social Norms* (New York: Russell Sage Foundation, 2001).

Social norms determine the priority of information exchanged within the group and what to say and not say.[22] In particular, as society becomes more personalised, people exchange much common knowledge and current information. At the same time, however, they are hesitant to ask about personal life and values under the excuse of respecting the other person. Metaphysical content or value-oriented information is considered very personal, and it is deemed rude to impose these values and ideas on others. As a result, it is rare for urban groups to bring in outside information unrelated to work, and it is considered rude to make individuals share their faith or private life. Therefore, modern people's indifference to others increases with their profession. Urbanites live in a flood of information, but the group's social atmosphere makes them accept only a select portion of information from outside.

Due to social standards and filters, urban groups actively absorb general social information and professional co-operation from both the inside and outside while blocking out value-oriented information and personal content. In this respect, urban groups can be said to be voluntarily disconnected societies. Here, voluntary disconnection does not mean forcibly blocking out information, but that groups accept only wanted information and block out what they do not want.

Non-believers in these voluntarily disconnected places are more likely to be alienated from the Gospel. This is because the group's strong filter blocks insiders from outside influences, naturally making it difficult to contact outsiders who have the Gospel. Suppose the atmosphere of a group is inherently hostile to Christianity or has no prior knowledge of it. In that case, the individuals in the group will usually have prejudices and negative attitudes. Even if there are Christians in the group, the social climate of the group keeps these Christians doing only their jobs, and prevents them from talking about their faith.

A group which is cut off from the outside and causes members who have the Gospel to stay withdrawn gradually becomes a neo-unreached group. This refers to a group disconnected from or hostile to the Gospel like the unreached people groups mentioned in traditional mission. Groups isolated by their social norm are either cut off from the Gospel or dismiss faith as something extremely personal.

A difference that these neo-unreached people groups have from traditional unreached people groups is that many Christians may present inside them alongside the other members. In other words, the problem is that these Christians live under the pressure of the group's culture and excessively competitive society, so they do not have any practical influence within the group. Furthermore, many of these Christians are not interested in religion due to secularism and pluralism and are tired of their faith. Furthermore, the dualistic worldview that all one can do in a sinful world is to make money and donate to the church also contributes to the flourishing of neo-unreached groups.

---

22 Cristina Bicchieri and Erte Xiao, "Do the Right Thing: But Only If Others Do So," *Journal of Behavioral Decision Making* 22(2), (2009): 191–208.

As such, newly formed neo-unreached groups are the combined result of the group's competitive and isolated atmosphere, the strong group filter created by the social norms, and the dualistic theology that gives Christians weak influence on society.

This emergence of neo-unreached groups is not only emerging within the workplaces but everywhere in the cities. For example, neo-unreached groups emerge even in the residential areas. No matter how close people live to each other, urbanites only interact with those with whom they already have a network. This means that most urbanites rarely step inside their neighbours' homes during the entire year. This has become even more pronounced as people own cars and become more private. Furthermore, if people of different ethnicities, occupations, and religions live in the same village, it is almost impossible to interact naturally because of socio-cultural differences. For example, if refugee families from Somalia settle in a town, villagers cannot expect to build a natural rapport without a planned approach because of the different networks.

These neo-unreached phenomena are no different in children's environments. Sharing certain religious beliefs in public educational institutions and public places is considered a rude violation of privacy and can even lead to legal problems in some countries. Urban families and kin relationships are not exceptions. Family members who live in different worlds during the day may find difficulties communicating with each other at home in the evening as they retreat into their own personal media and spaces. Although they live close by, the quality time they spend together is short. Relationships with relatives are more difficult, and if they meet only on special days and have shallow fellowship, spiritual exchanges with each other become unlikely.

As we have seen, the groups of cities are very well-connected and send and receive enormous amounts of information between each other. However, the information they do exchange is largely professional, with little sharing of personal values or beliefs. As a result, many groups in the city are (voluntarily) disconnected from the Gospel, and even the few Christians in them have difficulty revealing their religious influence. Eventually, cities produce neo-unreached groups, and churches lose influence over social groups.

Missiological Reflection: For the New Wineskin

> But new wine must be put into fresh wineskins (Lk. 5:38).

Will today's churches thrive in making a missional impact on changing urban groups? Can the urban church reconnect with the growing number of neo-unreached groups? Do urban churches know how to help the Christians inside the neo-unreached groups give off their fragrance? Unfortunately, approaching these neo-unreached groups with the church's current interests and leadership seems impossible. Besides, are we not losing even our existing Christians to these neo-unreached groups? What is sadder is that even if a Christian brings their non-believing co-workers to church, most churches do not know how to greet this person. This does not mean that the church is unfriendly to new people, is not enthusiastic about evangelism, or does not have a welcoming programme. Instead, it is as if a foreigner whom no one has seen before suddenly enters one's house.

In Jesus' parable (Lk. 5:37-39), new and fresh skins are required for new wine. The advent of urban society has burdened the church with the need to clothe itself in a new paradigm. Preparing this new wineskin was not an easy task. First, the animal must die and go through a complex careful tanning of the skin. A skilled person must review and carefully stitch the skin so that the contents do not leak. Preparing a new wineskin suitable for urbanites is an arduous task for an already established church. It means more than modernising church songs and having the pastor show up to worship on Sundays in jeans instead of a traditional robe. To prepare the new wineskins, we will examine what we urban Christians and the urban church must do.

Urban Christian's Doing: Go to Your Urban Groups

For urban Christians to wear new wineskins, they must appropriately manage their personal group packets, primary network groups, and secondary network groups as children of God.

First, urban Christians should re-examine the I-Centred Group Packet they have made before God. Christians have been given tremendous opportunities and power to choose many groups to belong within. However, we may use this opportunity selfishly for our own sake or as a tool to feed our sinful nature. Moreover, in the anonymous environment of the city, even within a group, one can live while hiding one's true face and background. For this reason, for Christians to choose their groups neglectfully means that they are using the God-given opportunities incorrectly and living a life excessively for themselves.

In this sense, the first step for an urban Christian to put on the new wineskin is to reconstitute their I-centred group packet in holiness before God. The kind of people one associates with makes up who one is. Therefore, one's selection of groups is God's providence and stewardship and one's obedience toward God's missional journey. Since the groups one is involved in are like food and nutrients that make one's body, both primary and secondary networks must be groups that are pleasing to God.

Second, new wineskins must have more quality relationships with primary network groups. Christians are first sent out to their primary group of families and kin. The city's excessive competition, consumerism, complicated and busy lifestyles, and secularism make urbanites focus less on their families and more on themselves instead. Furthermore, since the state has replaced the family for most social welfare functions, commitment and interaction within the family have greatly weakened compared to traditional societies. Jeong Byeong-Kwan explained this phenomenon, "The family, which comprehensively covered the functions of production and education, has been reduced to a minimal function of exchanging stability and affection in the city."[23]

Christians must not put off loving their family until tomorrow. For families, the home must be a place they want to come to and where they can talk about anything. The family of a Christian should be a community that other families envy. But such envy is neither about success nor promotion. Instead, when family becomes a place that repeatedly gives forgiveness, encouragement, love, and trust, nonbelievers nearby will desire it for their own homes. Not only this, but urban Christians should not forget the burden on their kin (Rom. 9:1-3). Relatives seem close in relationship, but they easily become uncomfortable when they come close. However, they can become more trustworthy than anyone else because of what they have in common. Particularly in a collective society, many people find their faith through the evangelism of their relatives. This is because the Gospel spreads through such trusting relationships.

Third, new wineskins mean becoming Christians who are sent to their secondary network groups. Christians are sent to their residential groups to meet with the residents and friends in their neighbourhoods. Gorringe explains the importance of neighbours as "People live in one place, work in another, and take their leisure in another. This is true, but the micro politics of education, health, transport, and even street design, remains obstinately local. [...] the importance of the local remains, especially for children, the elderly and their carers, as also for the owners of small businesses and the disabled."[24] Having just three families in our neighbourhood whom we could trust to watch our children would enrich our lives tremendously. In fact, the church has traditionally grown through neighbourhood evangelism. When one has a fragrance, it is natural for their neighbours to be the first to receive the beautiful scent.

The social and economic circles and virtual groups we participate in are also groups we have been dispatched to. Christians should consider their workplace, weekend cycle clubs, parental associations (PTA), the market, YouTube comments, and various online groups as the fields to which God has sent them. When we engage in these socioeconomic activities, we should position ourselves as apostles of peace, those who are holy, those who give harmony and joy, and those who provide comfort and encouragement. Therefore, it is fair to say that the real lives of the urban Christians, as those who are sent by God, begin on Monday morning rather than on Sunday.

---

23 Byung Gwan Chung, *도시교회 성장학[Urban Church Growth]* (Seoul: Chongshin DaehakGyo, 2009): 91.

24 Timothy Gorringe, *A Theology of the Built Environment: Justice, Empowerment, Redemption* (Cambridge: Cambridge University Press, 2002): 186.

Urban Church's Doing: Urban Nurturing and Urban Missions

For the church to wear new wineskins, they must first renew the meaning of nurturing people.[25] This new concept of nurturing means helping believers act as light and salt as they live within the city groups. The church must also humbly acknowledge that it is difficult for it to cover the members' diverse networks by itself and must be able to co-operate with other mission agencies and social organisations.

First, urban churches need to shift the way they nurture to an urban style. This does not mean completing a set of church programmes. Rather, it refers to supporting people to live as salt and light in the field of life where they spend the most time. This is far more than just adding new content or using trendy programmes; it means focusing on helping members live correctly in their networks. To have such a nurturing system requires changing the contents, education patterns, educators, and the field of education. First of all, nurturing activities and the topics of Bible study must be related to the field of life. Otherwise, the sheep and the shepherd will live different lives.

Traditionally, the church's nurturing was based on the theory of *Ordo Salutis*. In other words, it was based on the principle that every believer must pass through a sequential process that begins from living as a sinner, then conversion, sanctification, and finally glorification.[26] The *Ordo Salutis* theory lays a rich biblical base for the discipleship process and is still a fundamental framework for the upbringing of believers today. However, its weakness is that it weighs heavily on the religious maturity of the individual believer, and this maturity is based almost entirely on church activities and knowledge. Such training is very helpful in producing workers to help the church's ministry or to nurture other believers of the same type, but there is a great gap between this and the pattern of being salt and light in the field of life. Compared to traditional nurturing methods, nurturing to live a life of example within the field of life requires a much greater emphasis on who urban Christians are, what God is doing in our city now, and equipping us to be a part of what is his work. Of course, this does not mean that the traditional value of the *Ordo Salutis* should be undermined. However, because growth and sanctification occur not only within the church, but in every aspect of the believer's life, the nature of the urban church must also provide for growth in all the places where urban people live.

Therefore, compared to the traditional nurturing strategy, this nurturing to become salt and light gives greater weight to discovering who we are as urban believers and what God currently is doing in our city, and equipping Christians to participate in his work. Of course, this does not mean that the values of the traditional *Ordo Salutis* theory are weakened. Instead, because growth and sanctification apply both inside the church and in every part of one's life, the urban church's nurturing must cover the aspect of the believer's daily life.

---

25 Hiebert and Meneses, *Incarnational Ministry*, 327.

26 Handrikus Berkhof, *Christian Faith: An Introduction to the Study of the Faith* (Grand Rapids, MI: Eerdmans, 1979): 478.

Urban nurturing also requires a change in education methods and educators. In the traditional church's pedagogical approach, the instructor is the expert while listeners do not know the content, and therefore the instructor does most of the speaking. However, life-centred education allows everyone to be an instructor and listener. In this educational environment, an educator of authority is not just someone who studies the theory in advance and repeats it for teaching, but someone who can set a real example of the subject or can introduce the listeners to better and broader resources. In particular, the principles and testimonies shared by those who have experience in the field for decades are words of wisdom, not just knowledge.

This approach overcomes the limitations of the text-centred and pedagogical approaches, allows the participants' fields to become the starting point of their Bible study topics, and enable their studies to be directly related to urban life. Furthermore, their education becomes an andragogical approach as they are taught by Christians who have lived in similar environments.

Second, the church must train its members to work as salt and light in their neighbourhoods and residential networks. Many Christians spend time at home and in their neighbourhoods. Children, students, the self-employed, part-time workers, the elderly, and housewives can always be found in the neighbourhood. We may not necessarily invite them for dinner, but there are many things the church can do to nurture Christians to be kind, sympathetic, and trustworthy people to their neighbours.

Helping believers to live as salt and light beyond their families and in the economic, social, and political networks is another task of urban churches. For this to be possible, the church needs to convert a significant portion of its programmes to be field-centred rather than church-centred. Field-centred means making the centre of training the place where the members want change.

The problem is that the social distance between the groups is too great for the traditional church system to affect these urban groups, and the groups' barriers are too strong to overcome. For this reason, the church should review co-operating with mission agencies who have already worked with the professions, interests, regions, and cultural groups related to church members so that they can exert a positive influence on such fields. Even now, many Christian organisations are active in social groups, such as workplace missionaries and politicians' breakfast prayer sessions. However, it is true that these Christian gatherings are becoming another church or a Christian ghetto. Therefore, mission agencies must also change to the new wineskin, as follows.

First, mission agencies must clarify that, for Christians, the co-workers in their groups are their primary field. In other words, we must have a sense of mission that it is God who sends us as Christians to connect with our present towns, workplaces, and clubs. Defining these fields becomes the basis for the contextualisation of the ministry because the Gospel should be the good news that gives them hope and trust. This good news is realised when one fully understands the culture, needs, and circumstances of one's group.

Second, for the contextualisation efforts of mission agencies to be sustainable and effective, their leadership must fit into the context and become an organisation that receives co-operation from a larger structure. A mission organisation with a new wineskin must first have leadership with a different background from that of a traditional church. In other words, instead of pastors or church workers, leadership should consist of senior Christians who have been engaged in the field for a long time. They may have less ministry experience than the church's pastors, be biased theologically, or have weaker moral standards. However, they know and can experience the problems that Christians and non-Christians face in their field better than anyone else. They also know who their juniors respect and how to guide them to become followers of the Lord in their environment.

Mission agencies need to form alliances with similar mission agencies to help each other. For example, groups of various Christian artists are united to work under the umbrella of an Artist Mission. This united mission organisation must have an advisory group of missiologists, church pastors, and elders who can provide theological and practical advice to each member group to contextualise and help develop leadership and textbooks properly.

Third, since mission organisations must create much more diversified contexts than ordinary churches, they require co-operation with mission experts. This contextualisation work creates a dialogue between the Bible and the given circumstances and provides the organisation with the groundwork for appropriate goals, activities, identities, programmes, and training content. Unlike the traditional church nurturing methods, the contextualisation work of mission agencies is centred on objectively understanding the environment of the field, interpreting its meaning through God's eyes, and discovering what the good news is for the people of the field.

Such co-operation is possible only when churches, seminaries, and mission agencies view each other as subjects for co-operation for the kingdom of God rather than as rivals. This kingdom-level perspective allows institutions to see each other as valuable associates to fill the city with God's glory instead of focusing on their own organisations.

As we have seen, God allows urbanites to participate in countless groups. These groups enable us to survive and thrive as we make new neighbours and friends, even in an urban environment filled with loneliness and anxiety. The many opportunities gained through these groups are a wonderful gift from God to the urban churches so that people within the groups can forgive one another and come to know the Gospel.

Theme 3: Urban Space and Time

Stepping into Unfamiliar Places for Reconciliation

5. Re-Read the Urban Narratives

Story Box 3[1] – Otto Re-read the Düsseldorf

Mr Otto, from an ethnic minority, runs a small store in the Flingern area in Düsseldorf, Germany. Shortly after Mr Otto opened his shop in Flingern, he realised that the place was full of ex-convicts and violence, meaning that even the police avoid the area. As expected, many customers spoke harshly and were overbearing, such as: Peter, a pimp who ran a brothel in Hamburg; Lux, who was detained in the police centre numerous times; Ike, who got into fights almost every week; and many unemployed foreigners living on government subsidies.

As time passed, Mr Otto attained the freedom to joke around with some of these people and share long conversations with them. At the end of every conversation, Mr Otto never forgot to mention that he is a Christian.

Eventually, Mr Otto was no longer just an outsider from an ethnic minority in the Flingern area but a kind shop owner of good faith. One day, Peter, who pimped in Hamburg, gifted a German Bible to Mr Otto. Interestingly, the Bible was full of extensive illustrations and looked valuable. The gift surprised Mr Otto because Peter showed minimal interest whenever he encouraged Peter to attend church. This made Mr Otto wonder, what made Peter present such an impressive gift? Peter also demonstrated a change in attitude toward Mr Otto. He suddenly began to address Mr Otto using the honorific *Sie*, a word that Peter had never been heard using. Usually, using honorifics is not considered a big deal in German society. However, it was a tremendous change for a former pimp who never used honorific words to use such language to a member of a small minority and the owner of a small store.

However, the most significant change happened to Mr Otto himself. Before this, customers were just people who said insignificant greetings when paying for goods. But Mr Otto was now able to see his customers as creations of God with stories, wounds, and common sincerity. Thankfully, this change in perspective became a cycle of virtue, and Mr Otto began treating them like his younger brothers, and they, too, treated Mr Otto like a cherished older brother. As a result, whenever Mr Otto faces a challenge, members of the neighbourhood

1 Mr Otto's story is a real example of elder H in Düsseldorf Missioni Church in German. Doctor Son Gyohoon is the senior pastor of the church and he gave permission to use the story in this book.

come and help him as if it were their own business. Now, Mr Otto's business has become a much more meaningful place than just a store.

Over the past 22 years, every surrounding street and corner around Mr Otto's store has served as a narrative box that consists of Mr Otto's story, aspirations, worries, and anxieties. The locals consider Mr Otto as a part of their whole and cannot imagine Flingern without his store. They are accustomed to Mr Otto being always present in the store, ready to greet them with a bright smile. They all expect to hear "you should go to church" at the end of a conversation. The store's counter holds a collection of the countless stories of Mr Otto's lonely customers. And when Mr Otto attends a funeral of a Flingern friend of 22 years, he is convinced that rather than simply running a store, he has been gaining people in his life. Although others may avoid these ex-convicts, locals are aware that there is a store owned by a brother from a minority, a place that helps anyone to open up. The store is more than a store; it is a space that tells stories about people's lives. Although Flingern, a village full of violence and ex-convicts, may be dark, Mr Otto's store serves as a small lighthouse that creates stories and friendships between many people.

People Connect and Disconnect in the Urban Space and Time

As seen with Mr Otto, time and space are not just environments to live within. For him, his store in Flingern is more than a place to make money but a place to collect life and stories, a place to remember his time with people, and a place that accumulates the past 22 years of his life. As such, space and time are mediums that connect people to others, and we reinvest these meanings back into space and time. As a result, people gain a sense of belonging through time, space, and memories, and through empathy, creativity, and wounds. In this way, time and space provide us with memories and narratives, and we place those stories into the built environment.[2]

A city is full of artificially built environments, such as buildings and roads. What does God think when he sees us making subways and highways or constructing other environments like parks and offices? Would he think that we use developments to build high walls around us to mark our territories, boast about our class superiority, and contain our privileges? Would he not see development being used for demonstrating superiority and inferiority rather than for sharing? God expects the city to be a place to be "fruitful and multiple"' (Gen. 9:1) and desires that the cities become a space for meeting and reconciliation. Such meeting indicates the breaking down of barriers that have separated people and a petition to shake hands for reconciliation.

In this chapter, we will study the phenomenon of modern cities that use the space and time God has given them as a medium for division. To do so, we will begin by asking the questions below. Let us examine how our cities rebuild the walls that Christ has broken down in a social network perspective.

2 Gorringe, *A Theology of the Built Environment.*

- What is the relationship between built environments and worldviews?
- How do urban time and space affect society?
- What role does urban space play in dividing people?
- What role does Virtual Space play in connecting urbanites?

In the final Missiological Reflection, we will share the way Christians and churches can act to enable the city to become a time and space for restoring the lordship of God.

Built Environment as Extensions of People

Can you imagine a city without buildings? Today, great facilities, factories, parks, and highways of cities serve as an environment for life, in other words, a built environment. The built environment refers to "The buildings, infrastructure, landscaping, and in-between places that we create for ourselves".[3] As such, urban buildings do more than their primary function; they form our surrounding environment as we breathe, sleep, and work.

As the term "built environment" suggests, surrounding facilities and buildings create an environment and a culture for people. Just as cultural anthropology regards form as a vessel containing meaning, people mould their meaning and values into the shape of the city's time and space.[4] As such, the built environment refers to buildings and the consensus of people, which indicates that the city's space is a social product. Therefore, it "is never empty; it consistently embodies a meaning."[5] In other words, urban spaces already contain different meanings depending on "the meaning of space, use of space, and user of space, without neutrality."[6] The meaning and value bestowed in space and time thus become a message that makes people think and act accordingly when they enter such a space. For example, people act reverently in a national cemetery but dance freely in a club because each place contains a message that prompts people to act appropriately. Therefore, "the built environment is not a passive container of or a background for urban life, but plays a critical role in shaping, expressing, and validating the meanings and practices of urbanites."[7]

Built environments are spaces where people express elements of their worldview such as priorities, class, and spiritual realms. In other words, cultural factors have a crucial influence on the structure and utilisation of urban spaces. For example, the location and appearance of temples, the direction and height of buildings, the location and structure of low-class people's housing, and so forth

3 Jacobsen, *Sidewalks in the Kingdom*, 167.

4 Charles H. Kraft, *Anthropology for Christian Witness* (Maryknoll, NY: Orbis, 1996): 132–47.

5 Henri Lefebvre, *The Production of Space*, trans. Donald Nicholson-Smith (Cambridge, MA: Balil Blackwell, 1991): 154.

6 Lefebvre, *The Production of Space*, 154.

7 Deborah Pellow and Denise Lawrence-Zuniga, "Built Structures and Planning," in Donald Macon Nonini (ed), *A Companion to Urban Anthropology* (Chichester, West Sussex: Wiley-Blackwell, 2014): 85–86.

are all characteristics of the city and are tremendously cultural products. This is why when we experience a foreign culture, we feel awkward as we notice different buildings and alleys and various unfamiliar signs and symbols. But ,on the other hand, built environments seem predictable and natural within common cultural backgrounds. This is because urban spaces "impose upon us ways of thinking and doing which reinforce existing patterns of social life".[8]

The built environment also contains social meaning. It is a crucial survival base for those who live in the city and a place where they realise their ideals. It is both a personal and a communal place. Therefore, the built environment portrays the efficiency, creativity, ideas, priorities, health and nutrition, politics, and economic conditions of those who utilise it.

The built environment is a good representation of the social priorities and situations of its users. Social priority refers to the priority of policies such as social order, political hierarchy or status, and even the allocation of finite resources. For example, although spaces like coffee shops and restaurants facilitate social interaction, banks and ticket booths prioritise functionality.

The city's structure reflects its ruling class' social priorities and situations. When designing cities, urban designers generally consider the city's compartments, infrastructural locations and functions, sacred and secular divisions, defence and war facilities, and notions of gender and social identity. For example, the ruler may prioritise visualising authority and power over convenience or efficiency as they design palaces and city halls. In addition, cities that experience instability or fear of outside invasion prioritise safety and defence facilities, emphasising police and military efficiency. Henri Lefebvre saw such dynamics as an ideology.[9] Such ideologies of space are everywhere from "the moment we emerge from our front door, drive to the out-of-town shopping centre or visit the local post office. In the built environment, social relations are inscribed concretely in space."[10] Therefore, the built environment shows that the understanding of buildings is "the understanding of the cultural, the political, economic, social, technological, artistic, and cultural anthropological background."[11]

A macro view is not enough to fully understand the city's culture and worldview. Reading with a micro view helps us discover internal dynamics and cultural elements and uncovers facets which cannot be seen or understood using a macro view. For example, in a macro view, we see that cities worldwide have similar external appearances as if they were some sort of siblings.[12] It is

---

8 David Harvey, *The Urban Experience* (Baltimore, MD: Johns Hopkins University Press, 1989): 250.

9 Lefebvre, *The Production of Space*, 128–29.

10 Gorringe, *A Theology of the Built Environment*, 27.

11 Enoch Kim translated this sentence. Yu Hyunjoon, *What the city live with?* (Korean), Ch'op'an (Sŏul: Ŭlyu Munhwasa, 2019): 16.

12 S.M. Lod, *Theorizing the City: The New Urban Anthropology Reader* (New Brunswick, NJ: Rutgers University Press, 1999).

complicated to distinguish cities when we view them from their centres or concentrated areas with high buildings. However, a micro-view shows that all cities "vary from one epoch to another and from one society to another."[13] The built environments go beyond their functions to express the culture and worldview of their architects and users, because they are the result of the belief systems of their rulers and architects and the expressions of their versions of space.

The history and external influences of the city also contribute to the city's culture. For example, houses of celebrities, war-torn areas, and former slave trade hubs greatly influence the city's image. Capital, new ideas, and new settlers from the outside also change the appearance and culture of the city, along with imported resources, ideas, and settlers. External influences not only bring in foreign-styled restaurants and architecture but also change consumption patterns, transportation facilities, and even the expansion of airports and roads. Modern cities have increased their exchanges with the outside world tremendously due to globalisation and the mobile media revolution. As a result, built environments in the cities around the world, in the macro view, have functions and shapes like that of each other.[14]

As we have seen, the built environment of a city reveals the culture and worldview of its people, the passion and ideology of its rulers, and what we and our society are. Just as Marshall McLuhan called the media "The Extensions of Man", the built environment is "The Extensions of People."[15]

Urban Times: Made of Socio-Temporal Narratives

A city is a spatio-temporal unit that the accumulating stories of its current and long-time residents have created. People input stories into urban spaces, and the stories tend to resurface at any given time and enter the thoughts of modern residents. For example, five years ago, I visited a university that had produced six Nobel Prize winners in chemistry and physics since 1972. Since then, I have never viewed that university in the same way.[16] Such a history has a tremendous influence on the attitudes and thoughts of the junior researchers who practice on

---

13 In the 1990s, scepticism arose in urban academia about the macroscopic approach to understanding cities mainly based on their appearances and functions. For example, people think Jerusalem, Mecca, and Athens in Greece are all sacred cities, but no one thinks these cities are cities with the same meaning. George E Marcus, "Ethnography in/of the World System: The Emergence of Multi-Sited Ethnography," *Annual Review of Anthropology* 24 (1995): 95; A.M. Orun and Xiangming Chen, *The World of Cities: Places in Comparative and Historical Perspective* (Malden, MA: Wiley-Blackwell, 2003): viii.

14 J. John Palen, *The Urban World* (New York: McGraw-Hill, 1992): 339–56.

15 Herbert Marshall McLuhan, *Understanding Media: The Extensions of Man* (London: The MIT Press, 1964).

16 The University of California, Santa Barbara, has produced six Nobel Prize winners since 1972.

the same campus today. Likewise, there are countless layers of accumulated stories underneath every place, and my realisation that day only uncovered one of them.

The future also creates significance in today's places. For example, when a couple who just had their second child walk through the front yard of a hospital, they picture the beginning of a new future for their family. This may be the location where the father decides to take on a second job, and for the firstborn, a place where he develops a new sense of pride for his baby sibling that permeates into his social life.

Like this, conversations between the urban time and space continually reshape their narratives and make a multi-dimensional meaning.[17] As falling water gradually cuts rocks, "time thickens, takes shape and materialises by space, and space acquires meaning and is measured by time."[18] That is why the city's image "is perceived as becoming and circulation with time, combination and recombination of people, society, and entities."[19]

Time and space contain stories created by communities and individuals: "A social form and a social practice, throughout history space, has been the material support of simultaneity in social practice. That is, space defines the time frame of social relationships."[20] For example, people are reminded of the same objects when they pass the streets, monuments, museums, and statues of a neighbourhood, because the long-preserved significance of places serves as a social memory that helps the community remember the same story.[21] When the historical meaning embedded in a place meets the community, it becomes a social memory, which can bring people together to think about the same thing. Therefore, a city is a hub of socio-temporal units that conversations and communities have developed over thousands of years.

The place is like a station that links the stories of the past with that of the present and the future. For instance, for young Christians, the tomb of a martyred missionary is more than just a place of the past. Instead, it is a place with a

---

17 Russian philosopher and literary critical Mikhail Bakhtin introduced the word chronotope as a concept integrating time and place. Bakhtin thought that a variety of people, time, place, culture, politics, and economy contributes to the meaning in combination, as well as one factor in explaining any existence or certification.

18 M.M. Bakhtin, "Forms of Time and of the Chronotope in the Novel: Notes towards a Historical Poetic," in M.M. Bakhtin and Michael Holquist (eds), *The Dialogic Imagination: Four Essays*, University of Texas Press Slavic Series (Austin, TX: University of Texas Press, 1981): 84–258.

19 Mike Crang, "Time: Space," in Paul J. Cloke and Ron Johnston (eds), *Spaces of Geographical Thought: Deconstructing Human Geography's Binaries*, Society and Space Series (London: SAGE, 2005): 199–220; Mike Crang, "Rhythms of the City: Temporalised Space and Motion," in Jon May and N.J. Thrift (eds), *TimeSpace: Geographies of Temporality* (London: Routledge, Taylor & Francis, 2001): 190.

20 Manuel Castells, *The Rise of the Network Society*, 2nd ed. (Oxford; Malden, MA: Blackwell, 2010): xxxi.

21 Paul Connerton, *How Societies Remember*, Themes in the Social Sciences (Cambridge: Cambridge University Press, 1989).

powerful message that can transform the lives of today's Christian youth. A place is also where people create future stories. The story of the martyred missionary will continue to live on when these young Christians in the future bring their children to the same place and tell them how the missionary's story had transformed their lives.

The time and space of a city also depend on who remembers it and who lives there today.[22] Mr Otto's store in Flingern, introduced earlier, may be a simple store to others. However, for Mr Otto, it is a narrative box that contains 22 years of stories and life. In addition, even if it is the same place, people create different stories according to their ethnicity, region of origin, social class, and individual tendencies. Even in the same place, the significance and story constantly change and acquire different outfits depending on time and people. Therefore, other patterns and values are created depending on the time, community, and storyteller. History is not just a fact of the past but a narrative of its interpreters. And as this narrative develops, history develops with it. Therefore, "places are anchored in time, and time, in turn, may be said to unfold in space. It is thus impossible to understand space without the necessary temporal dimension."[23]

As such, people in the past, present, and future utilise the same place to meet others and create stories and, as they listen to the stories of the past, they individually create their own. Today's stories will capture the thoughts of people who will come in the future and become the ingredients for their new stories. Therefore, urban space is a socio-temporal unit where time, place, and people meet.

Urban Spaces: Made of Socio-Spatial Narratives

A city is a socio-spatial society where people are actively creating stories.[24] Unlike space, an empty area, a place is a designed area with purpose, such as a building or a train station. Traditionally, people have interpreted the space as a physical space, such as parks and fields. But ever since Einstein introduced the theory of relativity, the concept of space has expanded not only to time and experiences but also to digital space and mental and emotional realms.[25] As such,

22 Maurice Halbwachs, Francis J. Ditter and Vida Yazdi Ditter, *The Collective Memory* (New York: Harper & Row, 1980): 133.
23 Ondřej Mulíček, Robert Osman and Daniel Seidenglanz, "Urban Rhythms: A Chronotopic Approach to Urban Timespace," *Time & Society* 24(3), (1st January 2014): 304.
24 Socio-spatial perspective incorporates a number of different factors that can account for development and change. This concept was inspired by Henri Lefebvre (1991) and has developed into socio-spatial perspective theory. Lefebvre, *The Production of Space*.
25 The concept of space has developed in a wide variety of ways, including virtual spaces such as logical and abstract concepts, mathematical spaces recognised through drawings or ground, artistic spaces to express emotions and emotions, social spaces related to society and human relations, and political forces. Cornelis van de Ven, *Space in Architecture: The Evolution of a New Idea in the Theory and History of the Modern*

the concept of space encompasses the idea of place and even contains philosophical significance.

Beyond its simple function, utilising a space means establishing a relationship between people and space. Even in the same space, people add their meanings and approaches based on their values and functions. For example, the meaning and significance behind the same house change dramatically when one goes from being a monthly tenant to a homeowner.

Like urban time, the meaning of space is created through social consensus.[26] Therefore, space is a social product created from social consensus, and people further strengthen and develop the meaning of the space as they engage in related social activities. As a result, space is not just a place for individuals but a place for conversation with society. The concept of space is thus bigger than just a place where people come to do activities. Space not only contains the actions of individuals, but it "constitutes a part of social relations and is intimately involved in our daily lives. It affects the way we feel about what we do. In turn, people alter space and construct new environments to better fit their needs. Hence, a dual relationship exists between people and space."[27]

Due to the social characteristics of urban space, the city becomes a space that undergoes constant change. Sociospatiality is a consented social product born in the process of people forming and living in society. The social construction of space is the social, psychological, and functional transformation of space – through people's social exchanges, memories, images, and daily usage of the material setting – into scenes and actions that convey symbolic meaning.[28] Therefore, interacting in space is not just the activities of individuals but interaction with related societies.

Social consensus instils value and power dynamics in space, which results in costs and benefits to those involved. For example, social consensus grants a house in a good location higher economic and real estate value. Also, in reverse, the value of these assigned spaces affects people's social lives. For example, people who own these expensive houses will be able to join a community of

---

Movements (Assen: Van Gorcum, 1980): 35–42; K. Michael Hays, *Architecture Theory Since 1968* (Cambridge, MA: The MIT Press, 2015).

26 Nancy D. Munn, "Excluded Spaces: The Figure in the Australian Aboriginal Landscape," 22(3), (1996): 446–65; Stuart Alexander Rockefeller, *Starting from Quirpini: The Travels and Places of a Bolivian People* (Bloomington, IN: Indiana University Press, 2010); Theodore C. Bestor, "Supply-Side Sushi: Commodity, Market, and the Global City," *American Anthropologist* 103(1), (2001): 76–95; Setha M. Low, *On the Plaza: The Politics of Public Space and Culture*, 1st ed. (Austin: University of Texas Press, 2000); Deborah Pellow, *Setting Boundaries: The Anthropology of Spatial and Social Organization* (Westport, CT: Bergin & Garvey, 1996).

27 Tim Cresswell, *Place: A Short Introduction* (Hoboken, NJ: Wiley, 2013).

28 Setha M. Low, "Spatiality: The Rebirth of Urban Anthropology through Studies of Urban Space," in Donald Macon Nonini (ed), *A Companion to Urban Anthropology* (Chichester, West Sussex: Wiley-Blackwell, 2014): 20.

other rich people and associate with them as elites. Like this, society affects space, and, in return, space affects social life.

The city's space is like a vessel that holds social relations and meaning. People mediate the space to create their human relationships, community values, economy, power, resources, preferences, and more. As a social product, social space results from society's culture, functional elements, and symbolic messages. Therefore, space is a medium that represents the society and the people in it. Furthermore, and mainly because a city contains numerous artificial facilities and places, a city is a sociospatial place where many spaces with social meaning are densely integrated.

As we can see, the social and spatial characteristics of urban space indicate that the city is not complete but is instead in the process of change. As city space continues to pick up new outfits from the stories of its residents, society and space create their own unique spatial culture. The city is thus a sociospatial space where people constantly input new stories.

Urban Places: A Mosaic of Different Narratives

Place refers to a space identified for a specific purpose or activity, such as houses, offices, and temples. Because of its purpose and usage, a place is much more social than a space.[29] Today, urbanites conduct most of their activities in urban buildings. Places are where people pursue activities necessary for their lives, such as self-actualisation, the pursuit of passion, relationship-building, or production.[30]

Subsequently, the city is a space full of places. Because urbanites spend most of their lives in places, Christopher Day argues that the buildings in a city are like our third layer (human skin being the first and clothing second). This is because the built environment, like our skin, "performs many functions: it breathes, absorbs, evaporates and regulates, as well as enclosing and protecting."[31] Places are not just part of our lives, but they have a message in them. "Land always tells a story of power and wealth, and whatever stories of community, belonging, or exclusion occur on that land are always layered over and interconnected with the politics and economics of the land."[32] Because of the meanings in them, places have many categories according to their purpose and role. Under a social contract, places are distinguished based on public and private elements, sacred and secular, or power and gender. People go to these

29 Jaffe and Koning, *Introducing Urban Anthropology*, 24.
30 Tim Cresswell, *Place: A Short Introduction* (Hoboken, NJ: Wiley, 2013).
31 Christopher Day, *Places of the Soul: Architecture and Environmental Design as a Healing Art* (London: Aquarian, 1990): 63–64.
32 David P. Leong and Soong-Chan Rah, *Race and Place: How Urban Geography Shapes the Journey to Reconciliation* (Downers Grove, IL: InterVarsity, 2017): 114.

differentiated places and give them the voice they deserve according to socially agreed upon expectations.[33]

Public Places and Private Places

Although the difference between public and private space is not always clear, typically "public space" refers to more open, accessible, and collective urban spaces, while "private space" refers to more bounded and restricted home spaces."[34] A public place is an open common space where most people can participate in social life.[35] Public places play an essential role in the composition of the city, as they create the commonalities among its people that are necessary for cities to form.

People create opinions in public places; they discuss, develop relationships, and collaborate.[36] As we know, the *agora* was a public square in an ancient Greek city-state (*polis*) where citizens met to discuss.[37] As a result, Greeks were able to gather in public places to discuss, collaborate, and participate in politics, which was why they could develop political institutions such as democracy.

Public places activate social relationships.[38] For example, to move around, people pass through public places and meet others on the way. They also come out to public places and collaborate with others for hobbies or economic gain. Therefore, public places are representative environments that forge social relationships.

Public places breed activities with materialistic characteristics. For example, people meet others at coffee shops while generating production and distribution in offices and factories. Politicians hold large public gatherings in town squares to win support from the masses. They use public places such as police stations or district offices to promote their governance and political propaganda.

Compared to private places such as their homes, people develop less sense of ownership and responsibility for public places. For example, people might damage benches in parks and drop litter on the streets. This is because people are not liable for treating public places like their own spaces. And, because people can exploit these spaces but evade responsibilities, in public places, people often

---

33 The criteria for classifying urban places vary depending on scholars. For example, public and private places; sacred and profane places; commerce, governmental and residential places; signs verses art; hierarchy verses egalitarian places. Among these, this book will deal with the five categories that fit the direction of the book.
34 Jaffe and Koning, *Introducing Urban Anthropology*, 56.
35 Iris Marion Young, *City Life and Difference* (Princeton, NJ: Princeton University Press, 1990); Richard Sennett, "The Public Realm," in Gary Bridge and Sophie Watson (eds), *The Blackwell City Reader*, 2nd ed. (Chichester, West Sussex: Wiley-Blackwell, 2010): 267–72.
36 Jürgen Habermas, *The Structural Transformation of the Public Sphere: An Inquiry into a Category of Bourgeois Society* (Cambridge, MA: The MIT Press, 1991): 27–31.
37 Don Mitchell, *The Right to the City: Social Justice and the Fight for Public Space* (New York: Guilford, 2003).
38 Jaffe and Koning, *Introducing Urban Anthropology*, 58–60.

desire to be part of the crowd rather than be the protagonist. Another reason for the diffusion of responsibility is that public places have vital freedom and anonymity. Most people are strangers in public places. As a result, people's behaviour is very different in public compared to in private. Although they may feel less constricted in their actions and words, people evade responsibility because strangers surround them.

Interactions in public places are affected by a range of factors much more extensive than just their immediate surroundings. In public places, people meet others from various backgrounds in the world and collaborate together. Thus, these people receive global information through connected networks and multiple forms of media. Therefore, a public place is where people exposed to such global and macroscopic information interact microscopically with others for the purpose and value of an individual or group to which they belong.

Private spaces have different characteristics from public places. Unlike public places, private space refers to a place that gives a different kind of freedom and responsibility to a person or small group.[39] In other words, people act freely in private spaces but must also take responsibility. Surprisingly, the city is filled with personal spaces.[40] Unlike traditional societies with solid communities and limited individual spaces, the city's culture, infrastructure, and private vehicles enable people to live separate lives. Urban environments guarantee private lives, due to a culture that respects "my" space such as my life, my time, my friend, and my plan. The home is the most representative private place. The home serves as much more than a place to eat and sleep. It is a place where people relax, spend time with their family, invite friends, make food, and maintain moral values and faith that may differ from outside.[41]

The development of private spaces in urban society is because workplaces, social activities, educational institutions, and retail areas are separated from residential areas. For this structural reason, urbanites perform functional and business tasks in public spaces, but are reluctant to bring these tasks into private spaces.[42]

Residential areas are also sociospatial and socio-temporal places. The shape and functions of a house demonstrate the culture and personality of its users. People build houses in accordance with their culture and wield them in cultural ways. Houses have their own rules, which permeate their structures and shapes. "Interior design tells us something about people's identities, how they see themselves and how they want to be seen by visitors."[43]

---

39 Walter Brueggemann, *The Land: Place as Gift, Promise, and Challenge in Biblical Faith*, Overtures to Biblical Theology (Philadelphia, PA: Fortress, 1977: 5.
40 Refer to Chapters 1 and 2 for research on urban privacy.
41 Lewis Mumford, *The City in History: Its Origins, Its Transformations, and Its Prospects* (New York: Harcourt, Brace & World, 1961): 220.
42 Cox, *The Secular City*, 145–50.
43 Jaffe and Koning, *Introducing Urban Anthropology*, 30.

There are some places, however, that are categorised as public places but feel like private places. These include regular coffee shops where one spends time alone for reading, or one's work desk with personal photos. In these places, people act personally but are also aware that they are in a public place. Notably, the house churches presented in the Bible are also places where public and private affairs overlap. A house church is literally a place where a personal family and a public church are combined. It is a place where the exclusive concept of family expands beyond the physical household into the family of Christ, which allows us to call each other brothers and sisters. Such expansion allows the house church to become a unique and beautiful space where public relationships can transform into personal relationships. Originally, a family involves a limited number of people who love and break bread. However, when a family expands into a church, it is also extending exclusive family privileges such as love, bonding, invitation, and community to outsiders in a public place with the guidance of the Holy Spirit.

Sacred Places and Secular Places

There are sacred and secular places for distinguishing urban places. In sacred places, people think and behave appropriately, while they may act differently in secular places. Urban areas are also affected by these distinctions. There are numerous religious facilities, buildings, shrines, and monuments in both city centres and their outskirts. It is important to note that religion alone does not separate the sacred and secular. We act more reverently in front of statues of historical figures in grand museums. We act more cautiously around a jinx and are mentally affected by areas with a history of unfortunate events. We know to behave appropriately and seriously when we reflect and make our New Year's plans, when we visit a teacher we respect, and when we hear the sirens and share a moment of silence on Memorial Day. As such, our lives are full of sacred and secular times and places.

Religion has played a vital role in the birth and revival of the city. Since the dawn of humankind, people built temples or shrines in spiritual places where they thought they could encounter God, and held feasts and festivals throughout various seasons. In the Bible, Bethel (Gen. 28:19; 35:14-15); Shiloh (Joshua 18:1; 21:2); Mizpah (1 Sam. 7:5-6); Gilgal (1 Sam. 7:16); and Ramah (1 Sam. 7:17) were all places where people experienced God, which gradually developed into cities.[44] The religious appeal of these spiritual places caused many to gather, and the need to maintain the religious facilities and rituals resulted in settlement.[45] As such, "cities have started as the gathering place for a community

---

44 Ronald Edward Peters, *Urban Ministry: An Introduction* (Nashville, TN: Abingdon, 2007): 35.

45 Mary Hancock and Smriti Srinivas, "Spaces of Modernity: Religion and the Urban in Asia and Africa," *International Journal of Urban and Regional Research* 32 (2008): 617–30; Irene Becci, Marian Burchardt, and José Casanova, *Topographies of Faith:*

experience of the divine-human encounter."[46] The temple was usually located in the city's centre, and religious leaders made people live in the city to maintain the temples and religious events. The settlers then formed families and conducted farming and economic activities. As the number of settlers increased, the supply of governmental and administrative ministries maintained such growth.[47] As such, religion provided the basis for ancient urban development. Even today, perhaps there lies a holy past beneath the city's surface that awaits an opportunity to share its stories.

Today, spiritual and sacred places are not limited within church and mosque buildings but permeate every corner of our lives. They exist around us in many forms: through the small incense altar in front of a restaurant, the cross hanging next to a bus driver, the closet prayer room in one's house, the prayer room in an airport, the coffee shop rented out for Sunday worship, or a company conference room that is used for early Friday morning Bible study. In addition, sacred places expand beyond physical spaces into new spaces such as virtual communities, religious radio broadcasting frequencies, or virtual Bible studies.

Opposing these sacred places are secular places. Secular places are much more difficult to define than sacred places. Usually, people imagine secular places as bars or brothels. However, secular notions vary greatly depending on culture, religion, and philosophy. When someone you distrust tries to touch you in the East, you would say, "Get your dirty hands off me!" Muslims in China might consider fly-infested halal beef in the marketplace to be cleaner than the packaged pork in a modern Costco market. As such, people perceive what is good, bad, sexual, and vulgar depending on the lens of religion or belief. People define sacred and secular places with prior-experienced values, philosophy, history, and events.[48] Like other places, people give these places meaning, formed by community consensus.[49] Although the place may have initially exerted a mystic power or have been associated with memories of the miraculous, it is the community's consensus and meaning that determines whether the place is sacred or secular. A secular place must have secular experiences, memories, and procedures to instil social consensus and meaning for the community to define it as a secular place.

Christianity, influenced by dualism, has long regarded structures other than churches to be secular spaces.[50] People have thought that the area inside the

---

Religion in Urban Spaces, International Studies in Religion and Society 17 (Leiden: Brill, 2013).

46 Peters, *Urban Ministry*, chapter 4.

47 Harvie M. Conn and Manuel Ortiz, *Urban Ministry: The Kingdom, the City & the People of God* (Downers Grove, IL: InterVarsity, 2001): 35.

48 Emily A. Schultz and Robert H. Lavenda, *Cultural Anthropology: A Perspective on the Human Condition* (St. Paul, MN: West, 1987): 350–54.

49 Gorringe, *A Theology of the Built Environment*, 40.

50 John Archer, "Colonial Suburbs in South Asia 1700-1850, and the Spaces of Modernity," in R. Silverston (ed), *Visions of Suburbia* (London: Routledge, 1996): 52;

church, such as the pulpit or seats near the cross was the holiest place to meet God. Such amalgamation of the religious spaces and the concepts of sacredness and secularity has been deeply rooted in the Christian mentality. As a result, people embed religious sacredness and secularism in places rather than in people and community. Furthermore, dualism has caused us to interpret our daily and social lives negatively, and naturally it reduces the scope of the place of God.[51] As a result, some Christians even treat their workplaces and financial institutions as places of the god Mammon, as they stimulate human greed.

The philosophical and theological attitude to distinguish the sacred from the secular according to the functions of place and buildings drives us further into spiritual stratification. In other words, spending more time in church becomes spiritual, while people who devote more time to companies and families are seen as secular or wasting their lives. Furthermore, people who work in secular environments are reflected poorly and bestowed guilt, shame, and judgement. As such, people distinguish the sacredness and secularity of a place according to its meaning and purpose.

Power in the Place

People know who has power and how guests should behave in a familiar place. There, people naturally act according to the rules of the place. As such, all places carry the message of power, and those who read it submit to it.

Whether they are private or residential, all places have this message of power. In a private space, the owner bears responsibility and authority. Owners use their power to generate the expected function and meaning of their places.[52] In these places, the message of power created by the owner permeates to the corners of the smallest spaces. For example, the owner decides where is sacred, where to sit at the dinner table, where is clean, or where one can lie down. Of course, because these criteria are highly cultural concepts, people of common culture are already familiar with the dynamics and can generally accept them without conflict. Individuals and communities thus emit power, or operating principle, and implement the message of power in each place and space.

Public places, such as government institutions or business offices, demonstrate the message of power more evidently. People determine how much power is invested in the public place by location, cultural implications, priorities, or ruler's will. The rulers and leaders of society use their power to animate their vision, values, relationships, abilities, resources, and aesthetic tastes. As a result, public facilities such as urban structure, transportation, security, and comfort systems act as indicators of the leaders' ideologies and philosophies. For

---

Sigfried Giedion, *Space, Time and Architecture: The Growth of a New Tradition* (Cambridge, MA: Harvard University Press, 1974): xxxii.

51 Nicholas P. Wolterstorff, *Art in Action: Towards a Christian Aesthetic* (Grand Rapids, MI: Paternoster, 1997): 82.

52 Lefebvre, *The Production of Space*, 85.

example, the streets of Paris, France, which radiate from the Arc De Triomphe, reflect the thoughts of Napoleon III. Fearing a civil revolution, he installed the Arc de Triomphe in the centre so police forces could quickly subdue rebels from all angles.[53] The shapes of buildings also show the ideologies of the ruler. Some rulers erect extraordinary, grand, and coercive buildings to establish authority and differentiate themselves from the citizens.

The location of a place may be a message of power. For example, in ancient Asia, one's status was determined by residential proximity to the throne, as powerful and high-ranking dignitaries lived close to the royal palace. The image of the region where the place is located also reflects the dynamism of the force. Each place contains its message of power: Beverly Hills, a high-performing school district, Harlem in New York, or a tiny garret with no sunlight.

A place's cultural implications and symbolism may show the message of power. People expect spiritual power from old and famous religious sites, ponder life lessons inside historic buildings, and wear black suits when attending funerals. In the Old Testament, the Israelites considered Jerusalem as more than a region; it was the spiritual homeland and source of the nation, symbolising the chosen people. Therefore, the Israelites' loss of Jerusalem as a result of war was much more impactful than the loss of other surrounding cities.

The background and culture of a city and the will and ability of its rulers determine where that city's power is primarily distributed. Some cities prioritise functions such as economy and production, while others invest in cultural aspects such as artists or historical traditions. If buildings and facilities are designed for the privileged and disregard disabled or minority groups, the city is considered a place that spends on the powerful. Furthermore, gates and checkpoints symbolise power. If one must go through a series of doors to meet someone, then it means they are a person of high-rank, and having multiple security check facilities indicates the safety requirements of the tasks completed within.

Thus, "from the great strategies of geopolitics to the little tactics of the habitat,"[54] the city is governed by the message of power, and people act following this principle. Therefore, such a message of power maintains communities, prevents chaos, and creates efficiency by enabling predictable relations. On the other hand, the message of power also discriminates and divides people into groups under the guise of efficiency. As a result, people associate places with status. For example, people often associate places with a certain social group, such as women, Black people, Jerusalem natives, or celebrities.

Gender and the Place

There are many places in the city where the space is divided by gender. Other than restrooms, certain places are designed for specific genders. For example,

---

53 Yu Hyunjoon, 도시는 무엇으로 사는가, 73–76.

54 Michel Foucault, *Power/Knowledge: Selected Interviews & Other Writings 1972-1977*, edited and translated by Colin Gordon (New York: Pantheon, 1980): 149.

we first divide masculine spaces from feminine spaces and then label the rest as mixed-gender spaces. Certain genders dominate in a pub at night or a mall on a Monday afternoon. In these gendered spaces, people naturally express more exaggerated views and biases regarding their own and other genders, and such expressions are socially accepted.[55]

Traditionally, men have been dominant, through power, social status, and economic strength, in public spaces, or outdoor places. Therefore, these have naturally been designed and utilised mainly from the male perspective. Considering that almost all who design, build, and repair cities are male, it can be said that cities themselves are created from the male perspective.[56] Ironically, males build the houses, streets, roads, and shopping malls where women spend most of their time. The failure to consider women's perspectives often results in consequences such as long lines for the women's restrooms in parks or concert halls. Perhaps the men who designed these buildings believed that providing equal facilities would result in equal opportunities.

Similarly, despite walking on the same street at night, women tend to feel more fearful and pressured to return home early.[57] As a result, when they stray further from social life, they are "impacted by violence, or threat of violence, just in the atmosphere around them."[58] Masculine spaces go beyond baseball stadiums or bars. For example, some white-collar workplace offices enforce high barriers for women recruits and have thus become masculine spaces. If family culture focuses on educating boys first, it is natural that fewer women qualify for jobs that require higher education.

For urban space to have become masculine-dominated, social, cultural, religious, and traditional factors have played a major role. Traditionally, women could only perform social activities other than domestic labour when society had a great need or met certain conditions. For example, women's participation in society, such as in the labour force, temporarily increased during wartime. However, once the war was over and the baby boomers were born, women returned home.[59]

Increased income does not necessarily result in more social activities for women. In the United States, the urban housing problem and the yearning for home ownership developed suburbanism. Suburbanism moved people away

---

55 Daphne Spain, "Gendered Spaces and the Public Realm," in Judith N. DeSena (ed), *Gender in an Urban World* (Leeds: Emerald, 2008): 9–28.
56 Gerald D. Suttles, *The Man-Made City: The Land-Use Confidence Game in Chicago* (Chicago, IL: University of Chicago Press, 1990).
57 Jan Newberry, "Women's Ways of Walking: Gender and Urban Space in Java," in Judith N. DeSena (ed), *Gender in an Urban World* (Leeds: Emerald, 2008): 9–28.
58 Jocelyn A. Hollander, "Vulnerability and Dangerousness: The Construction of Gender Through Conversation About Violence," *Gender and Society* 15(1), (2001): 83.
59 Erving Goffman, *Relations in Public* (New York: Basic Books, 1972); Richard Sennett, *The Uses of Disorder: Personal Identity & City Life* (New York: W.W. Norton, 1992): 173; Griselda Pollock, *Vision and Difference: Femininity, Feminism and Histories of Art* (London: Routledge, 1988).

from the city and alienated women from social and economic life. For women to join in with social activities, the family had to have two cars in the household and make long commutes to the city.

The advancement of social facilities and cultural perceptions and the development of home appliances and technology reduced the effort for domestic labour, and cities once again opened the door for the socialisation of women. As a result, the employment rate of married women with children in the United States has steadily increased, rising from 28% in 1955 to 62% in 2000. (See graph).

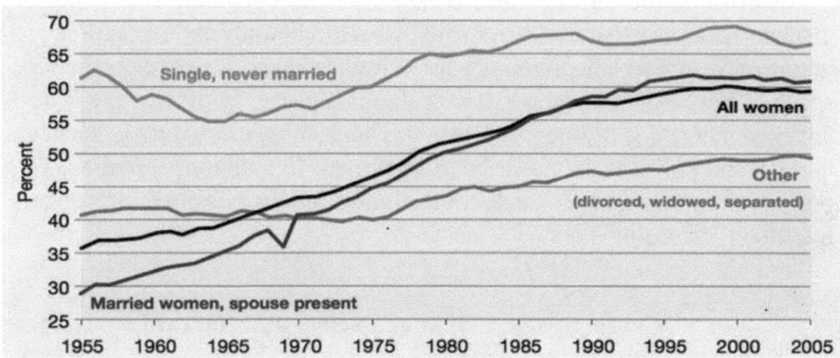

Figure 12: Labour Force Participation of Women in the USA, 1955–2005[60]

As more women entered society and acquired jobs, many places were no longer only spaces for men. Even the previously mentioned white-collar offices are now transitioning into mixed-gender spaces due to the arrival of many women.

Nevertheless, urban spaces are still dominated by masculine spaces. As a result, women's expression of femininity becomes somewhat distorted and is expressed in ways that are imagined and desired by men. The city is full of media, billboards, and postings of sexual expression, and female sex workers and sex shops supply the streets. The overflowing sexual expressions are a form of commercialisation rather than just a commodification of sex. Furthermore, the city enables such freedom of sexual expression because the city contains more strangers and atmospheres that respect individual freedom and expression. Individuals in the city, therefore, experience less pressure than those in traditional societies.[61]

---

60 Data from 1955–1975 comes from the US Census Bureau, Statistical Abstract of the United States [Available at: https://www.census.gov/library/publications/1955/compendia/statab/76ed.html], [Last accessed: 25th December 2023]; Data from 1976-2005 comes from the Bureau of Labor Statistics [Available at: https://www.bls.gov/], [Last accessed: 25th December 2023].
61 Ara Wilson, "Sexuality," in Donald Macon Nonini (ed), *A Companion to Urban Anthropology* (Chichester, West Sussex: Wiley-Blackwell, 2014): 193.

Due to their openness toward sexual expression, cities are places where those with diverse sexual identities, such as homosexuals or transexuals, are vocal and active. Cities are places where sexual minorities can socially present their identities and demand rights. Conflicts with supporters or opponents also occur mainly in urban spaces. In cities, people who admit to non-heterosexual identities such as gay, lesbian, bisexual, intersex, genderqueer, or transgender create their own culture, protect their rights, and maintain their networks.[62] In conclusion, cities are relatively more generous in terms of gender space than are traditional societies.

Meanwhile, the virtual world remains steadfast regardless of gender space disputes. Contrary to traditional reality, where male-only and female-only spaces merge into gender-integrated spaces, virtual spaces preserve gender-specific spaces. For example, there are cultural spaces, movies, and consumer advertisements for women, and movies and consumer adverts, such as war movies and political dramas, often target men. In addition, extreme TV sports programmes and sensual and combative video games revitalise spaces for traditional masculinity.

Virtual Space: Extended Society and Narrative

Virtual reality is a computer-simulated place or environment where users can interact via an interface. "Virtual reality," "virtual space," or "virtual environment" are similar concepts that people often use interchangeably.

Humans have always sought to secure various spaces. Besides discovering new worlds and expanding empires, we have constantly created virtual worlds. As we envision an ideal society, dream of forming a lovely family, and imagine ourselves as the protagonist of a fairy tale, we immerse ourselves into our imaginary worlds. Such creating of the imaginary world is thus as old as humankind. Adding the technology and social network dynamics to the imaginary world, numerous people made it possible to create and operate new worlds in their perceptions.

The online environment facilitates access to information and distant people and allows society to enter the information age.[63] The information age has brought enormous changes to people's lives and thoughts, one of which is the change in the concept of space. Traditionally, the concept of space only referred to the "space of place", but now we also recognise the "space of flow." This space of flow is created by the movement of human thoughts and streams of

---

62 Anthropologists have researched the activities and life patterns of these sexualities. A few leading scholars are Wilson and Voss. Barbara L. Voss, "Domesticating Imperialism: Sexual Politics and the Archaeology of Empire," *American Anthropologist* 110(2), (2008): 191–203; Ara Wilson, *The Intimate Economies of Bangkok: Tomboys, Tycoons, and Avon Ladies in the Global City* (Berkeley, CA: University of California Press, 2004).

63 Castells, *The Rise of the Network Society*, 2010.

signals, which provides the material support for simultaneous social practices communicated at a distance with the help of technology. The space of flow is not visible, but it creates a space that we can recognise: a virtual space.[64] By using the space of the streams of signals, people have extended society to online spaces.[65] As a result, the space we live in extends beyond the real world and into our thoughts delivered through media. Therefore, we can describe the virtual space as a world of our perceptions that have been created by our interpretations of the existing world rather than a world that was previously non-existent. Just like in the space of places, people perform "production, transmission and processing of flows of information" in the space of flows.[66] In virtual space, people transcend time and space and enjoy more accessible and comfortable spaces than in the real world.

The most significant forces that power and develop virtual space are the virtual citizens of virtual society. We call these people citizens because they perform social activities and, because of the nature of virtual spaces, can participate relatively freely and equally in their society. People more actively participate in virtual societies because the Web 2.0 era enables more openness, sharing, and collaborative environments. In virtual spaces, people can broaden their awareness and influence by sharing, rather than monopolising, information. Such a culture of sharing has resulted in a culture where people can obtain high intelligence and collaborate simultaneously. As a result, publishing, media, journalism, education, commerce, political activities, religious activities, hobbies, personal PR, and relationships with others have changed drastically.[67] In this way, participation, sharing, openness, and collaboration have shaped virtual space into a platform where people can freely discuss and generate opinions and leadership roles. Just as people gathered and discussed in the public space of Athens, such active and participating citizens of this democratic, equal, open, and collaborative virtual space primarily drive the development of virtual space.[68]

As in traditional cities, people are the main creators of substance and meaning in the virtual world. Therefore, the nature of virtual space is also socio-spatial and socio-temporal. These similarities enable virtual space and the real world to interact easily. Therefore, interpreting the virtual society as evidence of the collapse of the real world or as a competing target of the real world is a misunderstanding of the two worlds. Citizens can travel between both worlds to meet, discuss, and produce because they are the common subjects of both worlds.

---

64 The term cyberspace, a term similar to virtual space, first appeared in William Gibson's novel, Cyberpunk, Neuromancer. William Gibson, *Neuromancer*, Reprint (New York: Ace, 1987).

65 Wellman, *Networks in the Global Village*; "The Community Question. "

66 Castells, *The Rise of the Network Society*, 2010: Kindle Location 653.

67 Matthew Fraser and Soumitra Dutta, *Throwing Sheep in the Boardroom: How Online Social Networking Will Transform Your Life, Work and World* (Chichester, England; Hoboken, NJ: Wiley, 2008): 195–210.

68 Fraser and Dutta, *Throwing Sheep*, Chapter 8.

Just as Herbert Marshall McLuhan described the media as "an extended man," virtual space can be considered an extended space of our own.[69]

For The Place You Are Standing Is Holy

After the emergence of the Reformation movement and Existentialism, there was a slow but sure change in the dualistic influences that had traditionally affected Christianity. Later, Paul Tillich,[70] Karl Barth,[71] Dietrich Bonhoeffer,[72] Harvey Cox,[73] and others also developed theologies for secular places. This resulted in the theological attitude within some Christian circles that God must be the owner of any space. This integrative perspective broadened the Christian perspective, which had long been restricted to dualism, and became the basis for changing our attitude toward the space around us.[74]

Because all the spaces of this world are affected by the fall, no place is holy enough to be purely devoted to God. However, the issue is not of the land itself, but the people associated with it. Depending on who is there, a land that was once holy may become cursed, and even a cursed land can become a holy place at any time. Moreover, God is the ultimate owner of all places in the universe, and any place where he works is a sacred space that belongs to him. Therefore, there is no place in this world where God does not need to be glorified. As Abraham Kuyper said, "There is not a single inch of the whole terrain of our human existence over which Christ [...] does not proclaim, 'Mine!'"[75] So, all creations in the city must become sacred and belong to God. Whether it is a brothel or a cursed land, they all must exist for the glory of God. No matter what evil spirits or cursed history the land had before, places with God's presence become holy.

In the Old Testament, Jacob slept on the ground in a certain place after leaving his home to go to Haran. In his dream, he saw an angel and confirmed the promise of God. When Jacob awoke from his sleep, he thought, "Surely the Lord is in this place, and I did not know it." He was afraid and said, "How awesome is this place, this is none other than the house of God, and this is the gate of heaven" (Gen. 28:16-17). On that day, the "certain place" (Gen. 28:11) in the desert that had only meant loneliness and fear to Jacob suddenly became the sacred place of Bethel (Gen. 28:19). To be precise, that certain place had always

---

69 McLuhan, *Understanding Media*, 30–32.

70 Paul Tillich, *On Art and Architecture* (New York: Crossroad, 1987).

71 Karl Barth and Edwyn Clement Hoskyns, *The Epistle to the Romans* (London: Oxford University Press, 1968); Karl Barth, *Letters, 1961-1968* (Grand Rapids, MI: Eerdmans, 1981).

72 Dietrich Bonhoeffer, *Letters and Papers from Prison* vol. 8 (Minneapolis, MN: Fortress, 2010).

73 Cox, *The Secular City*.

74 Gorringe, *A Theology of the Built Environment*, 1–17.

75 Abraham Kuyper, "Sphere Sovereignty," in James D. Bratt (ed), *Abraham Kuyper: A Centennial Reader* (Grand Rapids, MI: Eerdmans, 1998): 488.

been God's place, and He had always been there. However, to Jacob, he was only able to recognise God's presence through an encounter with Him.

A similar case happened to Joshua in Jericho. To Joshua, Jericho was a place of death and war. But the commander of the Lord's army told him, "Remove your sandals from your feet, for the place where you are standing is holy" (Joshua 5:15). At that moment, the land of slaughter turned into the holy land. Even when Moses, who lived as an ordinary shepherd, came upon the bush on Mount Horeb, God said, "Remove your sandals from your feet, for the place on which you are standing is holy ground" (Ex. 3:5). At this moment, Mount Horeb, where Moses had raised his sheep and lived an everyday life with his family, became holy ground.

As Jacob realized at Bethel, God is not only present in every space we pass through, but He is the Lord of it. Therefore, no matter how secular and cursed "certain places" of our space are, they become a Bethel once we open our eyes. In this way, the holy land refers not only to the people, the past, the spiritual experience, or the culture of the land, but also to who owns it. Therefore, the first thing that Jacob, who began the next chapter of his life, Joshua, who faced a fierce battle, and Moses, who rescued the nation from Egypt, needed to understand was that they were now stepping on holy ground of which God was the owner.

Recognising God's sovereignty over space is the basis for reconnecting and reconciling disconnected people. National borderlines, hundreds of years of boundaries between villages, colleagues we do not want to encounter, and factions within organisations are all divisions that separate and bring hostility between people. To repent from these traditions and structures and treat others with God's heart, the first thing to do is realise that God is the only owner of this land. Even if the space is a brothel or belongs to hostile people, we cannot judge the value of the land.

Missiological Reflection: Reconnect Them, for They Are Mine!

Since the city's time and space are socio-temporal and socio-spatial, their meanings are given by the people. Thus, to properly understand the inherent meaning of space, we must read the people who pass through it with the eyes of God. Therefore, the church must escape its dualistic concept of space and its building should not be confused with the temple. Because God is holy, wherever God works is the object of our activities and missions.

Urban Christians Reading the Holy Places with God's Eyes

Urban Christians should strive to maintain a holy life wherever they are in their time and space. To do this, we must first try to read the space we are in with God's eyes. The space in the commuter bus we ride every morning, in the office where we work hard every day, and at home where we think we can live our lives however we want should also become a sacred space owned by God. Reverend

Robert Boyd Munger's book *My Heart Christ's Home* has inspired numerous Christians to spiritual repentance and rededication because it taught them that Christ is the owner of their homes and rooms.[76] God wants the space to be purified and reused regardless of a place's past or the competition, achievements, and anxieties surrounding it. Just as the Lord told Peter, "What God has cleansed, no longer consider unholy" (Acts 10:15), God wants to cleanse our spaces. Despite being born in a filthy stable, Jesus was a man without flaws and sins. No one says that the stable in Bethlehem is dirty because it is the holy place where Jesus was born. Likewise, even if our space has an impure background, it can become holy when we recognise again that Jesus is the owner, that it is, a space with Jesus who has no flaws or sin. Richard Niebuhr said, "What we learn from Scripture is that every day is the day that the Lord has made; every nation is a holy people called by him into existence in its place and time and to his glory; every person is sacred, made in his image and likeness."[77] As such, the space in which we live is not ours, but a space where Jesus proclaims: "Mine!"

If urban Christians had a Bethel, Jericho, or Horeb moment like the Old Testament characters, the streets that we pass, the places where we fight fiercely, and the places we live our daily lives would become holy places where God is the Lord. For Mr Otto, introduced earlier, receiving the Bible from Peter was a kind of Bethel moment.

In this way, reading the space with God's eyes instead of one's own is crucial. Looking through God's eyes means to see the space and the people in it as God sees them and to have His heart. To do this, we must be able to go to the place and humbly listen to the people. This is the best way to overcome the prejudices and misunderstandings about them. Just as Jesus came to us and lived with us, we must also visit them and talk to them as equals. Treating them as outsiders and making no effort to remove prejudices will disconnect us from them. This disconnection between people is what the enemy wants to see (Jn 8:44) and is the work of the flesh (Gal. 5:20).

Naturally, those who see the city through God's eyes have God's same vision for the city. Even if it seems wounded and distorted, our eyes will focus on God, who dreams of a transformed city.

Urban Church's Identity: The Semi-Public Church Model and the Yard of the Church Scattered Throughout All Living Spaces

During the daytime on weekdays, it is not easy for outsiders to enter the church. Iron gates and high walls block the church, and one must pass through several gates to reach the main sanctuary. Even if an office worker wants to visit during their lunch break to see the pastor, no one is inside. As a result, church buildings

---

76 Robert Boyd Munger, *My Heart: Christ's Home*, Rev. ed. (Downers Grove, IL: InterVarsity, 1986).

77 H. Richard Niebuhr, *Radical Monotheism and Western Culture: With Supplementary Essays* (Louisville, KY: Westminster/John Knox Press, 1993): 52.

in many cities are distanced from the outside world.[78] On the other hand, Korean Buddhist temples are open on weekdays and have small gardens and benches, so outsiders can easily enter. They are located in the centre of the city so that ordinary people who are tired of life can freely visit and relax. Mosques in China and Central Asia typically have front yards; for local Muslims, this place is like their own front yard. Inside the temples, there are always people inside to meet. Although these Muslims may be uncomfortable with outsiders entering their area, if visitors are polite and introduce themselves, they will usually be kind to guide them around the front yard.

The church is usually empty, except on Sunday mornings when numerous believers come at once. These very few short hours on Sunday mornings are so crucial to the church that all its facilities and human resources are organised around this time. Consequently, gatherings are often inconvenient for times other than on Sunday morning. Because the spatial structure and activities of the church were adapted mainly to Sunday's internal activities and functions, the church is unavoidably separated from the surrounding community.

For churches to become more accessible to outsiders, it is worth bringing up Paul Hiebert's semi-public space model for the church. This semi-public space is a kind of neutral territory for outsiders to visit freely. For example, customers can try on clothes displayed in a department store because the department store is neutral and open territory. Although an owner is present in this neutral territory, others temporarily use it as if it were their own. Moreover, urbanites are already familiar with semi-public spaces such as offices, parks, and coffee shops. This tendency is easily revealed when encountering the Gospel or choosing a church. People do not usually go to places they consider to be someone else's space be told about God, except for those who are in desperate situations. However, it is not as uncomfortable to talk about God with others in a neutral territory if they use it as if it were their own space. Hiebert explains the church model as a semi-public space as follows:

> One thing is clear: many city folk will not come to a church, even for evangelistic meetings. They see the church building as religious territory. To enter it is to make a first positive step to becoming a Christian, a step they are not ready to make. They may be willing to look at Christianity, but they will do so only in the safety of some neutral territory where no pre-commitment is needed. They just want to window shop the Gospel.[79]

If this semi-public space becomes easily accessible and achieves favourable results, even the outsiders can feel comfortable and accessible in the space. For example, large hardware stores in the United States sell various building and construction materials such as pipes and wood so that consumers can repair the electrical or water supplies of their house. Fathers who visit the shop to buy supplies to repair broken parts of their homes often stand in front of the displayed

---

78 Yu Hyunjoon, 도시는 무엇으로 사는가, 161–65.

79 Hiebert and Meneses, *Incarnational Ministry*, 331.

items, unsure of what to do because this is unusual work for them. Fortunately, these stores have experienced staff in every section who help customers. While the workers can be seen organising and cleaning their sections, their primary role is to make consumers happy by solving their problems. The reason people come directly to the store instead of ordering online is because they do not fully understand what is going on in the electrical area and are in a hurry to get it fixed as their families are experiencing inconvenience. Therefore, in addition to giving advice about the repairs, these experienced staff members provide the fathers with the praise and exclamation of their families later. In other words, these workers make the hardware store a fun weekend playground for fathers. As a result, they feel as though this store is their own space and sometimes even buy expensive equipment that they do not need. Likewise, if the church becomes a semi-public space with friendly people which is accessible to outsiders, its likeability will increase tremendously.

The nature of the church that the Bible refers to focuses on the meeting of people rather than the concept of space. For example, the church is described as "For where two or three have gathered together in My name" (Mt. 18:20) or as the body of Christ (Eph. 1:23). Therefore, the church can be divided into groups of two or three people not only on Sundays but also on weekdays, in the office, with neighbours, in the coffee shop, and in the virtual space. The place where we stand is a holy place, and the urban church must now seek to change all spaces into sacred places where people can meet God in creative ways. This is how urban churches that believe any place can be transformed to be God's holy sanctuary should present themselves.

6. Crossing Over Your Boundary for Reconciliation

Introduction

Do social classes still exist in the 21st century? Are inequality and group discrimination appropriate words to use for a city culture that values a democratic and equal society, people's dignity, and equal opportunities? Although different from the caste system of the past, even a modern democratic society cannot avoid the issue of status.[1] We identify others' status by judging their vehicle brands, neighbourhoods, morning coffee, where they go on vacation, workplaces, and the parties they are invited to. Stratification often creates misunderstanding and disconnect in people's relationships and eventually cuts them off from each other. In addition to stratification, the fact that people are divided into groups also creates the risk of conflict and building walls between people. When these walls are built, people naturally develop a sense of territory. This makes one strongly distinguish oneself from others and avoid entering others' territory.

The division between people is not simply about people being divided, but is also a spiritual phenomenon. Severance is an evil that creates division, a sense of superiority, jealousy, personal blasphemy, and real-life discrimination. Division separates people and causes prejudice and hatred, trampling on the divine dignity of one another and eventually making each other evil. In other words, severance causes one to view the other as an object that can be treated destructively instead of someone equal to oneself.

This chapter will look at the relationship between the division of people and space and time. Additionally, we will reflect on what kind of person Jesus is in the face of this division and competition. We will also examine what the Bible says to us who are trying to break the indifference, anger, and glass ceiling that division creates, and fighting against the class system. As a result, we will see the vital roles that reconciliation, forgiveness, courage, and service to others have in the urban ministry. To this end, this chapter will be structured in a way that answers the following questions:

1. What creates groups and boundaries between urbanites?
2. What are the characteristics of the severance phenomenon that is present in all classes of the city?

---

1 Hiebert and Meneses, *Incarnational Ministry*, 287–95.

3. What opportunities has God given to reconnect the disconnected urban classes?

In the final missionary consideration, let us discuss the needs of courageous Christians who cross the boundaries between groups for reconciliation and forgiveness and the urban churches that seek places of conflict.

A City Filled with Boundaries

Multiple groups co-exist within the city. Each group has a group boundary that separates the inside from the outside. Since the city is made up of groups of people, it can be said that cities are naturally filled with these boundaries. Group boundaries are not formed naturally but are all formed by opinions agreed upon by people with some intention or concept in mind. In Chapter 5, the fact that the neighbourhood of Flingern became a violent and notorious place means that the minds of the people had divided the inside and outside of the village into places where there is and is not notoriety. Now, let us see how the boundaries that people have drawn affect their own society.

Place Making and Place Identity

People give names to places around them, small or large. For example, every place and room in an office building has a name such as copy room, CEO office, and bathroom, and every town and region has a name. This type of behaviour, which involves the assigning of names, is called "place-making."[2] Place-making is a conceptual behaviour in which people show interest in a place with no particular purpose or use and assign meaning and use to it. For example, in 1851, Jim D. Savage (1817–1852) and Doctor Lafayette Bunnel (1824–1903) "discovered" Yosemite Valley and put it on the map.[3] This does not mean that Yosemite Valley did not exist before the discovery as it has always been there. But Yosemite became a symbol for travelling and making memories and a national emblem because people gave it the name Yosemite and embedded the word into people's psyches. As such, assigning names to places means that these places now become part of our lives and are granted a proper status within society's politicised discourses.[4]

Place-making is a behaviour that creates "place-identity" for the location. Place-identity is created by multiple factors. Among these factors are its history and geographical attributes. For example, the name Foothill Village describes the region's natural environment, and San Francisco is named after a respected saint, thereby attempting to determine the city's identity in a certain way. Place-identity is not something created by one or two individuals but rather through a consensus within a community context. If the community has an agreement,

---

2 Jaffe and Koning, *Introducing Urban Anthropology*, 23–25.

3 Lafayette H. Bunnell, *Discovery of the Yosemite, and the Indian War of 1851* (New York; Chicago, IL: F.H. Revell, 1892): 41.

4 Tim Cresswell, *Place: A Short Introduction* (Hoboken, NJ: Wiley, 2013).

place-making can happen quickly. For example, in the 1970s, the refugee camp created in Jaesongdong in Busan, Korea for Vietnamese refugees, known as "Boat People", symbolised the Cold War and the unfortunate refugees of Communism. However, after these Boat People moved to other places, Jaesongdong's significance shifted to representing the friendship between Korea and Vietnam, who went through hardships together.

Political situations and ideology also contribute to place-making. For example, the name of Saint Petersburg in Russia is a Germanic image. During World War I, the Russian government changed it to Petrograd to have a Russian image. Ten years later, it became Leningrad to symbolise Communism. Still, in the early 1990s, they changed the name again back to Saint Petersburg.

Lastly, "zoning", a geographic indicator, also contributes to place-making. Zoning is like a numerical system assigned to each region that a government uses to manage regional characteristics efficiently. For example, a specific code is assigned based on weather, wildfire-prone areas, and pollution. Most national and city governments develop such zoning systems for functional division of regions and city-planning. Often, such zoning systems create images of the people who live in the area.

As such, complicated factors, such as location, history, consensus of a community, political and social situations, and governmental policy, create place-making and place identity. This place-identity is not permanent just because it was determined so at the time but is constantly going through transformations.

Places, Symbols, and Groups Are Integrated

Place-making induces people to do place positioning as well as give place identity. Place positioning is a state in which the people perceive an agreed-upon idea that a place is to be used in a certain way because it belongs to a certain type of person. For example, it groups a place with a person, such as men's and women's restrooms, tool shops with men, sewing factories primarily with people of colour, and ghettos with poor minorities. Because of the symbolism of a place, it can be predicted who is there and how they behave in such a place. As such, place-making is more precisely socioplace-making because geographic space is closely related to social symbols.

Socioplace-making creates a social image. In people's minds, the images of a place and the people of that area gradually solidify, eventually causing people to think that people in that area are such and such. Thus, they create a certain image of the people by combining the place and its people. For example, one may think that a Thai co-worker is used to the hot weather, which leads them to believe his desk can be placed where the air conditioner is weak.

An agreed social awareness further creates a social symbol for a certain area and the people associated with that area. For example, localisation divides commercial and residential areas, but as a result, it induces people of the same race, economic background, or those with similar occupations to live close together.[5] In such instances, the area comes to symbolise a neighbourhood of poor people, celebrities, or a certain race. In the previous case of Mr Otto, people branded the Flingern area as outdated and of poor quality.[6]

Furthermore, people create connotations about an area and its residents that they think of whenever they mention them. For example, consumption pattern is an important social symbol that shows the social status of people. For urbanites, consumption is a culture, not just a trade of goods and commodities, because people with different social positions are bound to have different lifestyles and consumption patterns. People feel a sense of belonging to their group and class through consumption. Therefore, the environment and buildings in a particular area are symbols that describe the groups and classes of the people who use them.

On the other hand, the places and symbols created by people of a specific place serve to reinforce the identity of the groups and classes that created them. In particular, when people with the same background – such as a specific ethnic group, class, or age group – live together in an area, the identity of the place is further strengthened and the people there create a spatial norm that can only be used there. This spatial norm has unspoken promises that make people think a certain way when they are there.

When a society begins to observe a spatial norm, the space comes to have a spatial regime, such as thoughts, actions, manners, and power structures that must be prioritised for that space. By this spatial regime, people agree upon what the normal state and acceptable behaviour are. Spatial regime refers to a space in which the people in it follow the norm and normal behaviours that they set. In other words, a differentiated system unique to that region is created in the society of that region. Once the spatial regime is agreed upon, it is natural for people to come to live and think according to the rules of this place. This spatial regime makes people interpret the same symbol or shape differently depending on the place. For example, the Hui, a Muslim minority in China, wear white hats or multicoloured Muslim scarves on their heads that symbolise their ethnicity on the streets. Ordinary Chinese people think differently depending on where they meet these Muslims. If they encounter them in a Muslim village, the Han Chinese think of them as ordinary Muslim restaurant workers or labourers. On the other hand, if they encounter them in an area of a mainstream ethnic group, they are on guard to think of them as unique people who do not eat pork, or, in extreme cases, Islamic terrorists or pickpockets.[7] They evoke different thoughts about the same people depending on the region because the Chinese have set different spatial norms and spatial regimes in each region. Spatial regimes and spatial norms come into play in places considered to be the domain of specific people, such as a workplace only for men, a church only for white people, a cafe for young people, and a park for the elderly.

---

5 Tim Cresswell, *Place: A Short Introduction* (Hoboken, NJ: Wiley, 2013).

6 Jacobsen, *Sidewalks in the Kingdom*, 87–88.

7 The typical view of Chinese towards Hui Muslim in the text is the result of the author's observation in 16 years of experience.

As such, urban places are social spaces that bring people from the same background together and create regional characteristics. These local groups create symbols that can shape themselves and create spatial norms to maintain their society. These regions, symbols, and groups become the causes and effects of each other and act as symbols to indicate the region and its people.

Social Positioning and Boundaries

The previously introduced zoning and placemaking are based on comprehensive and accurate data with considerable objectivity. The problem is that this localisation policy does not end with introducing a mere conceptual phenomenon but also establishes the social positioning of the people involved. Originally, this localisation policy was created by the city government for administrative efficiency, but in reality, it goes further than this to become a boundary that judges the image of the region and the society. As a result, people go from what the area is like to what the people there are like. Furthermore, regions give social positions and add value judgements to those people such as how good and bad people there are. For example, people do not think of ethnic minorities in poor neighbourhoods at the same level as elite residents in a neighbourhood where space science researchers live. As a result, people come to believe that the region and its society become one, making the area and its people stratified.

This stratification creates social boundaries between people and makes them see each other as different groups. Further, this social boundary is a kind of territorial mark that prevents other people from entering the area. For example, there is a local agreement in a wealthy neighbourhood that pushes out those who do not fit in.[8] This division between people forms prejudice, hostility, and boundaries toward each other. While people who identify with each other form a community, they become distinct, competitive, and hostile to those different from themselves.[9] This boundary and noticeable difference in social status create classes, no matter how modern a society is.

As such, there are countless borders between groups, whether they are differences in regions and backgrounds or classes. People are well-acquainted with these invisible borders and know how to only go to familiar places without overstepping them. These boundaries often create efficiency, but when these divisions between people become fixed in place, hatred and prejudice between people increase, and this phenomenon is not pleasing to God (Gal. 5:20; 2 Cor. 12:20).

Segregation Continues

In the era of globalisation, cities worldwide resemble each other, just like similar products or franchise restaurants. Not only that, but the media allows people

8 Jacobsen, *Sidewalks in the Kingdom*, 29–32.
9 Leong and Rah, *Race and Place*, 39.

around the world to hear the latest news at the same time. In this big picture, people today are interconnected with events and situations around the world. However, if we look on a local scale, we are grouped by different religions, classes, races, educational backgrounds, and economic levels.

A city is essentially a collection of divided entities. In ancient times, the outside and inside of a castle were divided by a wall, and divisions were also made inside the city so that people could live separately. In fact, rather than the walls and fortresses dividing the people, the boundaries and discrimination between people have come to create such physical boundaries. This phenomenon of division between people is always present in our daily lives. For example, even in the same office, people group together with those of similar backgrounds or may only do business with certain ethnic groups. In addition, signs indicating one's territory, walls dividing houses, surveillance cameras that prevent outsiders from entering, and entrances that require permission to pass separate those who can and cannot enter. This kind of disconnection makes people feel alienated and isolated, which causes them to make comparisons and have prejudices against different groups, leading to anger and hatred.

Winners' Segregation: The Space Behind the Wall

Winners know how to close themselves off from the outside because they have to protect the property and vested interests they have acquired. Since ancient times, the rich and powerful have separated their space from other classes of people to protect their vested interests. To distinguish the houses of the nobility from the common people, they built walls or roads between them. In some places, people of high social status located their residences closer to the royal palace. In colonies, people built tall towers in areas reserved for foreigners to prevent locals from entering.

The reason people with power and wealth set outward boundaries is usually because of the fear of crime and, more generally, of others.[10] Usually, those in superior positions have always had to protect themselves from external threats and do not want their privileges to be violated. This type of appearance can be easily found in modern architecture. For example, a gated community separates residents from the outside by having closed circuits and passwords that only insiders know.

Nowadays, the exclusivity of powerful people toward other groups is revealed in terms of culture and service rather than the physical. For example, convenience facilities, transportation facilities, decorations outside the house, and community activities are mainly installed and operated for mainstream groups.

Ironically, globalisation accelerates the disconnection of the haves from the have-nots. The haves not only face threats from those who live nearby but must

---

10 Low, "Spatiality," 23.

also compete with new trends and various other superior groups of the world.[11] The haves further separate themselves from the weak for fear of being encroached upon by the stronger and to maintain their vested interests.

Losers' Segregation – Those Who Have Nowhere to Lay Their Head

Lands and places mean more than just places to work and live; they are a means of creating enormous economic benefits for people. It is why people compete to secure a better area. People make great efforts to occupy expensive land, places where good education is attainable for their children, an office with a great view, and VIP seats at restaurants. People who have failed in this battle for space are gradually removed from opportunities and success, alienated from others, and fail to even secure a space for themselves to live. The losers who have failed in this race are a marginal group of the city, and they tend to live as a group in the same area. Marginal groups either fail to secure their own space, or even if they do, they create a high boundary between themselves and the outside world. Examples of a marginal group include ghettos, slums, shantytowns, squatters, and ethnic enclaves.

A slum refers to "a concentrated, densely settled area where housing is inadequate, residents are poor, and community functions are lacking."[12] Houses in a poor neighbourhood here refer to those built without a city government's permission. Since this neighbourhood is built ignoring proper procedures, a slum cannot expect sufficient social facilities. The reason why the slum has many shabby houses that are falling apart is not simply due to a lack of building materials, but rather a combination of insufficient public facilities, outdated medical facilities and educational environments, various domestic problems, and indifference, making residents poor and repairs difficult.[13] Fortunately, the population living in these slums has gradually decreased, from 40% of the world urban population in 2000 to 30% in 2014. During this period, "more than 320 million people gained access to either improved water, improved sanitation, durable housing or less crowded housing conditions".[14]

A shanty town is also a type of slum, but it is characterised by the illegal occupation of migrants from other regions. In their new settlement, migrants live with poverty and dysfunction in all aspects of their lives. They make a living through manual or simple labour, and the entire family usually lives in a place not far from the head of the household's workplace.

As such, slums and shantytowns do not have the economic capacity to follow the housing policy promoted by the government, so they end up building their residences illegally. For this reason, a slum population is usually common in

---

11 Low, "Spatiality," 23.

12 Mark Gottdiener and Leslie Budd, *Key Concepts in Urban Studies*, SAGE Key Concepts (London; Thousand Oaks, CA: SAGE, 2005): 135.

13 Gottdiener and Budd, *Key Concepts*, 136.

14 United Nations, "The Millennium Development Goals Report 2015," (New York: United Nations, 2015): 60.

emerging economies that have experienced rapid growth, whereas a shantytown is found in industrial cities with many transients or in cities in developed countries with many immigrants.

Ghettos and ethnic enclaves have some of the characteristics of a slum but consist of a specific race or ethnic group. While poverty is the cause of a slum's separation from society, ghettos and ethnic enclaves are separated from society because these regions are "occupied by a group segregated based on religion, colour or ethnicity."[15] However, in reality, the factor that drives people to live in a ghetto is still poverty, just like a slum. The origin of the word ghetto is unclear, but its traditional image was the poorest and abandoned Jewish population in a town or city. After World War II, black people in the United States inherited the image of a ghetto when they migrated from the south to large cities in the north and settled in one area.[16] Later, ghetto changed its image once more as an immigrant neighbourhood where foreigners immigrate to developed countries to adapt socially.[17]

Ethnic enclaves have characteristics similar to ghettos but differ from the mainstream society regarding ethnicity and culture. What separates them from a ghetto is that the next generation of ethnic enclaves moves into mainstream society. Migrants need and want to live close to each other because they lack the resources and economic power to survive. In this respect, the ethnic enclaves of migrants act as a kind of buffer between the new mainstream society and immigrants. Because of this role, ethnic enclaves create a unique subculture. Many first-generation immigrants spend most of their lives in this subculture, isolated from the outside world. They do shopping, economic activities, social gatherings, and even run churches only among themselves. Meanwhile, globalisation has narrowed the gap between ethnic enclaves and their homeland on the other side of the globe. As a result, ethnic enclaves became a hub of transnationalism. Ironically, some of these ethnic enclaves are cut off from the city, but exchanges with their mother countries become very active.

Finally, the homeless are most likely to be considered the losers in the race for urban space. The homeless are "those who cannot afford shelter by themselves."[18] They do not have a steady place to live, so some are forced to sleep rough in public places like roads, gates, parks, and subways. Those who live in illegal houses in a slum are far better off than the homeless with absolutely no place to stay. In recent years, more and more people carry all of their possessions in a car and live in it as their home. They go to work normally during the day but live in their cars after work.

---

15 Abercrombie, Hill, and Turner, "Dictionary of Sociology," 165.

16 Abercrombie, Hill, and Turner, "Dictionary of Sociology," 35.

17 Louis Wirth, *The Ghetto* (Chicago, IL: University of Chicago Press, 1928): 4.

18 Gottdiener and Budd, *Key Concepts in Urban Studies*, 49.

The most direct cause of the rise in homelessness in developed and developing countries is the "undersupply of affordable urban housing."[19] Soaring housing prices in cities create a group who cannot afford a place to sleep. In addition, national disasters such as the subprime mortgage crisis (2007) and the IMF (International Monetary Fund) bailout request for financial aid cause many people to lose their independence and become homeless. In addition, people become homeless due to reasons such as inequalities, poverty, loss of housing and livelihood, lack of decent job opportunities, forced eviction, lack of social protection and health care, domestic violence, accidents, mental illness, substance abuse, loss of employment, and gangs.[20] The homeless are a group often cut off from all parts of society.

Segregation in the New Places: Revitalisation, Suburbanism, and Mass Housing Development

Urban expansion and redevelopment rejuvenate an old city and increase its function and efficiency. As a result, it also changes the people and culture in it. Such transformation of a city can be viewed through process theory where the city itself is a process.[21] A city's expansion and redevelopment process can be divided into three main categories: revitalisation, suburbanism, and a mass housing plan.

First, revitalisation is an urban planning project with governmental authority that changes the existing urban environment when existing facilities cause functional impairments and there is a risk of deterioration of the city.[22] The reason for revitalisation is not only because buildings are old and the city has a long history, but also because it is necessary to meet the needs and demands of modern people. However, revitalisation also threatens the self-esteem and psychological support of the original residents. Some of the existing residents in urban areas have lived there for generations. For them, it is a place where the souls of their ancestors or their history and traditions reside, and the religious temples of the people built by their efforts are their very existence. However, this spatial cleansing disguised as revitalisation scatters residents and separates traditions and communities.[23] Their cultural heritage is in crisis. As land prices rise due to revitalisation, developers desire to bring in economically profitable buildings, such as shopping malls, rather than cultural assets.

---

19 Janet Ward, "Mayors Want Homelessness Back on National Agenda," *The American City & County* 115(2), (2000): 4.

20 "Affordable Housing and Social Protection Systems for All to Address Homelessness," Commission for Social Development (United Nations Economic and Social Council, 2019): 6.

21 Conn and Ortiz, *Urban Ministry*, 165–68.

22 Noh Choonhee and Kim Iltae (노춘희, 김일태), *DosihakGaeron (도시학 개론)*, (Seoul: Hyungsul, 2004): 210.

23 Gillette, *Between Mecca and Beijing*.

Revitalisation inevitably raises the rate of inflation and real estate prices in the area. This is due to middle class incomers who purchase run-down housing at cheap prices "and the subsequent upgrading of the property and massive rise in property values."[24] As a result, the phenomenon of gentrification appears when original residents who lived in the area cannot endure the changes or costs and leave. Gentrification naturally exchanges its landowners for people with completely different social networks and the ability to enjoy new trends and higher prices. As a result, the scattered previous residents are forced to forget their traditions and memories and are cut off from a community with a rich history and traditional heritage. As such, revitalisation plans cut off the original residents from society once again.[25]

The second type of urban development is suburbanism. A suburb refers to somewhere between the city and its nearby rural area.[26] Typically, suburbanism means a policy of developing new residential areas on the city outskirts for dispersing the city population. The development of the suburban area was a type of revitalisation project that started after the 1930s, especially in developed countries such as the United States, to solve the problem of overcrowding and housing in the urban areas and to achieve economic effects from large-scale development projects. Until the 1950s and 1960s, a suburban area acted as a sort of bedroom community that people only slept in, and they worked in the city during the day. However, as transportation and technologies developed, the suburban area developed into another significant living zone like the city. Adults in the suburbs commute downtown by car, and families use the educational, medical, and consumer environments near residential areas.[27]

The emergence of suburbanism created a new custom and culture that is neither urban nor rural. Because it is far from work and there is sufficient physical space between houses, the culture in the suburbs is very private. It also changed the family culture. The development of home appliances reduced housework and society's changed perception of the female workforce allowed many women to start working. Such increased economic power elevated the position of women in the family and promoted a more equal domestic division of labour.

The rise of the suburbs also created another type of segregation. As mentioned previously, living in a suburban area requires paying a high price for a home and the ability to commute downtown. As a result, it ended up becoming available to only a limited number of people. In the United States, some real estate agents prevented black people from buying homes in white areas and banks often denied them mortgages. As a result, suburban residential areas saw a dramatic increase

24 Tim Cresswell, *Place: A Short Introduction* (Hoboken, NJ: Wiley, 2013): 93.
25 Leong and Rah, *Race and Place*, 142.
26 Gottdiener and Budd, *Key Concepts in Urban Studies*, 154.
27 Mark Gottdiener, Randolph Hohle and Colby King, *The New Urban Sociology*, 6th ed. (New York: Routledge, Taylor & Francis, 2019): 125–28.

in segregation for cities and a concentration of white people[28] who were cut off from a busy urban life as home prices and maintenance fees increased. This structure further reproduced and reinforced a system that segregated people into different cultures, education, public services, and economic environments.

The third type of urban development is conurbation, or the development of new cities. Cities with dense populations build residential areas on a large scale in small towns or rural areas adjacent to a large city, rather than reclaiming wasteland. The idea behind this model was to disperse the population to the city's periphery, avoiding the overcrowding of people and social facilities in a single city. For this, government attempts to supply housing efficiently by building large numbers of houses of the same type in the affordable areas near the city.[29]

Because of the space limitation, the typical house type in the conurbation is clustered high-rise apartment buildings. The government's mass housing efforts have had the positive effect of reclaiming the suburbs and providing modern housing for many people. However, in the same way as gentrification, the development of the new outskirts also benefits outsiders who can purchase and maintain these facilities rather than existing residents. As a result, segregation of the original residents continues here as well.

On the other hand, high-rise apartments make people easily separated from one another. Residents adapt to the residential environment unilaterally designed by the architectural firm. Residents of high-rise apartment buildings have little say on the design of the structures in which they live. Both the inside and outside of the living environment are geared towards enabling a large population to live efficiently, but individual creativity and affinity with nature are ignored. Most apartments are designed with a nuclear family unit and indoor living in mind. As a result, life becomes completely individualistic as a family unit, and residents lead a life separated from neighbours and nature.

People in the outskirts of cities must spend much of their time on the road or railway. The economic and social facilities of many traditional cities are still located at the heart of the city. This forces the majority of the population in the outskirts to commute to the city centre for long hours every day. They have limited room for any other activities because so much time is spent on work, competition, and commuting. This leads people to live a uniform daily life in a uniform environment, alienated from neighbours and communities, separated from friends and family, and perhaps even from their dreams.

As such, urban redevelopment – such as revitalisation, suburbanism, and the construction of new cities – played a significant role in improving places considered outdated and ineffective. At the same time, these redevelopment plans inevitably changed place identity and the people, norms, and regimes. In addition, it should not be forgotten that the redevelopment process that was meant to provide a convenient and efficient residential environment unintentionally alienates and separates some people.

---

28 Gottdiener and Hutchison, *The New Urban Sociology*, 128.
29 Gottdiener and Hutchison, *The New Urban Sociology*, 98.

Racial Segregation

Economic and political power in multi-ethnic societies is greatly influenced not only by individual abilities but also by background and ethnicity. This is because there is already a substantial economic and political imbalance between the peoples. It also leads the same ethnicity or race on the same level to usually live in the same area. When buying a house, the socially weak are at a further disadvantage because the mortgage loan conditions differ according to economic ability.[30] Furthermore, the fact that one does not live in a good neighbourhood means a lack of housing opportunities and all the facilities and environment in the area, such as good quality health care and children's education.[31]

Such high levels of urban residential segregation greatly reinforce the poverty of minorities.[32] This is because the division of residences by group structurally disadvantages ethnic minorities in both education and employment opportunities. Such disparity is a major cause of poverty and differences in income levels by race. Furthermore, this environmental gap naturally increases the incidence of crime and violence. This makes the residences even more marginalised and there is a fall into a vicious cycle that once again brings deterioration in the living environment, health, and education level. As such, residential segregation and systemic racism become causes and effects of each other and finally fall into a discriminatory structure between the social classes as a whole. This causes barriers between classes to become higher, making it difficult for people in the lower class to climb the social ladder.

Since this racial separation problem is not caused by just one or two factors, but a combination of structural issues, historical experiences, and individual efforts, society, churches, and individuals should create a virtuous cycle by starting with what they can do. Just as a tall chair should be given to a short person, so it is necessary to provide advantageous benefits to those in structural difficulties due to unfavourable positioning to help them get out of alienation.

As we have seen so far, there are countless boundaries between urbanites, whether they are successful or unsuccessful. This disconnection easily breeds alienation, anxiety, and hostility among people. The pervasive disconnection in cities is an essential clue to understanding how God views our cities and how we can work in partnership with God.

---

30 Camille Charles Zubrinsky, "The Dynamics of Racial Residential Segregation," *Annual Review of Sociology* 29 (2003): 194; Low, "Spatiality."

31 Flanagan, *Urban Sociology*, 287–88.

32 Douglas S. Massey and Nancy A. Denton, *American Apartheid: Segregation and the Making of the Underclass* (Cambridge, MA: Harvard University Press, 1993).

God-Given Stepping Stones for Reconnection

A sense of disconnection and alienation can easily lead to hostility, anger, and rivalry. The Bible clearly warns that outbursts of anger, dispute, dissensions, and faction are the deeds of the flesh, just like idolatry and immorality (Gal. 5:19-20). Furthermore, those who neglect this caution will not inherit the kingdom of God (Gal. 5:21). Taking it one step further, for those who truly want to have love, joy, peace, patience, kindness, goodness, and fruitfulness (Gal. 5:22), it does not make sense to live with the dispute and factioning mentioned above.

To reconcile, we must first reconnect the divided. To overcome alienation and disconnection in the city and connect those who are divided, we must first figure out what God has planned for this work. Unbeknownst to us, God has already done many things in accordance with his divine plan. This section will discuss the urban middle zones where even awkward people can meet naturally, and the intersectionality that makes it easy to communicate with strangers to discover this holy plan.

The Urban Middle Zones: God-Given Spaces for Reconnection

There are many middle zones in cities that are different from private spaces, such as homes, and public spaces, such as offices. In these middle zones, people naturally engage in relationships that cannot be fulfilled in private or public spaces. For urbanites who must meet people outside their own family for personal acquaintance or purpose, this middle zone is a kind of buffer; it is emotionally natural and comfortable, and is a place where they can meet their personal and business needs. This middle zone has two types: the third place and the urban junction.

The third place is neither home nor workplace, but a place where people gather for the purpose of meeting. Traditionally, people have welcomed guests at home. Inviting someone into one's home means trusting the other person and feeling close enough to allow them into one's own private space. Also, inviting a guest into one's home means that it is a relationship where the host does not mind exposing their culture and worldview to the guest. In the act of welcoming guests, there are not only language and cultural factors but also manners and etiquette and the power relationship between the two. Usually, guests are expected to show some respect for the host's traditions or religious beliefs. Therefore, to be invited to someone's home means not only visiting someone else's house or territory but also entering the ethnic and religious sphere to which the family belongs. This means that inviting guests to one's home does not happen in uncomfortable relationships but with people of good rapport who have the same ethnic or religious background or good trust and friendship. While the guests one meets at the workplace are usually only business connections, the guests who come to one's home are a mixture of work and personal acquaintances and therefore form very different relationships from people one only meets at their workplace.[33]

As society becomes more urbanised, inviting guests into one's home has become rare and more burdensome. First, the physical distance between places of social life and home has grown too far. In the past, most of one's social life took place close to home, so guests naturally lived close by as well. But now, guests must come from afar by car or public transport. Moreover, a busy city life where people work all day and have various plans on weekends makes inviting guests burdensome. Additionally, modern people who have become accustomed to individualism or familism are not happy to see others come into their personal domain.

Being an urbanite does not mean they lack a place to invite guests. In fact, urbanites can interact with guests more abundantly than in any traditional village. Ray Oldenburg introduces the third place as a place for urbanites to casually meet guests and hold informal public gatherings. This third place is an informal place that takes the burden off inviting people to one's home – for example, coffee shops, bookstores, bars, and hair salons – and avoids a formal or work atmosphere like a company space. This third place is "marked by a playful mood, [...] [and] is remarkably similar to a good home in the psychological comfort and support that it extends."[34] People sit face-to-face together in the third place and socialise or work mainly through conversation. Therefore, the people who meet in this third place are people who have built up some trust or have a reason to meet.

Perhaps for modern urbanites, this third place is also a place that shares some of the roles of a house church in the past. This is because people feel comfortable in this place and can have deep conversations and share life with someone who accepts them. It is common to see people studying the Bible together in coffee shops all around the world on Saturday mornings. One may also often see middle-aged couples sitting in a restaurant on a Thursday evening, introducing Jesus to another person.

A second model of the urban middle ground is urban junction, introduced by Eames and Goode.[35] This urban junction is an urban space where even people who do not know each other well and have different backgrounds can meet naturally. Of course, there are places where one avoids conversations with strangers as much as possible, but there are other places where one must interact with others. For example, introduced earlier, Mr Otto's shop is visited by anyone who needs it, regardless of their personal background. Cities are full of intersections, like hobby gatherings and shopping malls, where even strangers can be together.

---

33 Ray Oldenburg calls this meeting an informal public gathering. Ray Oldenburg, *The Great Good Place: Cafés, Coffee Shops, Bookstores, Bars, Hair Salons, and Other Hangouts at the Heart of a Community* (Cambridge: Da Capo Press, 1999): 9–19.

34 Oldenburg, *The Great Good Place*, 42.

35 Eames and Goode, *Anthropology of the City*, 216.

Urban junctions can be broadly divided into four types. First, there are situational urban junctions such as hospitals, government offices, parks, and restaurants; temporary places where people prepare and work together regardless of individual relationships, such as sports stadiums, national foundation day events, and Children's Day events; and structural formation where people with the same interests gather and achieve a common benefit for a political activity, a leisure activity, or a club. Finally, there is a recently popularised urban junction known as the cyber and modern space, which includes computer repair shops and virtual spaces.[36] Whereas the third place mentioned above is where one meets people they already have basic trust in, an urban junction is where one can meet people from entirely different backgrounds who do not know them well. It is a place where people meet because of activities they have in common, or for a common purpose. Thus, the many different urban junctions in the city make it easier to interact with people other than those from the same background.

In this way, urbanites come to middle zones such as urban junctions or third places for their own needs and purposes. It could be a workplace where one's dreams come true, a recharge station that shares the same interests and emotions, a place with friends who accept and encourage each other, or a quiet place to rest. Among these, the third place and urban junctions within virtual reality are on the increase. If there are common interests and goals, one can meet anyone from all over the world online and naturally receive interest and help from small groups.

The well where Jesus asked the Samaritan woman for a drink of water (John 4) is also a middle zone. Although Jesus and the woman were of different ethnicities, regions, religions, statuses, and genders, the two people with a common need for water came to the well, and the conversation that started naturally on the topic of water was the starting point that led the woman to know the Messiah.

Jesus, as one who seeks to turn division and separation into reconciliation and forgiveness, appears as one "who made both groups into one and broke down the barrier of the dividing wall" (Eph. 2:14). The increasing urban junctions can be an important meeting point through which the influence of peace and reconciliation can flow if used by Christians appropriately. If this message of reconciliation is spread throughout the multicultural society, it would be a message of good influence. Although the boundaries and distrust in cities might be increasing, the Jesus of reconciliation and forgiveness allowed urbanites to meet in such numerous places.

Intersectionality: God-given Potentials for Reconnection

Intersectionality is the theory that there are several social identities within a person, all of which can represent that person, and that the image of a person can be stronger when two or more identities are combined, depending on the

---

36 Kim, *Mission Strategy in the City*, 141–43.

situation.[37] The status, advantage, or disadvantage that a person can receive in society is formed when various identity factors such as gender, social class, academics, background, and race interact.[38] For example, if a black woman in the United States is involved in a criminal trial, she could suffer much more because of the prejudice against women on top of the prejudice against black people. It is the theory that a person standing at the intersection of two streets is in much more danger than when crossing a regular road because of the vehicles coming from multiple directions. There are institutional, symbolic, and individual dimensions to a person's identity. Among them, a person with more than one unfavourable factor in society is much weaker and more disadvantaged than a person disadvantaged by only one.[39]

If we perceive this intersectionality theory as information flow and social networks between urbanites rather than as an individual social advantage or disadvantage, we can see an unexpected possibility for communication. There are numerous elements of identity within a person, such as ethnicity, region, gender, religion, educational background, hobbies, occupation, and income. Communication with people far more diverse and distant than before is possible if we connect them with the identities and interests inherent in people. For people to communicate, there must be a common ground to act as a foothold between them.[40]

If they have even one thing in common despite their different backgrounds, they can communicate with each other. Each time the elements of common identity increase, the two can expand and deepen their interactions. For example, people who went to the same high school, are related to each other, and speak the same language have more commonness that they can empathise with than people who only speak the same language.

This concept of intersectionality easily explains how people in cities with dual-layered cultural sets can communicate with people from different backgrounds.[41] As mentioned in Chapter 1, modern urbanites functionally have dual social layers that have clear separations. On the inside layer, they maintain the traditional identity that they inherited from their ancestors, and on the outside, they maintain the social identity they acquired while living in society. In this social identity, urbanites contain various pieces of identity that let them live in society and interact with others from different backgrounds.

---

37 The term intersectionality was first introduced by an American critical race researcher and black female sociologist, Kimberlé Crenshaw.

38 Crenshaw stated that the social pressure that one receives is the result of one's various backgrounds and social perceptions. Kimberlé Crenshaw, "Demarginalizing the Intersection of Race and Sex: A Black Feminist Critique of Antidiscrimination Doctrine, Feminist Theory and Antiracist Politics," *University of Chicago Legal Forum* 1(8), (1989): 139–67.

39 Patricia Hill Collins, "Toward a New Vision: Race, Class and Gender as Categories of Analysis and Connection," *Race, Sex & Class* 1(1), (Fall 1993): 25–45.

40 Smith, *Creating Understanding*, 23–40.

41 For deeper understanding of the dual-layered cultural system, see the Chapter 1.

Table 1 is an example of how Mrs Baker, Mr Liu, and Carlos come to have an identity within the main networks of urbanites mentioned in Chapter 3 – residential, ethnic, and socio-political networks – and how their identities relate to each other. These three people come from completely different ethnic backgrounds but belong to the same group in some residential and socioeconomic groups (grey boxes). Here, Carlos and Liu have never met, and they have absolutely nothing in common regarding ethnicity, interest, or even occupation. But Mrs Baker in the middle meets Carlos every Saturday morning at the bike club. She also meets Liu twice a week at meetings between real estate agents. So, if Liu tells some good news to Mrs Baker, she may even pass it on to Carlos, whom Liu does not know. As such, the various social identities of urbanites can exchange information even between people who do not know each other, through those who play an intermediary role.

<table>
<tr><th></th><th>Carlos</th><th>Mrs. Baker</th><th>Liu</th></tr>
<tr><td>Ethnic Groups</td><td>Puerto Rican</td><td>American White</td><td>Asian American</td></tr>
<tr><td rowspan="2">Residential Groups</td><td colspan="2">Cycle Club</td><td>Church</td></tr>
<tr><td>Parents and Teachers Association</td><td>Volunteer for Community</td><td>Badminton Club</td></tr>
<tr><td rowspan="2">Socio-econo-Groups</td><td>Stock Investment</td><td colspan="2">Real Estate Co. Agent</td></tr>
<tr><td>Barista in a Coffee House</td><td>A Member of the Republican Party</td><td>Internet Asian American History Club</td></tr>
</table>

Table 1: Intersectionality and the Communication Channels

Since many social activities can take place in cities regardless of individual backgrounds, this shared identity element has made it possible to interact with various people much more freely. In addition to this, the numerous physical environments known as the middle zones that the city provides make it much easier to talk to and share information with strangers. Figure 13 is a conceptualised diagram assuming that urbanites with such dual cultural structures interact and spread information in public places such as intermediate areas or companies. Everyone has two layers: one consisting of elements of the original culture and the other of social activities. A larger inner circle means that one's original cultural element is stronger. For convenience, the two letters set in parentheses expresses each person's original and socio-cultural elements. First, Carlos (A, B) meets with Mrs. Baker (D, B) in the middle of the diagram at the cycling club regularly. Although the two have entirely different original cultures – A and D – they share a common identity (B) in that they cycle regularly, so they often meet and share important information. At company meetings, Mrs Baker (D, B) regularly meets Liu (C, B), a colleague at her real estate company. All three people at the top of the diagram possess the cultural code B, a social promise used in the city, meaning that there is always a possibility that important information can flow between them regardless of their original cultural elements in the inner circle. On the other hand, the Coffee Shop

Owner (A, E) and Cousin (C, G) have thick inner layers, limiting their receiving of information from the urban society. Despite this social distance, (A, E) is frequented by Carlos because Carlos works for the café owner as a hired barista, and they came from the same hometown. (C, B) also accesses the information thanks to a cousin of Liu's. Although they are not very exposed to the mainstream urban society, accessing the new information is still possible, because of the middle ground and network.

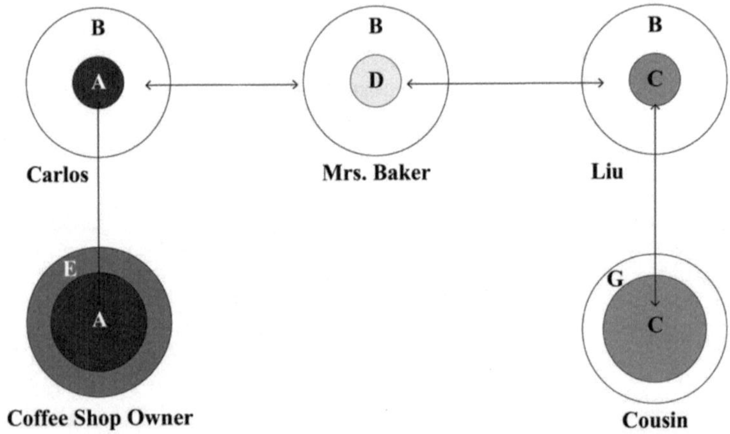

Figure 13: The Intersectionality and Diffusion of Information

God gave us common elements in our identities that allow us to understand and empathise with others so that we can break down the walls between the divided and discriminating urbanites. Adding to this, although their backgrounds may differ, urbanites with a double cultural structure have the potential to spread important information quickly and efficiently, thanks to the abundant intersections and intermediate zones they possess. As a result, even a person in the corner of a city can connect with the broader world and even influence other peoples and social classes.

In this way, although our enemies (evil spirits) set up high barriers between people to divide and foster hate, the missionary God has sent people and environments throughout the city to reconnect them. Although past generations have competed and hated one another for hundreds of years, God wants our generation to share the good news and to stop repeating such destructive relationships. Therefore, middle zones and intersections are both a gift from the missionary God to urban Christians and also a heavy responsibility.

Missiological Reflection: Missional Reconciliation in the Urban Junctions

> Now the deeds of the flesh are evident, which are: immorality, impurity, sensuality, idolatry, sorcery, enmities, strife, jealousy, outbursts of anger, disputes, dissensions, factions, envying, drunkenness, carousing, and things like these, of which I forewarn you just as I have forewarned you that those who practice such things shall not inherit the kingdom of God. But the fruit of the Spirit is love, joy, peace, patience, kindness, goodness, faithfulness (Galatians 5:19-22).

The city is constantly at war, despite no shots fired. People compete for possession of spaces, creating spatial regimes everywhere, and there are winners and losers in the fight to occupy each other's spaces. Although the city is prosperous and glamorous from the outside, we understand it alienates others. It is a class society that divides people, thus disrupting communication, and neutralises the efforts of the weak.

Jesus, too, descended from Heaven into a powerful class society. However, he neither preached about class struggles nor the trampling nor alienation of others for success. Instead, Jesus taught us to live as peacemakers in a divided world full of distrust and hate. In other words, Jesus expects us to begin the work of forgiveness and reconciliation in an urban society full of hostility and strife.

Now we will meditate on Jesus, who took the lead in knocking down these walls. In addition, let us see what urban Christians and churches of Christ can do in such a divided and grim society.

Urban Believer's Doing: Crossing the Boundary for Reconciliation

The fact that the division of space is also the division of humanity leads us Christians to read human divisions and schisms through a spiritual dimension. Grouping by class or race or by the principle of a homogeneous unit is a very natural phenomenon that allows society to function effectively.[42] The problem is the divisiveness, injustice, and violence created within these groupings. These sentiments become building blocks of hatred and indifference and continue to raise walls between different groups.

There is a spiritual element to divisive grouping. Division does not simply divide people, but it collectively and structurally creates means of human sinfulness such as division, superiority, jealousy, personal insult, and discrimination. Satan seeks to stimulate such human evil to achieve his ultimate goal to steal, kill, and destroy (Jn 10:10). Division allows people to justify discrimination and destructive treatment toward others. This tramples our innate divine dignity, and we are left as children of evil. Division also prevents us from achieving results that can only be achieved through co-operation and trust.

---

42 C. Peter Wagner and Donald A. McGavran, *Understanding Church Growth*, 3rd edn (Grand Rapids, MI: William B. Eerdmans, 1991): x; 223.

Division blocks communication and thus inhibits the ability to share good news and opportunities, which ultimately prevents the flow of the gospel. In addition, division results in the rejection of missionaries and prevents Christians from mingling with those from other classes. Consequently, the distrust and hatred that result from division are ultimately acts that obscure the glory of God and enable the work of Satan.

Second, before attempting to heal divisions, Christians in the city must pay attention to Jesus, who came to reconcile the divisions on Earth. Jesus himself is our peace and has made both groups into one. This peace is not soft or naïve; rather, it was powerful and proactive enough to break down the high and solid dividing wall that seemed impossible to overcome (Eph. 2:14).

Third, urban Christians must traverse through the rubble. Jesus may have torn down the dividing wall, but this does not mean that both sides have been connected. Simply observing Christ's work will not bring the two together. If Jesus broke down the wall with a hammer, our role is to cross over it. Just like Jesus came down to this Earth from Heaven, connection only begins when one courageously crosses over the broken wall to the other side.[43] This means we become the bridge builders. However, David Leong advocates that we must thoroughly reflect upon ourselves before building a bridge, as the real barrier is embedded in our attitude of prejudice and indifference.[44] The first step of crossing is to clearly acknowledge and repent of the barriers within us: anger, contempt, and discomfort.

Fourth, Christians who cross over the broken wall must pursue reconciliation. For, as Jesus is peace, we are also called to come as peacemakers. Simply crossing over to achieve "my work" cannot be considered a mission; we must reconnect and reconcile with people across the chasm. Reconciliation is a laborious and difficult act that requires one to approach unknown people with an incarnated and humble attitude. Furthermore, the process involves the act of removing the darkness that exists between both parties and allowing the light to reign.

Through the city, God offers Christians the opportunity for reconciliation and the physical environment to do so. This is because God has created a multitude of in-between zones in the city and intersections that allow for communication between people with various backgrounds. Reconciliation is both the beginning and destination of the mission because, without reconciliation, it is impossible to approach the unknown with the Gospel. Moreover, reconciliation is an ongoing task that must persist even after evangelism; receiving the gospel involves reconciliation with those we dislike, including people groups with generational feuds and hatred.

---

43 Leong and Rah, *Race and Place*, 103; 105.
44 Leong and Rah, *Race and Place*, 102.

Urban Church's Doing: Church Spaces for Public Use, and Reconciliation

What do the high-rise apartment buildings, slums, virtual spaces, and gentrification phenomena tell urban churches? What is spiritual rest for urbanites who are economically polarised, who excessively sacrifice their lives for careers and achievements, and fail to know the lives of their family despite living together? What should the church do in this convenient yet difficult, connected yet separated, urban society?

To reach these urbanites, the church must go to them first. A good shepherd does not wait for the flock to come but goes to where the flock is. To become such a church, urban churches may apply some of the following practices to their use of space.

The first is to open up some of the church's space to the non-believers of the neighbourhood.[45] If the church overemphasises a dualistic posture towards its space and isolates itself from the so-called pagans/heathens outside the church, disconnect from the community is not surprising. Churches usually struggle to share their space with their neighbours because they think they have too little space even for their own use. Lack of space is something most churches deal with. However, the real reason why the space feels too small is because of the church's Sunday-centred system. Maximum numbers of believers gather for various activities in a very short period. Especially in countries where inner-urban real estate prices skyrocket, considering the space for others is unrealistic and the church spaces become like an assembly line in a mass-production factory. However, this space is often empty for the rest of the week and just waits for the following weekend.

As a result, the church ignores the neighbours' needs and separates itself from the community. Unfortunately, if the church is isolated from the outside, the interaction opportunity through the church building's spatial existence is almost extinguished. Just as a mountain sanctuary is reserved only for special occasions, today's busy urbanites are unlikely to access church unless they have a special occasion. On the other hand, if the church shares its space with the community of non-believers, if it can hold events in conjunction with the neighbourhood, and if the church yard is used for children to take piano or English lessons after school and for seniors to receive health checks, the church space can become not only a place to engage with the community, but also a neutral, semi-public place that can go one step further in reaching the lost sheep.

Second, churches need to have more flexibility with the usability of space. In other words, if the concept of church is limited to the church real estate, then it automatically creates geographical distance from people's daily lives. In other words, visiting the church becomes a challenge for the busy modern urbanites especially on the weekdays. In fact, the Bible says, "For where two or three have gathered together in My name, I am there in their midst" (Mt. 18:20). The church mentioned in the Bible is not about the space, but about who the owner of the

---

45 For the meaning of semi-public space, see the Missional Reflection in Chapter 5.

meeting is. What if the church space could be divided into several pieces and be placed wherever the sheep were? This way, church can exist on weekdays and wherever the urbanites are: in the downtown office, on the lawn, and even in the virtual space. By these principles, many semi-public places can become churches as long as Jesus is the owner. If there is a small prayer room or a small worship place in the inner-city office buildings, it becomes a place to meet with God. If these small churches can connect by phone to a chaplain or elders experienced in the workplace, they can become spiritual centres for counselling and prayer. In this way, churches can divide their space into small pieces and place them where sheep are and work.

Thirdly, the urban church should intentionally seek to be in places of conflict.[46] A city always experiences divisions and hostilities because of its diversities, competition, and conflicts. Because of this, the best mission strategy of urban churches is going to the middle of conflicts and becoming a bridge of reconciliation and forgiveness. Being a bridge means that the church gives alternative answers to worldly values and commits to building new alternative communities.[47] To do this, the church must protect its members from falling victim to the anger and division that the city constantly spews out, or from absorbing worldly values as they do, because the shepherd's mission is to protect the sheep and feed them the right food. The shepherd's mission is to protect their sheep and feed them healthy food. Just as David fought and rescued his sheep from the lion and bear (1 Sam. 17:34-35), the shepherd must protect the herd by boldly coming to the places of conflict. Such good shepherds do not side with the powerful or use their sheep for their own success. Instead, they bravely confront the forces that harm their sheep. Whether it is a conflict between the church members, someone who disrespects another race, or governments that enforce evil laws, the urban church must not keep silent or ignore such unhealthy environments for their sheep.

A church that walks to the middle of conflict means that it stands between two divided sides and painfully becomes a bridge of reconciliation and forgiveness. Such a brave action is an exercise of the church's function called *diakonia*. This *diakonia* refers to healing the sick and filling the gap for reconciliation to strengthen the organism.[48] Walking into conflict means that the church goes beyond a personal level of reconciliation to include educating, campaigning, and persuading stakeholders to resolve conflicts between groups, regional and racial discrimination, and legal or structural contradictions. Contradictions in the legal or structural system are like a playing ground with a steep incline; it is almost impossible to solve at an individual level. However, the story changes when organisations like churches step in. In particular, the church should not overlook legal inequalities and discrimination by social stratification or innate factors such as race, gender, appearance, or health. Although no one

---

46 Leong and Rah, *Race and Place*, 116–19.
47 Leong and Rah, *Race and Place*, 160.
48 Cox, *The Secular City*, 211–14.

wishes to stand in the middle of conflict, shepherds who truly love their sheep must take it as their responsibility. The church is able to be involved in the conflicts of this world because Christ also came in amongst our hate and conflicts and broke down our walls.

THEME 4: URBAN FLOWS

GOOD NEIGHBOURS TRANSFORM THE CITY

7. Promotion or Failure? Flows to Get Urbanites Moving

Story Box 4 – Urban Flow Washes Away Bias

In Istanbul, Turkey, Alp is one of the countless people who work around the clock to achieve success, advancement and status. Alp is the son of a Christian family. Originally from the countryside, he is a white-collar worker at a company that produces car parts. Alp works tirelessly because of his belief that he must succeed, and lately has even been working on Sundays except for church hours. However, while he tries to achieve that success, he cannot help the thought that he is always hindered and discriminated against. Whenever that happens, Alp feels frustrated that he was born into a minority and blames the ethnic majority because they seem to succeed and secure better homes with less effort. Furthermore, the conflict between employee groups after the last mass layoff has once again deepened the rift between ethnic groups within the company.

Once, at a business dinner with Emir, an ethnic majority colleague from another department, Alp found out that Emir lives with his mother, who has Alzheimer's. Emir explained that the burden of his mother affects his marriage, and he is now considering divorce. Alp felt sorry that Emir, who was always sincere and bright, lived with such a hard burden.

The next afternoon, Emir came to Alp to thank him for listening to him as it made him feel much relieved. After that, Alp gained the courage to confess that his mother-in-law also had the same disease. He then shared with Emir his efforts to ensure that his mother-in-law's health problems did not jeopardise his own marriage.

This caused Alp to change his perspective on the colleagues around him. The people he had previously seen as competitors or as partners who he only had to work with were now people who were no different from himself. To Alp, Emir had been just a part of the majority ethnic group who had much baggage and feelings. However, the more Alp talked with Emir, he began to sense that there were far more similarities with himself than differences. Like Alp, Emir also worried about his future, was afraid of failure, and was hiding his heartache and wounds behind a smile in the workplace.

Introduction

Cities receive people from all over the world, along with information, thoughts, and trends. These people, goods, and ideas move around the city in the same way that nutrients enter the body, providing a driving force for change. The city's change causes people to succeed, think better, and create new consumer lifestyles and trends. Someone's acclamations after landing a good job, someone who has newly moved in, Wi-Fi antennas in every household, and new department stores and coffee shops create change in people's lives. The city's driving force for change makes people dream new dreams and gives them opportunities to succeed and move up the social ladder.

On the other hand, this force for change also creates competition, fear, distrust, and feelings of defeat. People spend their entire lives immersed in their work to climb the social ladder set by the city. Unfortunately, with a few exceptions, most are trapped by a glass ceiling and cannot better their social status. Successful people and the city's splendid consumption culture shown in the media keep them in the frustration that they are not successful and in the fear of failure.

The city's dynamics for change give people a desire for success and a fear of failure, leading them to believe they must "move or lose!" In the example above, Alp got the good job he had hoped for, but this hard-earned luck made him more anxious so that he could not help but work even harder. He must try hard so that he is not looked down upon and can overcome his low social class, being a member of an ethnic minority from the countryside.

This and the next chapter are studies on urban flow, which we can say is the driving force of urban change. This flow is about opportunities and resources, the force that creates people's successes and failures, and ultimately, the environment that creates hierarchies in society. Here, we will analyse, from a sociological perspective, what drives people to hope for success and causes the sense of urgency that they should not fail. To this end, this chapter will begin with the following questions:

- What is urban flow?
- How is the hierarchy between urban classes created?
- How does the urban flow affect social classes?
- Why do the city's excessive opportunities make people more anxious?

In the final reflection, we will look at the missional attitude that urban Christians and churches should have toward the success and anxiety of urban citizens.

The City as a Node of Flows

A city is like a free, constantly changing creature. For a long time, urbanists have regarded cities using the concept of space as fixed places. This fixed perspective allowed early urban studies to develop into many shapes. These included using demographics to establish policies according to the size of the city, identifying sociological differences between urban and rural areas, studying urban lives through ecology, and considering anthropological perspectives.[1] On the other hand, this concept of fixed space makes the city look like a model made of plastic Lego bricks, with a fixed shape that can be made according to its designer's plan. As a result, we tend to believe that we can sufficiently interpret the causes and effects of urban phenomena using a formula or principle.

Over time, a view that saw the city as a process emerged. From this process point of view, the city is not fixed but rather a dynamic space in which various elements are constantly active and changing like a living organism. In other words, a city is a process that changes every moment.[2] The fact that a city can be in the process of change means that it is connected to the outside world and constantly receives external energy and influence. A vast amount of materials, human resources, and information from the outside moves around the city and makes it come alive. Setha M. Low introduced this flow of energy supplied to cities as "urban flow". This urban flow refers to "circuits of labour, capital, goods, and services moving ever more rapidly through space, time, and the Internet; […] of social production, reclamation, and the home."[3] Just like a river flows in to the city from the outside, then through the city, then out, the urban flow enters from the outside and creates consumption, redistribution, and reproduction throughout the city. Since this process is continuous, the city is not fixed but is in the process of change. After promoting the city as a vibrant and transformational place in this way, the urban flow again spills out of the city with creative new energy. Cities are influenced by the outside world, react to it, and exert their influence beyond themselves. Modern cities are well exposed to and influenced by their surroundings and the rest of the world. They determine how to absorb and respond to global influences at every moment. In this way, cities are the nodes to the flows that absorb and react to external influences and exert their influences outward.[4]

Commodities, People, and Thoughts Are Flowing

Countless commodities and human resources flow between cities, providing energy for change and vitality everywhere. Setha Low largely divides the numerous flows that travel through the city into people, commodities, and thoughts.[5] Firstly, the city has a constant flow of people. Cities are places filled

---

1 Simmel, "The Metropolis and Mental Life"; Cooley, *Human Nature and the Social Order*; William Isaac Thomas and Morris Janowitz, *On Social Organization and Social Personality: Selected Papers* (Chicago, IL: University of Chicago Press, 1966); Wirth, *The Ghetto*; Wirth, "Urbanism as a Way of Life"; Park and Burgess, *Introduction to the Science of Sociology, Including the Original Index to Basic Sociological Concepts*; Burgess, "The Growth of the City".

2 Conn and Ortiz, *Urban Ministry*, 165–68.

3 Low, "Spatiality," 15.

4 Gary W. McDonogh, "Flow," in Donald Macon Nonini (ed), *A Companion to Urban Anthropology* (Chichester, West Sussex: Wiley-Blackwell, 2014): 33.

5 McDonogh, "Flow," 33–44.

with "people flow," from people who repeatedly travel short distances – such as commuting to and from work – to immigrants from foreign countries. Relatively permanent changes in one's residence are called migration and immigration.[6] Between them, migration mainly refers to a permanent movement within the country, and immigration refers to when people "[…] travel into a country for the purpose of permanent residence there."[7] The influx of population through migration and immigration is a major cause of rapid growth in cities. Migration usually refers to the influx of people into the city from the outside, but with the recent development of suburbanism, there is also a phenomenon of de-urbanisation in which urbanites move away from the city centre to settle in the suburbs.

The second type of urban flow is commodities and finances. In the past, cities absorbed large amounts of food, raw materials, and goods from the surrounding farming and fishing villages and industrial complexes. Most cities now absorb commodities from all over the world thanks to their outstanding connectivity. As a result, the world's trade volume and circulation of goods increases at a tremendous rate. The global export volume of trade in goods rose from $1.9 trillion in 1985 to $19.45 trillion in 2018.[8] This change in flow was made possible because many countries had grown enough economic power, technology, and transportation to handle such a large volume of goods. On top of that, the reduction in international regulations on trade and the development of remittance systems also contributed. In particular, the flow of goods between countries moves across the borders much more freely than the flow of commodities.

The third category of urban flows includes thoughts and fashions. A city is where people come together to form creative and beneficial ideas. In other words, the city becomes a creative space that develops the arts, sciences, and literature and creates freedom, humanism, democracy, and ideologies.[9] Globalisation and abundant distribution networks within the city stimulate people's thoughts so that the city's creativity and passion can bear fruit. New information and fierce competition create new desires in people, and many facilities and services help them to fulfil their passions. Additionally, the revolutionary development of media and technology awakens people's long-dormant self-consciousness and civic awareness. For those who have long been

---

6 J.J. Mangalam and Harry K. Schwarzweller, "Some Theoretical Guidelines toward a Sociology of Migration," *International Migration Review* 4(2), (1970): 8.

7 Merriam-Webster, "Immigration", *Merriam Webster Dictionary* [Available at: https://www.merriam-webster.com/dictionary/immigration], [Last accessed: 27th December 2023].

8 Statista, "Trends in global export volume of trade in goods from 1950-2018". *Statista Website* Latest Release Date: August 2023. [Available at: https://www.statista.com/statistics/264682/worldwide-export-volume-in-the-trade-since-1950/], [Last accessed: 27th December 2023].

9 William Alexander Robson, *Great Cities of the World: Their Government, Politics and Planning* (London: Allen and Unwin, 1954).

trapped in traditional groups, cultures, or countries, this globalisation and urban flow provide the energy to create new ideas, preferences, trends, desires, distribution networks, and relationships.

Commodities, people, and thoughts flow like water in and out of the city. In addition, human interaction and the desire for success are the driving forces that push these urban flows like a pump. On top of that, globalisation and modern technology significantly increase this driving force of the flow.

These urban flows – commodities, people, and thoughts – flow together to become the cause and effect that stimulate each other and cause more flows, rather than moving independently. First, the flow of goods and materials stimulates several different flows to follow alongside it. This is easy to understand just by thinking about the production and distribution of a pair of jeans. For a pair of jeans to reach the hands of a consumer, various companies and distributors must connect. Moreover, suppose the leaders decide the factory is to move abroad; in that case, farms, chemical plants, and consumable factories that provide raw materials, as well as the labour market and finances, will undergo tremendous changes. In the overseas factories, the expatriate and local employees have thousands of intercultural experiences. As a result, they share one another's culture and consumption patterns. It also affects the flow of commodities, with global chain restaurants, consumer goods, and branches of famous schools flowing to the other side of the globe for families of the expatriates.[10] On the other hand, the abandoned factory back at the original location impacts subcontractors, labour markets, and financial markets, resulting in social tensions and an economic crisis in surrounding cities. Furthermore, the political perception there also changes. Even in the production of a single pair of jeans, the goods move, and countless flows accompany it as they create shifting dynamics around them.

The spread of ideas and thoughts also creates complex flows. As society becomes pluralistic, thoughts, philosophies, religions, values, and trends that had stayed only in one area easily spread to various cultures and regions. When a flow of thought such as a particular idea, religion, value, or trend spreads, the transportation and distribution facilities that make it possible and the traffic between related materials and people increase. For example, the spread of the Islamic faith goes beyond just the spread of religion but also increases the exchange of physical and human resources with the Arab people, thereby improving the language and political and economic status of the Arab ethnicity. On top of that, the flow and consumption generated by millions of Muslims on pilgrimage every year create tremendous economic effects.

The movement of people also creates complex flows. Immigrants and international students do not merely bring technology and academics, foreign philosophy, values, tastes, and entertainment come with them. As a result, people come to like food and trends from other regions and encounter new values and

10 Ulrich Beck and Ciaran Cronin, *The Cosmopolitan Vision* (Cambridge: Polity, 2006).

philosophies. We can see this phenomenon in domestic migration. For example, young couples who enter the urban labour market from the countryside also significantly contribute to spreading urban goods and ideas. They send cash from the city to their parents in the countryside and provide their children with opportunities to study in the city.

Intra-Global Flows

Cities are the spaces most directly affected by globalisation because people move from city to city, and information and commodities gather where there are many people. Nonini describes a modern city that encounters global flows, saying that it is a "city […] region made up of complex interrelationships of places and a space of flows dependent on the whims of global capital."[11] Cities are not unilaterally affected by globalisation; they also exert their influence on other cities around the world. As a result, cities become agents that lead globalisation.

Globalisation connects distant objects and issues, thereby correlating them with each other and, in the end, directly and indirectly affects many people around the world through various phenomena.[12] Globalisation has created a connected relationship of people, goods, and ideas across the globe. That is why people's "everyday activities are more influenced by events at a great distance" due to globalisation.[13] It has made it possible to connect the scale and scope of flows within the city, between multiple cities nationally, and worldwide.

Technological advances and international co-operation made it possible for flows to act globally. Tremendous advances in science and technology, such as transportation and communication, have made it easy to move and connect resources even from opposite sides of the planet. Transportation facilities such as container terminals and airports, technologies for mass production, food production, health and medical treatment, banking and currency transfer, and media development all make it possible to connect globally.

International co-operative organisations and treaties also contribute significantly to the development of flow on a global scale. For example, when countries enter into a Free Trade Agreement (FTA) or form an economic bloc like the European Union (EU), exchanges between the countries increase tremendously. Political and economic blocs based on historical relationships and language, such as English, Chinese, Arabic, Spanish, and French, also increase exchanges. On top of that, as technology advances, interpretation and translation become easier, and the gaps between nations become closer. Political or co-operative organisations such as the United Nations (UN), the World Trade

---

11 Low, "Spatiality," 25–26.

12 In this section, only connection, one characteristic of globalisation, is dealt with. For others, refer to the following: Bryant L. Myers, *Engaging Globalization: The Poor, Christian Mission, and Our Hyperconnected World*, Mission in Global Community (Grand Rapids, MI: Baker, 2017): 33–51.

13 Alan Smart and Josephine Smart, "Urbanization and the Global Perspective," *Annual Review of Anthropology*, 32 (2003): 263-285: 265.

Organization (WTO), and the World Health Organization (WHO) also connect all human beings in the world with each other under the theme of health and common benefits.

Transnationalism, which emerged due to increased immigration, is another driving force behind global connections. Immigrants, who act as bridges between their home countries and the countries where they have settled, create transnational ties throughout the world, through which the import and export of food and goods, as well as travel, economic, financial, and political influences, can flow. Ethnic villages in the cities overseas are representative of these transnational places. For example, in the Jewish or Chinese sections of major cities around the world, the shops, restaurants, and plazas run by such people are always popular.[14] This environment creates a tremendous exchange of goods and people between the two countries: the home country and the country of the those who have newly immigrated. Transnationalism changes not only immigrants but also their places of origin. New technologies, trends, consumer goods, and information introduced by immigrants put their hometowns in the global arena. Such connections make cities in the world become the entrance and exit of global flows.

Societies and Flows Are Integrated

A city is a society of people or a node of interaction. The difference between urban flows and natural rivers is that flows are introduced, distributed, and reproduced by the driving force of social necessity. In other words, the people take the initiative in importing, redistributing, and recreating flows. Conversely, flow moves people. Just as villagers gather by the river to do their laundry, urban flow brings people together, makes them collaborate and compete, and forces them to engage in creative and destructive actions. Interaction allows people to create new built environments, and these environments encourage people to have new interactions again. As Gary W. McDonogh said, "flows constitute a powerful tool in the imagination of human interactions. Nevertheless, 'flows' can never be divorced from human constructions of society and culture materialised in the city."[15] The built environments in the city are constantly changing due to its rich flows and interactions.

In this way, flows and society's mutual exchanges make the city something that is not fixed but rather "in the process of change." Just as humans are born, grow, work, age, and eventually die, cities live by consuming flow and engaging in creative activities. This view of the city in the process of change further makes it possible to see it as a space of flows as well as a space-time dimension. As a

---

14 P. Levitt and Schiller Gulick, "Transnational Perspectives on Migration: Conceptualizing Simultaneity," *International Migration Review* 38(3), (2004): 1002–39.
15 McDonogh, "Spatiality," 44.

result, the scope of the urbanism study expanded to include urban flows, various processes of change, and dynamics within the city.[16]

The worldwide network has a massive impact on the urbanites' lives. These connections with the outside world change people's perceptions and values and bring new possibilities and opportunities. The widespread sense of freedom and human rights has allowed people to exercise more opportunities and capabilities. On the other hand, this global connection also makes people's lives feel more insecure and exhausting. This is because people are forced to participate in the infinite competition and are exposed to a life of dehumanisation under the trap of materialism and successism. Global connections also cause people's social networks and social status to fluctuate. New opportunities can lead to a tremendous rise in status, while the privileged class may be eliminated or plummet in status. To keep up with the competition, people make the most of their social resources and put more effort than ever into expanding their social networks.

As we have seen so far, urban flows are like blood vessels, providing nutrients to all body parts. The urban flow functions complexly, having a cause-effect reaction rather than flowing on its own. This flow is not driven by its power but by the driving force of the needs of the society concerned and the designs of those who hold power. Globalisation has put all parts of the city under the network. Due to this globalisation, urban society's new thoughts and passions expand to a global level. On top of that, the technological revolution has allowed the network to operate and has compressed time and space to make it more possible to actualise people's desires. Therefore, the flow, urban society, and the urban network have a cause-effect relationship, becoming pumps and pipes that complement each other to send the flow through them.

Urban Flows that Solidifies the Classes

Class and social status have existed in the past and still exists even in societies that strongly value equality.[17] People live without breaking the balance of society by acting according to their status and knowing their hierarchical dynamics. Status divides people into groups and allows them different possession of information and power.

The limitation of the resources and opportunities creates the hierarchical order of society, thus the flow that members of society need, causing its distribution to be unequal.[18] Therefore, social class is a system in which repeated inequality

---

16 McDonogh, "Spatiality," 28–29.

17 Gary Ferraro divided societies into three categories according to the degree of equality: the Egalitarian society, which mainly practiced hunting or gathering, the Rank society, where resources were redistributed under the head and the Stratification society which can be seen in countries with industrial or market economies. Ferraro, *Cultural Anthropology*, 267.

18 Social stratification exists when people regularly experience unequal access to valued economic resources as well as prestige. In stratified societies, the chance in life

between groups becomes institutionalised.[19] Social stratification refers to a situation when such an unequal state spreads throughout society, and social hierarchy means the structure as this stratification solidifies.[20]

Among many social scales, the ability to possess society's scarce resources becomes a distinctive social scale for stratification. Karl Marx categorised society's scarce resources into economic capacity and productive capacity and divided the social classes into capitalist bourgeoisie and proletariat classes. Recent experts from Western society also consider economic ability as a status criterion. They, too, are accustomed to dividing the upper and lower classes based on their economic level.[21] However, society is too complex and organic to divide the classes based on economic flow alone, so classes are set through various measures other than the economy. For example, people create a hierarchy of people even with "religion, ethnicity, or symbolic differences, and on the possession of political power".[22] Also, heritage, education, leadership, ability, and unique talents – for example, in acting, music, art, or oratory – define the society's cultural status.[23] For people who maintain a high cultural standard, society grants the status and privileges of the so-called noble lineage, and the people around them respect it. Legal status guarantees a much stronger status. For example, qualifications such as citizenship, military superiority, and immunity are protections and benefits that the state guarantees. In this way, class is a dynamic relationship between differentiated groups that everyone is already familiar with, even if it is invisible.

Flow Strengthens Social Stratification

Hierarchical societies distribute people into status. Flows often strengthen the structure further but can also induce social change. Social class is a social structure, a culture, and a solid system formed over a long history. Therefore, society considers it a natural order to follow.

---

of obtaining economic resources and/or prestige is much higher for some individuals than others, resulting in economic and political differences, inequality, and differences in rank that produce groups on different social levels. Spradley and McCurdy, *Anthropology, the Cultural Perspective*, 151.

19 Han Wansang and Han Gyunja, *People and Society* (Seoul: Korean Broad-communication, College Depart Press, 2011): 236.

20 Han Wansang and Han Gyunja, 236–37.

21 W. Lloyd Warner and Paul S. Lunt classify America's classes based on economic ability as upper, lower-upper, upper-middle, lower-middle, upper-lower, and lower-lower. In contrast, Gottdiener divided the classes of Americans into The Wealthy, Creative, Suburban Middle, Working, Working Poor, and the Jobless. W. Lloyd Warner and Paul S. Lunt, *The Status System of a Modern Community* (New Haven; London: Yale University Press; Oxford University Press, 1942): 262–70.

22 Mark Gottdiener and Ray Hutchison, *The New Urban Sociology* (Boulder, CO: Westview, 2006): 140.

23 Eugene Albert Nida, *Message and Mission; the Communication of the Christian Faith*, [1st] (New York: Harper, 1960): 160–62.

Although the caste system has mostly disappeared in these modern days, people are still familiar with class and social status. The terms class and social status are conceptually similar, but people use class primarily when the distinction and social cohesion are strong. For example, Marxism uses the word class to illuminate the severance and confrontation between two groups, such as the bourgeoisie and proletariat.[24] Each class develops its social system and culture, including social resources, consumption style, life zones, and networks. When the system suits them, they become difficult to change once created. People of the same class have similar abilities in using social resources such as time, goods, social networks, and opportunities, so their social lives show distinctive patterns. For example, people's occupation quickly becomes a symbol of their class because people in similar occupations have similar life patterns.[25] Studies have shown that blue-collar workers have different life patterns from their white-collar counterparts both inside and outside the workplace.[26] Likewise, the upper class uses the lifestyle and consumer goods that suit their status to create and maintain their patterns.

Consumption activity is a representative cultural symbol that expresses people's social class. Although legally equal, people's jobs, cars, residences, grocery stores, favourite beverages, and even churches can indicate the difference in status.[27] In this way, people of the same class "consume in distinctive ways that reproduce their status."[28]

When consumption activities are connected to places, stratification between groups becomes more pronounced and visible. This is because people of similar levels tend to live in similar locations and have similar jobs. People place social factors such as gender, race, and status on people living in a specific area, i.e. a conceptual container, and, thus, create a unique image of the container. For example, some regions show poverty, disproportionate development, racial exclusion, and high crime rates. In contrast, others are predominantly inhabited by scientists and intellectuals, creating a sophisticated image of social privilege

---

24 In modern times, when the caste system has mostly disappeared. In this book, social stratification and class will be used interchangeably. Wansang Han and Gyunja Han, *Human and Society* (Seoul: Korea National Open University Press, 2011): 237–38.

25 Eames and Goode divided the division of labour in the city into social classes and small units. Within the social class are macro-structural, hierarchically ranked strata, defined in terms of their wealth, power and prestige. And the small unit was divided into different occupational groups defined by their specific role in their division of labour. Eames and Goode, *Anthropology of the City*, 198.

26 LeMasters found that blue-collar workers had similar patterns and standards of living, spending time at a pub with co-workers after work, or spending time with family on weekends, and found that this was also different from the life of white-collars. LeMasters, *Blue Collar Aristocrats*.

27 According to Claerbaut, there are at least three primary bases of stratification: occupation, income, and education. Also, Hiebert and Meneses, *Incarnational Ministry*, 287–95 cited wealth, power, and offspring of class as factors.

28 Gottdiener, Hohle, and King, *The New Urban Sociology*, 262.

and wealth. In other words, the strong hierarchies between people "result from an interaction between social factors and spatial organisation."[29]

The reason the class system continues to exist is that there is a powerful group who maintains it. The higher the class, the more powerful it is, and these people of power absorb as much of the flow as possible to protect their vested interests. They can quickly pre-empt the flow and use it to maintain their privileges rather than change it.

A more significant class imbalance means greater exclusivity for each class, which naturally causes a severe disconnection between the classes.[30] Such disconnection calls for prejudice and victim mentality toward other classes and raises the barrier between them. Such distrust and high walls become a much more severe problem for the kingdom of God and evangelism. Excessive hierarchical consciousness and monopoly of the flow cause hereditary privilege, the inheritance of poverty and grow hate and division among people. It also stimulates successism within urbanites, making even Christians a slave to excessive success. As a result, too many of the city's channels of good news are blocked and cannot flow, and even Christians who are supposed to serve as channels forget their responsibilities and it becomes difficult to navigate their identities. Eventually, the city will again be forced to mass-produce the neo-unreached groups described previously in Chapter 4.

Flow Strengthens Ethnic and Racial Stratification

In cities, various ethnic groups frequently encounter each other. Traditionally, in the case of multi-ethnic situations, while people can meet those from different ethnic groups, they do not need to have many encounters because their living areas and social ranges are so different. On the other hand, modern urban societies have many occasions when people have no choice but to face other ethnicities, such as in schools, during social activities, or in commercial districts. As a result, there is naturally more conflict and competition between different ethnic groups living in cities. This competition is also caused by attempts to seize the limited social capital and opportunities, otherwise known as the flow, and gain superiority. Ethnicities use their size, history and tradition, geographical advantages, human resources, and political power to win the inter-ethnic competition.[31] As time goes by, this inequality among ethnicities becomes solidified and institutionalised. This institutionalised ethnic inequality refers to "a system of ethnic relations and social rules that determines the unequal distribution of resources across different ethnic groups."[32]

As the ranks among ethnic groups become institutionalised, people's minds get familiar with an ethnic positioning and give high or low status to the

---

29 Gottdiener, Hohle, and King, *The New Urban Sociology*, 226.

30 Gottdiener, Hohle, and King, *The New Urban Sociology*, 226.

31 See, Donald Noel as quoted Philip Q. Yang, *Ethnic Studies: Issues and Approaches* (Albany, NY: State University of New York Press, 2000): 67–68.

32 Yang, *Ethnic Studies*, 61–62.

ethnicities. In some cases, this ethnic positioning is so pronounced that laws and institutions even guarantee this discrimination.

Occupation is one of the easy ways to know the social position of a particular ethnicity. Since society overall is operated by the system of the mainline society – including language, institutions, and connections – it takes much more energy for ethnic minorities with a weak social base to take advantage of opportunities in the city and move up the social ladder. Even with college education, they are less likely to be active in society because the social resources they need to get a job and promotion cannot be compared to those of the ethnic mainstream.

Moreover, if their daily lives stay mainly within the boundaries of their ethnic group, they cannot access information and opportunities from outside it. As a result, they tend to have similar occupations and live near each other. For example, suppose white people are mainly concentrated in high-income groups and office jobs, while minorities of colour are primarily engaged in taxi driving or tailoring. In that case, it can be seen that society has clearly defined ethnic roles.[33]

Once the ethnicities establish their position, they repeatedly absorb the flow that strengthens their identities, and as a result, the ethnicity's position becomes institutionalised and more fixed. This is not only because of the laws set by mainstream society but also because of the characteristics of the flows they absorb. For example, less educated ethnicities have a lower quality of information gained at a much slower rate than others. As such, the ethnic and racial positioning is the result of a combination of the order, worldview, and flow of society, and cannot be easily changed.

Social stratification is a very delicate and complex problem, so there are even more complex classes inside the same race and ethnicity. For example, even among immigrants, those who immigrated earlier when their motherland was poor may live in the lower classes inside ethnic villages for the rest of their lives. However, as the motherland becomes rich, immigrants tend to have higher education and come from professional and technical jobs. They, therefore, enter the middle class and get professional jobs from the start. They may also scatter into the suburbs or better school districts instead of settling in ethnic villages at the city's centre. As a result, there is a vivid hierarchical positioning even among immigrants of the same ethnic group. At the same time, as a group interacts with mainstream society, their financial and social status generally rises while contact with their ethnicity decreases.[34] This phenomenon is also present within the same race, where individuals live in different classes according to their abilities and social perceptions. For example, young educated black Americans who have successfully entered the middle class tend to live in the same neighbourhoods as

33 Gulick, *The Humanity of Cities*, 141–42.
34 Achor, *Mexican Americans in a Dallas Barrio*, 116–21.

white Americans and have the same consumption patterns and culture.[35] Eventually, a hierarchy is created within their race as well.[36]

Urban Flow Changes Classes

Flow can stiffen the existing social class, but it can also cause it to change. Just as water seeps through hardened soil, the city's flows change its solid social hierarchy. The resources of modern cities provide citizens with more information and social resources, which also gives them new self-awareness and civic awareness. As a result, social movements arise in places that have long seemed unchangeable. In this way, the urban flow provides the power to shake up the social classes.

Urban change is a natural outcome of a changed people and society. These visible changes include new buildings, products, and trends. Changes in society are possible through reforming the existing social order and authority, information flow, cognitive system and values, priorities, social status gaps, and self-esteem.

Above all, the universalisation of information creates changes in social classes. Expanding the supply of information makes it difficult for certain classes to monopolise information, and creates a new elite group familiar with the new communication pattern.[37] This information society not only changes the elite group but also spreads information throughout society previously monopolised by a few people of power.[38] This information becomes a social power that moves society. As a result, this advent of information enables society to move power more easily. In this way, the spread of information and power ultimately creates the power for social movement.[39]

In addition to information, society is also changed by the movement of populations, the spread of consumer goods, structural changes in industry and economy, and the political environment. Behind the changing environment, there is always a change in the flow supply. Just as the muscles do creative work when supplied with nutrients through blood vessels, the urban flow reaches every corner of the city and provides energy for change.

---

35 Ulf Hannerz, *Soulside: Inquiries into Ghetto Culture and Community* (New York: Columbia University Press, 1969): 38–57.

36 Steven Gregory, *Black Corona: Race and the Politics of Place in an Urban Community* (Princeton, NJ: Princeton University Press, 1998).

37 Manuel Castells, *The Rise of the Network Society*, vol. 1: Information Age (Malden, MA: Blackwell, 2000).

38 Manuel Castells, *The Informational City: Information Technology, Economic Restructuring, and the Urban-Regional Process* (Oxford: Blackwell, 1989); Castells, *The Rise of the Network Society*, 2000.

39 The case of Manuel Castells and Erik Swyngedouw presented here was inspired by the writings of Gary W. McDonogh.

Flow Shakes Urban Classes

Social class and status are created by a combination of the ascribed status inherited from parents and culture and the achieved status earned through one's efforts and misfortunes. Within status, there are classes and castes. Castes are systems that greatly limit social mobility because they are based on ascribed status rather than achieved status. Unfortunately, some caste systems still exert their power, even in modern cities. In India, for example, leather handling is a vulgar task, so the lower classes mainly handle it.[40] Naturally, the leather business becomes a lowly job, and poverty is passed down through generations for those who engage in this business.

Change in status refers to the social mobility of an individual or group.[41] Although very rare, status can even improve in traditional societies, through marriage, adoption, career advancement, donations, and significant contributions, and may also fall through the collapse of the family, natural disasters, and so on. For class mobility, while individual effort is important, society must also be able to respect individual efforts and achievements more than ascribed status. In addition, the diversified culture and subdivided society can provide abundant opportunities for status change. Transparent principles, laws, and fair opportunities to access resources are also crucial for status change.[42]

Since urban society has relatively abundant conditions for status change, urbanites can have more opportunities for social promotion. Because people work with unfamiliar people from different backgrounds, urbanites evaluate people by their achievements and performance, and the ascribed status is naturally less relevant. Furthermore, as the social structure is infinitely differentiated, individuals have various places to choose from, and power does not concentrate unilaterally on one person. Employers are also under pressure to be favoured in the workplace and treat the employees fairly and meritocratically so that they can win the competition.

The diverse differentiation of social structures requires numerous redistributions of social resources, and in this process, mutual exchange between groups increases explosively. Such a social atmosphere facilitates people's movement between classes and makes them desire higher status. This environment causes urbanites to strive day and night to work their way up the ladder to a higher status, such as financial success, advanced education, and connections with influential people.

---

40 Gregory, *Black Corona: Race and the Politics of Place in an Urban Community*; Owen Lynch, *The Politics of Untouchability* (New York: Columbia University Press, 1969).

41 Spradley and McCurdy defined the movement of social classes as "the process of gaining rank in a system of social stratification." Spradley and McCurdy, *Anthropology, the Cultural Perspective*, 160.

42 Han Wansang and Han Gyunja, *People and Society*, 252–54.

This change in traditional social stratification and individuals' voluntary efforts for social promotion is motivated neither by violent revolution such as class struggle nor purely by individuals' efforts only. Instead, it results from an urban environment in which flows move freely and a social system where many people can fairly access the flow.

Flow Shakes the Ethnic Hierarchies

Flow causes a visible change in long-standing ethnic positioning. One factor that triggers this visible change is the change in the national minority policy. In modern times, many countries have established systems that provide fair opportunities for ethnic groups who have traditionally been discriminated against. Some countries go further and implement minority preferential policies which give them more benefits. This preferential policy also changes the stereotype that surrounds ethnic minorities.[43] Ethnic groups who have been considered inferior can improve their social status by actively making use of an educational environment and equal opportunities for success. A rise in social status in such ways increases not only individual capabilities but also pride in one's ethnicity.

The openness and aggressiveness of ethnic groups also affect their positioning. People who quickly accept the national policy and seize opportunities gain power faster and secure superior positions compared to those who do not.[44] For example, as of 2000, the proportion of university graduates living in China differed significantly by ethnicity. While the proportion of four-year college graduates across the country was 3.7%, ethnic minorities had a higher proportion – with 5.1% for Mongolians, 4.7% for Manchurians, and 8.4% for ethnic Koreans – compared to the mainstream Han ethnicity (3.8%).[45] Because these ethnic minorities in northeastern China traditionally place importance on their children's education, they sent their children to college as soon as they had the opportunity. As a result, these ethnic minorities were able to gain access to good jobs and economic security faster than the mainstream people. However, it is almost impossible for the rise of a few elites to change the position of the entire ethnicity, because as people actively accept and benefit from the state's policies, they also easily forget their identity and culture and

43 While observing black people in the United States, Milton M. Gordon found similar phenomena to be generated in the minority of modern countries, and this was called liberal expectancy. This liberal expectancy refers to a phenomenon in which minority groups are able to free themselves by breaking away from the expectations that they traditionally receive (stereotyped expectancy). Milton M. Gordon, "Toward a General Theory of Racial and Ethnic Group Relations," in Nathan Glazer and Daniel Moynihan (ed), *Ethnicity* (Cambridge, MA: Harvard University Press, 1975): 84–110.
44 Horowitz, "Ethnic Identity," 111–40.
45 "National Bureau of Statistics of China," State Council Census Office, 2002: 563-567, https://data.stats.gov.cn/english/easyquery.htm?cn=C01.

become absorbed in mainstream society. Therefore, they often may not be able to contribute too much to the revival and status of their ethnic group.

In the case of immigrants, when the status of their home country changes, so does their own status in their immigrated home. Even those who immigrated as war refugees or from poorer countries undergo a rise in their national status to become natural immigrants when their country of origin's economic and political status improves. As such, urban change causes much shift in ethnic positions that may have been maintained for hundreds of years.

Usually, a change in ethnic position means a change in their occupations. Occupational groups that were once concentrated only on taxi drivers or the real estate industry may now work in various occupations in a similar way to mainstream society. Furthermore, this shift in status also causes changes in the people's area of residence, educational level, and consumption. In this way, many elements, including the state's policy, contribute to change in ethnic position. Like other changes, urban flow and supply of urban resources still play a major role in ethnic positioning.

Flows Shake Flows

The consumption and reproduction of urban flows are comprehensive indicators showing the social status of the city. What flows are produced and consumed are also indicators that can show the economic power, health status, and educational status of the people there. One example is a study on the correlation between drinking water quality and residents' social problems in Guayaquil, Ecuador.[46] Eric Swyngedouw noted that high-class communities carried water from afar to avoid drinking the local contaminated water. In contrast, the general public drank the contaminated water as they could not install irrigation facilities. The various diseases caused by contaminated water made the lives of the public, who were already suffering from poverty and lack of education, more impoverished, and kept them in the vicious cycle of increasing crime and family problems. As such, we can infer various aspects of society, such as health and education, just by looking at water quality flow.

The problem is that this flow of urban change is not created naturally like a river but flows only when there is a need and distribution in society. In a survey report, Swyngedouw said, "while the city cannot exist without the perpetual metabolic transformation of nature, this very transformation turns nature into a deeply social process in which nature, society and the city can no longer be separated."[47] In other words, the people make decisions about the movement of resources. Therefore, the will of the powerful is also the will of the movement of urban resources. If a society is distorted and driven by irrational forces, the supply of social resources also flows unfairly along irrational channels.

---

46 Erik Swyngedouw, *Social Power and the Urbanization of Water: Flows of Power* (Oxford: Oxford University Press, 2004).
47 Swyngedouw, *Social Power*, 175.

The fact that the flow substantially impacts the social structure means that change in flow supply has an absolute effect on the change in society. For example, when urban slums are newly equipped with water facilities, the impact goes beyond just convenient drinking water; it also makes their homes cleaner and flushes toilets, lowering the infection and infant mortality rate. In addition, as housework becomes more effective and women use their spare time for economic activities, their children can regularly attend school.

Information or new ideas change society more broadly and rapidly than water facilities. This can be easily seen by looking at the speed at which citizens unite, or news spreads following the introduction of online media.[48] For example, the preparation period for large gatherings and demonstrations has significantly reduced. Preparations for The March on Washington for Jobs and Freedom on 28th August 1963 took several months and approximately 250,000 participants. It later took over a year for their demands to be accepted, passed by the U.S. Congress, and signed by President Lyndon B. Johnson.[49] However, the 2010 Arab Spring rally that spread across the Arab world led by Tunisia, and the 2017 Washington Women's March that drew about 740,000 people to oppose President Trump, each took only a few days to plan and launch. Even the Hong Kong protests in 2020, which started with the Umbrella Revolution in 2014, saw people move from place to place almost in real-time – demonstrating that introducing new distribution channels dramatically changes the face of society.

Social transformation is only possible when effective flow changes are accompanied. In the past, various parts of the world have tried to make social changes with revolutions, new technologies, and policy propaganda. However, in many cases, despite achieving superficial achievements, it is rare for the sense of ownership for change in society as a whole to spread. Because so many elements are connected like spider's webs in current society, it is difficult to expect complete change from one or two efforts. For example, the water shortage and health problems of Guayaquil residents in Ecuador result from numerous difficulties such as urban poverty, high crime rate, structural lethargy, and racial discrimination.[50]

Unlike the mechanical change led by a few influential people, the introduction and expansion of this flow creates the power for change within the society, leading to a voluntary and widespread change within its members. This is because changing one flow channel causes another flow to change. Furthermore, it increases people's ability to better themselves and gives them hope and confidence toward change. In this way, according to its use, flow can be

48 "How online social movements translate to offline results", YouTube Channel: *PBS NewsHour*, broadcasted 10th June 2017. [Available at: https://www.youtube.com/watch?v=_DTOc1uMOIU], [Last accessed: 27th December 2023].

49 Drew D. Hansen, *The Dream: Martin Luther King, Jr., and the Speech That Inspired a Nation*, 1st ed. (New York: Ecco, 2003): 177.

50 Swyngedouw, *Social Power and the Urbanization of Water*.

mobilised to keep the existing social class in power or to change the solid structure of a society as water enters dry soil.

Everybody Run!

The opportunities and hopes the city provides for its people give them desires and dreams they have never had before. People envy and admire the Hollywood stars and tycoons they see on TV. Globalisation, the media revolution, the sense of freedom and equality, the expansion of social networks, and enriched opportunities help cities rediscover their possibilities.

The city motivates urbanites to run toward "success." As much as they give many people new opportunities, cities are competitive. For their success, urbanites work day and night and compete fiercely with each other, determined to sacrifice anything. As a result, rather than taking care of themselves and their loved ones, urbanites run towards the type of success applauded by society. However, in the city, individual efforts cannot quickly achieve better status. Because those with existing vested interests belong to their cartels, they tend to be wary of and exclude strangers entering their class by raising their status. Since the social classes are complex and interconnected, it is difficult to escape one's existing class and even more so to enter a higher class. The social classes are separated by a sort of glass ceiling that cannot be seen from afar.[51] Therefore, urbanites must risk everything to find a small hole in one side of this glass ceiling.

Ironically, this desperation for better status is stronger in the upper class than in the lower. Surveys have shown that in the United States, people in the upper classes are usually more exclusive toward those of other classes and try harder to maintain their status. On the contrary, it was found that the middle, lower, and marginalised classes have a lesser sense of alertness between classes and are less reluctant to move to another status.[52]

Another reason urbanites strive for success is their fear of failure. The fear that stagnating will leave them behind and cause their status to fall eventually makes urbanites give their all. This fear drives the desperation that takes away time to care for and share with others and the sense of urgency to deliver results. In the end, they think that they must either run non-stop or become a failure. Although information has increased and become more accessible, this desperation for success causes them to increasingly monopolise urban resources and not share them with others. This is because everyone is fixated on surviving within this move-or-lose society.

---

51 Originally, the word "Glass Ceiling" was used by women and small groups when trying to raise their status or to overcome obstacles while reaching for success. However, this glass ceiling is also a sad reality for all the underprivileged who strive to improve their status.

52 Warner and Lunt, *The Status System of a Modern Community*.

Missiological Reflection: Standstill and Discern Them

Urban flow can both strengthen and change the city's social class structure. Abundant flows provide endless opportunities for urbanites to change their status. As a result, they live with a passion for rising status and a fear of falling status. This passion and fear are no exception for Christian leaders. Successism causes churches to become preoccupied with becoming larger and more famous rather than pleasing the Lord. Although they think they are working for the Lord, their hearts are focused on "move or lose," just like ordinary urbanites. Such successism can easily make people destructive. In that sense, what kind of people should Christians be in a city filled with success, fears, aspirations, and sacrifices for better status? And what kind of existence should the church be to please the Lord?

Urban Christian Identity: Discerning the Genuine Success

What does the Bible say to urbanites who work day and night to improve their class and social status? First, God as the Trinity is the most original and fundamental model for community and relationship between classes. God is the Triune One, the community of three persons. Each of the three is divine, sharing together in, and together constituting, the one divine essence. Therefore, the one God is not an undifferentiated, solitary oneness, but subsists in a multiplicity – the three members of the Trinity.[53] By playing different roles, these Triune persons voluntarily serve different roles and do not claim to be equal with one another. Jesus said, "Jesus the Son is more than just the form that God took when he came to earth" (Phil. 2:6-7), and that "God the Spirit, who was sent from the Father by Jesus, testifies about Jesus" (Jn 15:26).[54] This Trinity model also sets forth God as the foundation for establishing the ecclesiological community. This is because the church is called to be a community of reconciliation in a world that is constantly dividing and building barriers. The church is a community that respects, reconciles, and co-operates despite differences in social roles and classes to realise the community's image shown by the Triune God on this earth.[55]

The Bible does not deny class but recognises its necessity for social order (Rom. 13:1-5). It even advises us to recognise our limitations and not to think of ourselves more than we ought – but to think wisely according to the measure of our faith (Rom. 12:3). Additionally, receiving a proper reward (Tim. 2:6) and ascending to a high position due to diligent efforts are considered natural in the light of the righteousness of God. In other words, hard work and sincerity are both the main driving forces for success and the principles of God (Thess. 3:6-10). Even in the Bible, those like Isaac and Joseph who receive God's blessings become successful and high-ranking people (Gen. 26:12-14; 39:2, 23).

---

53 Stanley James Grenz, *Theology for the Community of God* (Grand Rapids, MI: Eerdmans, 2000): 66–67.

54 Grenz, *Theology for the Community of God*, 483.

55 Grenz, *Theology for the Community of God*, 66–67.

The Bible knows how difficult social promotion is. Isaac's sudden success in farming, for example, was enough for the Philistines of the land to feel threatened. In the eyes of the settlers, Isaac – a foreigner and barbaric cattle farmer – entering the same social class would have naturally aroused resistance and alertness from the Sodomites. Jacob too lost the wells he dug to the Philistine settlers and received an order from King Abimelech to move away (Gen. 26: 14-25). In a similar example, Lot, who was only a cattle farmer, moves to the city of Sodom to change his status and become a member of its society. However, while Lot seemed to have been successfully accepted by the city society for a while, a conflict of interest reveals that the Sodomites did not regard Lot as one of their own and rejected him as an outsider again (Gen. 19:9). Likewise, characters of the Bible made tremendous efforts to move from class to class, while the existing forces often stood in their way.

However, the Bible wants us to distinguish between rising status and success. To urbanites weary of struggling for their status, the Lord explains what true success is. He says that just as a branch must abide in the vine, abundant life comes only when we live bonded to Christ (Jn 15:4-5). In other words, He teaches us that our success and satisfaction in life are, above all, a life abiding in Christ and nourishing by Him (Cor. 3:5).

How do the urban Christians live to abide in Christ and receive genuine nourishment from Jesus? The first step is to read oneself through the lens of God's providence, not by status. This is because, regardless of status, one's existence is impossible without God's providence. God knows well in what status and class one was born. Ascribed status, such as country of birth and ethnicity, parents and language, skin colour and body, is something God has already determined from when one was in one's mother's womb (Is. 49:1; Ps. 139:13). The given identities have a tremendous impact on modern people's class and social status, even in an urban society. If Christians do not acknowledge who they are and keep comparing themselves to celebrity appearances or successful CEOs, the true success Christ spoke of would be impossible to achieve. God's providence includes the change of status we have experienced in our lives. Whether it is the adoption of a war orphan, a sudden collapse of the family, a lucky instance through meeting an acquaintance, or a loved one falling ill with an incurable disease, God is providential amid the rapidly changing waves of life. A person who reads the providence of God with the eyes of faith is one who, like Job, can "sing praise to the name of the Lord, for it is the Lord who gave and the Lord took away" (Job 1:22).

Modern cities offer unprecedentedly rich and incredibly diverse flows. Advanced science and technology help urbanites connect with resources from every corner of the world. However, social classes still maintain high walls, and those in power can control resources and information. Christians should be able to protect themselves and know what real success they and their loved ones should have while striving to change their status day and night in their "move or lose" society.

Urban Church Identity: Discerning the Things to Change and to Continue

While urban flow enriches the lives of urbanites, it also spreads successism throughout society and stimulates distrust between classes. This crisis of the times makes the church warn its members against the prevailing philosophy of successism. This is because Christians are not born to earn achievements but to live for true success. Therefore, when people sacrifice today for a successful future and neglect their relationships with their loved ones, the church must teach clear Biblical lessons about success.

First, the church must take strict precautions to avoid falling for successism itself. We must ensure that seminarians' dreams for mega-churches and ministers' hard work every day and night are not for achieving the so-called great success. At the same time, the church must teach its members to respect and learn from successful people. Unfortunately, some churches have taught social success to be secular and snobbish. However, we must acknowledge and celebrate the success earned from such efforts because it is the result of their hard work.

Furthermore, the church must learn true success through the life of Jesus. Success in the church is fundamentally different from corporate success. The church is not meant to rule over and be exalted on this land but to be sent so that people can taste the kingdom of God. To serve the world, the church must be missional and contextual (Jn 20:21). For this purpose, the church must always be able to communicate with the neighbours, like Jesus, who incarnated while immaculate.

Second, the church should strive to become a community of those who have received citizenship in heaven, not correlated to their status in this world. The greatest thing about our status is our citizenship in heaven and that we have become new creations (Cor. 5:17). The Bible tells us, who spend our whole lives on this earth to raise our status and succeed, that we do not belong to this land. In this way, we possess citizenship of heaven, which is a status incomparable with the citizenship of Rome – which was envied by the people at the time of the Apostle Paul – or the citizenship of modern advanced countries (Phil. 3:20). To this end, the church must teach its members to live a life worthy of heavenly citizenship. This teaching refers to encouraging believers to let go of their worldly status and treat one another as brothers and sisters (James 2:1-6). The church must teach that the power structure outside the church or the prejudice between classes does not apply within the church.

Third, the church must understand the threat and opportunities that the urban resources will give. Abundant flows in the city naturally accompany the movement of people. People are affected not only by news from the other side of the world but also by ideological trends.

The urban flow transforms the church's surrounding area into new mission fields because immigrants settle around the church and people change and move quickly. This change in the surrounding environment causes the church to re-select what needs to change and what needs to not. Forms and traditions that once defined the church may now become obstacles in maintaining the church's identity. These obstacles become unnecessary stumbling blocks for those who come to the church. Therefore, the church must always be ready to tear down old walls by keeping its front door open and understanding the changes around it.

8. A Good Samaritan on Wall Street: In-Betweenness at the Flow Channels

Introduction

If a Good Samaritan were to help a collapsed man up in a parking lot off Wall Street, New York City, on a Monday morning what would that man look like? Would the person be sick or homeless, as this story is often portrayed in modern settings?

The Good Samaritan in the story of Jesus was a man who, upon seeing a man mugged and knocked down on the road to Jericho, treated him and allowed him to recover in a safe place at his own expense (Lk. 10:26-37). Unlike today's homeless, the mugged person was not so vulnerable until he was robbed; he was healthy enough to travel on the rough path between Jerusalem and Jericho. This dangerous road would only be taken when necessary; therefore, he was likely a trustworthy person, perhaps a tradesman or public official. He surely had dreams of success, responsibilities, and his own set of skills.[1] Unlike many homeless people, the person in the parking lot may have been in good health not long ago, with a clear purpose in life. The person could have been highly motivated, working from morning to night. This energetic person may have invested his spare time researching on the Internet and finishing a master's degree programme on the weekends. Whomever or whatever played the part of the robber had impacted the person enough to make everything worthless in one blow.

Today, urbanites live alongside myriad threats that could turn their lives upside down overnight. For example, they could be used and abandoned by the company to which they have devoted their lives; colleagues could outpace them; they may be discriminated against because of their skin colour, age, or gender; as a foreigner, they might repeatedly come up against obstacles that natives are never troubled by; they could divorce and go bankrupt; they could receive a terrible diagnosis from their doctor; a church bus full of children may get into an accident; a son could yell at his father that he will never become like his father;

1 In fact, all the people in the parable of the Good Samaritan (Luke 10:30-35) are fictitious persons; thus, I tried not to picture them in too much detail so as not to create an allegorical interpretation. Instead, I only emphasise here that the man who met the robber was from a different social situation from today's homeless people.

one could break down next to one's car after it has flipped over; parents may give up hope for their disabled daughter; a stock slump might wipe out half of a person's pension fund, or one may hear that their team will be reduced to 30% of its size.

Every day, urbanites set out on the road to Jericho in their ways, eager to succeed, and many fall helpless at the robber's sudden attack. Alp and Emir from the previous chapters also fear losing their hard-earned advancements and are forced to live more defensively. Although they appear to be untroubled and cheerful on the outside, they fight through each day, dodging the blades that threaten their success. Underneath their clean suits, they are hiding their bleeding wounds and suffering.

This chapter discusses how to be a good neighbour by understanding and using the city's flow in an urban society where everyone desperately tries to raise their status. For this, we will ask the following questions:

1. What kind of people are on the road to Jericho in the city?
2. How does a good neighbour connect the city's flow to those in need?
3. How can one become a good neighbour in the channels of urban flow?
4. How can one become a good neighbour to those of different social classes?
5. How must good neighbours approach competition and achievement?

Lastly, in the missiological reflection section, we will examine how God has given great proximity among urbanites for the emergence of good neighbours. Therefore, we will await the arrival of a new generation of leaders whose value has not yet been properly recognised.

Channels of Urban Flow: The Good, the Bad, and the Poor Are Gathering

Today, people are drawn toward information and resources, thus flow channels. Due to their desperation for success, urbanites look for channels with the best and most diverse flow. Just as people took the path to Jericho in search of success despite its risks, today's urbanites follow the path of good flow. As a result, such channels attract the good (the Good Samaritan), the bad (robbers), and the poor (the victim).

Where are the flow channels in the city, and how do they deliver to the people the things they need? Who benefits from the flow, and how do urban resource supply channels differ from those in traditional societies? The flow supply channels of modern cities differ greatly from those of traditional societies. Figure 14 is a left-to-right comparison of the flow supply channels of resources and information that an individual in an urban and traditional society can connect to. In both diagrams, there is a 'My culture' and a social class to which I belong, and above and below that are the social classes that are higher or lower than my class.[2]

---

2 The flow channels in Figure 14 are somewhat exaggerated to compare the characteristics of the traditional society and the city more easily. In reality, the two scenarios are more similar than pictured in the diagrams.

In the left diagram, most of the flow is circulating within the same hierarchy in the same culture. Flow paths to other cultures are very limited. These limited flow paths force people in the same tier and in the same group to rely on each other. Especially in culturally collective societies, individuals in the same hierarchy make decisions based on group opinion. These groups have a strong sense of "We" rather than "I" identity. As a result, individuals have the same resources and information as their neighbors. In a society like this, where people are segregated by class and ethnicity, and have similar channels, it is difficult to expect new information and resources to spread naturally to the periphery. The same is true for the gospel, which does not naturally come from the outside, and even if it does, it is even more difficult to spread to the periphery.

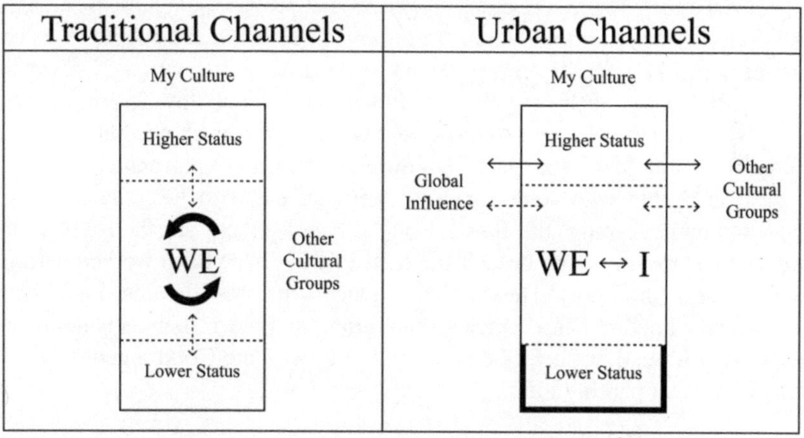

Figure 14: Flow Channels of Individuals in the City and the Traditional Society

The diagram on the right illustrates the flow channels of a modern city. The more urbanites focus on success and competition, the more information and resources they need. Because the flow inside the same class is insufficient, flow channels must also connect with other classes and cultures.

The type of flow distribution differs by social class. For example, members of the upper class, such as CEOs and politicians, need a large amount of information, requiring flow channels to connect with various people across cultures and nations. On the other hand, people in the lower class rarely divert the flow due to the simpler nature of their work or living conditions. As a result, inter-ethnic and inter-class interactions are rare.[3]

3 For example, Zang et al. reported the correlations between social class and their inter-class and inter-ethnic relationship in the context of the Hui Muslims in China as follows. "… the Hui that have frequent engage with neighbors are often the members of the higher status and more modern Hui groups such as state workers, professionals, and cadres. The lower status and more traditional Hui groups such as rural migrants are not necessarily

Although each culture differs, being I-centred – my opinion and decision – is relatively respected in the right-hand diagram. A secondary network of individuals that extends far and wide allows them to absorb flows from a wide variety of people. These individuals have excellent social skills, which is why they express their will rather than make unified decisions as a community.

Cities are strongly influenced by globalization, which means that urbanites are both citizens of a city and citizens of the world, connecting their flow paths to globalization. Plus, as the number of proximity groups increases dramatically in virtual communities, modern people's connection channels expand beyond the boundaries of location and time. In these enormous connection channels, people live with strangers but connect with others through hobbies, faith, workplace, and community associations.

Flow channels in modern cities are places that provide people with resources and opportunities to improve their status and therefore cause people to gather. Just as someone may sit on a riverbank and wash clothes amongst strangers, people always establish new relationships in the area of flow channels. Here, those who have the Gospel and those who do not, have no choice but to interact naturally despite being strangers from different cultural backgrounds.

Just as people who sought success went on the road to Jericho, today's urbanites gather around the flow channels. Among them are the robbers (the bad), poised to throw into despair the lives of those who have worked hard for their success (the poor). These robbers attack urbanites' dreams, loved ones, health and support, achievements, and pride to render them shameful and helpless. And ready to help the poor are the good – the Good Samaritans – in that Wall Street parking lot.

Three Good Neighbours for The Good Deeds

Just as the Bible tells of the Good Samaritan giving medicine and food to the poor man and bringing him to an inn, the goods of today also become a bridge and provide for the needs of those who cannot get up on their own. Christians who deliver good deeds and words also work as a bridge. However, this bridging refers to a much larger concept than simply providing someone with what they need. To let the good deeds be well-delivered and successfully diffused to those who need it, at least three types of people are needed[4]: an agent of change, that is, an outsider who transfers the goodness to the group; an early adopter, who first accepts the goodness within the group; and an opinion leader, who spreads

---

helpful neighbors." Zang, Lipman, and McKeever, "Ethnicity and Urban Life in China," 21.

4 In addition to these three characters, there are also spreaders who facilitate diffusion at each level and stage of the group, but we will not discuss them here as the focus of the text is on the first stage of the transmission.

the change.[5] A similar principle applies to Christian ministry as they deliver good news and deeds.

First, the agents of change are outsiders who deliver good deeds and influence insiders' decisions for change.[6] These agents of change visit and deliver the deeds/meet the needs with a humble and generous posture.

Agents of change go to people who have unmet needs and build trust and awareness of change.[7] Missionaries who travel long distances to share the Gospel or professors who teach new theories to international students to carry back to their countries are also agents of change.

The second type of good neighbour is the early adopter, who is the first to accept new outside resources and ideas. The term "early adopter" has lately been used to describe people who buy new technologies earlier or farmers who use new seed types. However, there are many more types of early adopters, and they have been around for a very long time. As mentioned in the former chapter, Isaac, who grew up in a nomadic tribe in the Old Testament, is an example. He was an early adopter who, born into a cattle farming family, bravely started to practice agriculture and achieved great success (Gen. 26:12-14). Other examples include Rahab, who broke the king's orders at Jericho to protect the spies from Israel and defected to Israel; Joseph, Nehemiah, and Esther, who settled in a new country; and St Paul, who absorbed Greek and Roman culture as an immigrant, and numerous Jews in Asia Minor who helped him and his team.

Typically, early adopters have relatively more formal education, have a scholarly manner, and are of higher social status. They demonstrate greater empathy, rationality, and intelligence and have a positive attitude towards change and science. Furthermore, they can cope with uncertainty, are predisposed to adopting new ideas, and are less dogmatic and less fatalistic.[8] In addition, the early adopters are relatively free from the constraints of conventional thought and have the courage to choose what they believe is right. This includes locals who import new cultures or accept the Gospel in the early stages of missionary work.

The third kind of bridge person is the opinion leader. These people can influence the attitudes or overt behaviour of other individuals with a relatively high frequency.[9] An opinion leader influences others daily as an insider. These individuals may have an official position; they may be an editorial commissioner for a broadcaster, a school teacher, or a government administrator. People with informal positions, such as the head of a household, well-trusted and highly

---

5 The three characters of bridging people are introduced in the following books. Kraft, *Anthropology for Christian Witness*, 339–401; Everett M. Rogers, *Diffusion of Innovations*, 5th ed. (New York: Free Press, 2003), 316–17; 368–73; 400–402.

6 Rogers, *Diffusion of Innovations*, 400–402.

7 Agents of change also diagnose the group's problems, explain how to create the will for change within the group and to take action, settle the change as the group's own, and set up an exit strategy.

8 Rogers, *Diffusion of Innovations*, 316–17.

9 Rogers, *Diffusion of Innovations*, 368–73.

educated people, or the president of a youth association, can also influence public opinions. Opinion leaders generally have a higher socioeconomic status, a more formal education, and greater exposure to the mass media. They tend to be more cosmopolitan, have frequent contact with agents of change, and are more innovative.[10]

The Bible shows such opinion leaders: Pharisee Gamaliel, who offered an arbitration plan as Peter and the Apostles confronted the Jews (Acts 5:29-40); and Apostle James who also altered the direction of opinion at the Jerusalem Council by proposing arbitration of the diet rule to the pagans (Acts 15:13-22). New trends spread effectively when opinion leaders have a positive attitude toward the outside. In the case of missionary activity, if opinion leaders welcome outside missionaries and allow evangelism, the Gospel will spread quickly. Conversely, if they persecute and spread negative rumours, the opposite will happen. This is also true in the commercial world; if opinion leaders spread a negative image of a new foreign product at the forefront of patriotism, the product will have great difficulty establishing itself in the market.

For information to flow between groups, there must be people to act as primary bridges. Just like the Good Samaritan, these bridges exchange the good that they have with others. The resources they deliver also include the good news that allows the poor of the city to restore the dignity of creation, have true hope and joy, and find the true master of their lives.

Becoming a Good Neighbour in Urban Flow Channels

In the Bible, a certain Jewish leader asked Jesus, "Who is our neighbour?" (Lk. 10:29). The leader was not asking about the concept of "neighbour," but rather about who they must love. Because Jews believed they were the chosen people, the leader already had the answer: Jews, not outsiders. Therefore, the parable of the Good Samaritan was not merely a heartwarming tale; it was a message that overturned the paradigm of what a neighbour was supposed to be for the children of God. While the Jews had thought that only those of the same ethnicity and religion could be considered their neighbours, Jesus said, through the analogy of the Good Samaritan, that a true neighbour has compassion for those in trouble. In other words, when the Jewish leader asked, "Who is my neighbour?" Jesus actually explained, "Whose neighbour should I be?" (Lk. 10:36) and told him to have compassion for those who encounter robbers, whoever they may be.

Being the truly good neighbour that Jesus taught is not simply being kind to others in a general sense; it is also about actively helping those in difficulty. People everywhere in modern cities are in danger and need help. So, what should today's Christians learn from the Good Samaritan?

First, a good neighbour in a city is a person who naturally performs kindness in the space where they live. The Good Samaritan and the robbed person were both on their way to Jericho. What the Good Samaritan did is very different from

---

10 Rogers, *Diffusion of Innovations*, 368–73.

the missions and charity of the church today. He was not carrying out a planned project; he was not on a week-long overseas mission or serving doughnuts and coffee to the homeless at the park in the morning. Unlike the evangelism and good deeds that have become projects and programmes in today's world, the Good Samaritan simply helped a poor person that he happened to meet on his way to Jericho.

We may do good deeds through church projects, but that does not guarantee that we are good neighbours. Projects are designed activities where people show up in their uniforms and do their assigned jobs; they do not necessarily require a change in one's heart. The road to Jericho is the best place to show one's true self because no one is watching. The priest, the Levite, and the Samaritan were not performing. Each treated the unfortunate victim exactly as they wanted, not according to their uniform. Therefore, the Samaritan's good deeds were not created by contrived programmes or plans but only reflected who he was.

We live across multiple human networks, including primary, residential, and socioeconomic groups. The things that happen in these human networks are part of our lives. Although we may do good deeds and share the Gospel with people outside of this network, we must first be genuinely good neighbours among our familiar groups in daily life.

Second, good urban neighbours prioritise, and have sympathy for, others. For example, in the movie Evan Almighty, Morgan Freeman plays a character who, despite being busy serving customers at the restaurant he runs, checks on a sad-looking mother who had left home. Freeman's first line to the woman was, "Excuse me, are you alright?" These words were the trigger that caused her to open up. Despite the rush of customers at the restaurant, Freeman's character stopped what he was doing, sat down next to her, listened attentively, and gave her some advice. Then he said, "I gotta run, a lot of people to serve!" and left. Although it took less than one and a half minutes, this conversation led the woman to return home to her family.

The main reason we find it difficult to do good deeds for those around us is that we lack the habit of paying attention to the personality and dignity of others. If we are too focused on our work, even the smallest good deed can feel like a burden. Like the priests and Levites on the way to Jericho, we may tell ourselves, "I am too busy for this". However, when we believe that the other person has similar characteristics, feelings, and dignity to ourselves, our sacrifices just feel like another aspect of daily life instead of "work" (Eph. 4:32; 1 Pet. 3:8).

Today, you can see many people waiting in urban middle zones for people to show them mercy – places that are neither fully private nor fully public, such as workplaces, neighbourhoods, and interest clubs. However, unlike the man lying bleeding on the road to Jericho, they generally have regular jobs, wear regular clothes, and chat like regular folk. Even when we sense someone is in need, we can quickly devise fifty such reasons not to help, such as wanting to respect their privacy or perhaps not wanting to get embroiled in a complicated situation.

On the other hand, sympathy and love make us brave to overcome our selfishness. A sympathetic heart gives us tremendous strength, which enables us to defeat our desires to be selfish. Courage does not come from mental or physical strength but is a power that comes from looking at people as Christ would have seen them. When it comes to someone we love, we do not try to retain our dignity and demeanour and instead persuade and give crucial advice. As Roger Schroeder puts it, the mission is "stepping into others' gardens." It is not enough to just look at the other person and maintain a superficial relationship.[11]

Third, our stereotypes of the robbed person and the programmed urban ministry become obstacles to us becoming good neighbours. We often think that the victim lying in the street is likely to be someone from a heterophilous zone and one with whom we have no acquaintance or previous encounter. However, the notion that the victim must be someone bleeding on the street blinds us from seeing the numerous people who have fallen around us. Some victims are very familiar to us: the people we meet daily who cover their bleeding wounds with clean clothes and attempt to get on with their lives. Suppose we broaden our idea of "victim" from only individuals in vulnerable classes, the homeless, and ethnic minorities to include "regular" colleagues we meet in our daily lives. In that case, urban missionary work will face a huge upheaval. Perhaps the urban ministry we are familiar with is too programmatic and its definition of "poor" too narrow.

Fourth, good neighbours build trust in everyday life. We are drawn to people we feel we can trust and pay more attention to the information they convey. This is because relationships with trusted people become an important information medium.[12]

There are several definitions of trust, but most definitions refer to a state of consistency regarding behaviour and thought, a kind of predictability and a feeling of emotional stability. The trust may arise in those in homophilous zones – those who are with us and not strangers.[13] This is because similar cultures, emotions, and daily lives create a common ground for trust to form.

The problem is that the victims in one's homophilous zone are not easily visible. This is because they are the people that we meet frequently in our daily lives and have various complex relationships with. For example, we must meet, compete, and collaborate with our co-workers on a daily basis. People tend to think that it is inappropriate to share their personal troubles with those they meet in the workplace. Therefore, they rarely reveal their wounds at work, in semi-public places like coffee shops, at badminton clubs, or on Internet platforms. Just as Alp from the previous chapters was unaware of his colleague Emil's sufferings for such a long time, people expose to others only what they wish to

---

11 Stephen B. Beavans and Roger Schroeder, *Prophetic Dialogue: Reflections on Christian Mission Today* (Maryknoll, NY: Orbis, 2011): 72–87.
12 Smith, *Creating Understanding*, 303–17.
13 Rogers, *Diffusion of Innovations*, 305–8.

show. The people who, like ourselves, live socially to pursue dreams and rise in status are the ones travelling to Jericho alongside us.

Becoming a Good Neighbour in Cross-Cultural Homophilous Spaces

Most cities today are multicultural spaces. We easily encounter other ethnic groups at work, in the classroom, and around our neighbourhoods. Situations that happened in mission fields in the past have now become part of our daily lives. On top of this, the city generally has its hierarchy. Where do the Good Samaritans work within this complex structure? To develop an appropriate model for urban churches seeking to share the Gospel in multicultural cities, we will first review the traditional missionary sending system. This is because sending a missionary to cross-cultural nations has many similar dynamics to working in multicultural societies.

Figure 15 is a simple diagram that compares the church's traditional foreign cross-cultural mission model and the modern urban ministry in a multicultural situation. On the left is a model that sends missionaries to other cultures without considering their social hierarchy. Here, missionaries from cultural group A go to cultures B, C, and D. Missionaries A1, A2, and A5 settle in D5, C2, and B1 groups, respectively. In this case, A1 and A5 must overcome ethnic and class differences, but A2 overcomes only one – culture. Missionary A5 goes to B1, who are a much higher class than themselves. Conversely, A1 moves from a high-class to a much lower-class individual, representing an incarnational mission.

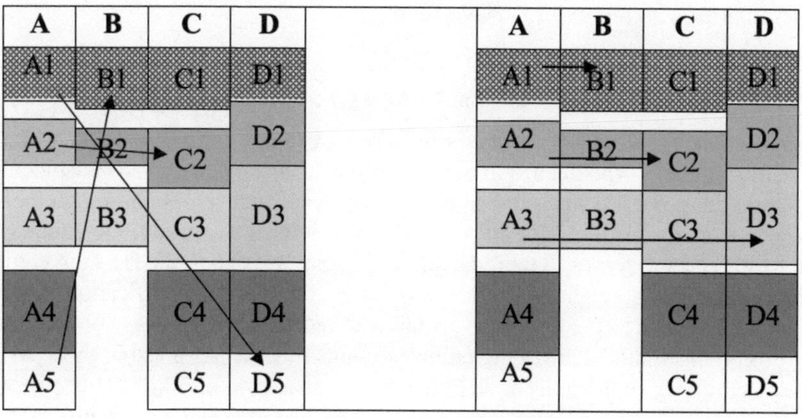

Figure 15: Cross-cultural Sending and Cross-class Sendings

The right side of the diagram illustrates intercultural evangelism within the same city. In the chart, Christians of ethnicity A contact other cultures B, C, and D in the same city. A1, A2, and A3 contact B1, C2, and D3, respectively. In a way, this can be described as meeting the people they already know and see daily. Each of A1 and B1, A2 and C2, and A3 and D3 are groups of people that encounter each other easily in their personal or work lives or are strangers who share similar lifestyles. Therefore, although they may have different cultural backgrounds, their interests and topics overlap in many ways. Despite cultural and perhaps language differences, A1, 2, and 3 have more in common than differences with B, C, and D.

Like the case of the Good Samaritan, good deeds are natural and effective only when within the same time and space and with a common ground that enables mutual understanding. To be a good neighbour within the same social class, business, hobby, or purpose in the same city may extend empathy while lowering cultural and hierarchical barriers. Wherever there is flow, it is expected that people with the same interests, skills, and social status will gather. In such an environment, A1 and B1, A2 and C2, and A3 and D3 will naturally meet. These good neighbours A1, 2, and 3 do not fit into or even need the title missionary.

Of course, overemphasising the efficiency of the mission – for example, going to the same social class – can contradict the ultimate spirit of the mission. It is true that if the missionary is from a class that is too high or too low compared to the people in the field, their work may become inefficient. However, because the fundamental spirit of mission reflects Jesus' incarnation, efficiency or convenience cannot be the first choice in mission work. No matter how many well-developed methods and technology we have, mission is still impossible without sacrifice. For example, the church must be careful not to deem missions to countries requiring greater funds as inefficient or to devalue the sacrifice of missionaries who report less visible fruits.

Isn't a B+ Also Great?

What would the Good Samaritan's high school report card have looked like? Usually, students who get a B grade are jealous of those who get an A. Students who get an A are jealous of those who get an A+. Students require much more flow to raise their A grade to an A+. So then, is a B+ a bad grade? Do adults go on to suffer great losses in their careers and social life due to the B+ they got in high school? Excluding careers that only accept the highest qualifications, there is plenty of space in the world for people who received a B+.

Promoting status requires incredible amounts of flow. As a result, those who look to improve their status have little scope to take care of others. However, if no one gives respect or value after achieving this exalted status, is it still an A+ life? If all one sees after winning the prize is fallen and bleeding competitors, what kind of person does that make them?

God has given Christians opportunities, abilities and good backgrounds, that is, good flow, to appoint us as a covenant to the people and a light to the Gentiles (Is. 42:6; Acts 13:47). Therefore, the flow that one is given is not meant for fulfilling only their A+ achievements.

What would happen if we dared to be satisfied with a B+ and used the extra energy for meaningful and good deeds? When we reminisce about high school friends from way back, when a colleague leaves the office for the next job, or when we leave our church as we move to another town, we more often regret that we were not better to others, not our B+ life. Spending time together is a God-given opportunity for love and help.

The extra energy from a B+ life allows us to live missional lives and care for those in need when we have opportunities, thus glorifying God. In other words, God gave us the opportunity to be like Christ, as "we who are strong ought to bear the weaknesses of those without strength and not [just] please ourselves" (Rom. 15:1-3).

Neighbours in cities do not emerge by chance; they must be consciously built. In urban life, the people next door, old friends from high school, and people in the office do not readily wait to be our neighbours. Jesus also said that a "good neighbour" does not automatically appear. To the Jews, whose sense of ethnicity sharply divided "us" from "them", Jesus defined a "good neighbour" as not a matter of ethnicity but of mercy (Lk. 10:26-37). In other words, our neighbours are made through our mercy. In addition, the Lord expects us to be neighbours not only to those we naturally like, but also to those outside our comfort zone. "If you greet only your brothers, what more are you doing than others? Do not even the Gentiles do the same?" (Mt. 5:47). Likewise, being a neighbour requires our hard work and courage.

When God gives us the authority and position to work with people, we must be careful not to use up all our energy scrambling for A+ results. Meeting people is a God-given opportunity. Just as income includes tithing, the flow that we receive must be used to fulfil both our own work and to help our neighbours.

Since urbanites work from early morning until late at night to ensure better flow and ultimately win the A+, it is perhaps natural that they cannot afford to take care of their colleagues who have fallen victim on the road to Jericho. The question is, are we Christians right to enter the same competition and give our all to the race? The priest and the Levite, who were busy with their lives and passed by the poor victim, may be the common urbanites of today. Meanwhile, the Good Samaritans continue to help others who we easily pass by, cleaning their wounds, putting them in their car, and taking them to a place where they can heal.

Missiological Reflection: Good Neighbours are Transforming Agents

People risk their dreams and lives for success. Christians and missionaries are no exception. Young Christians seek mentors and role models to succeed in society and faith. Pastors dream of ministering to big churches and becoming key instructors at seminars and events. If the idolisation of success powers such dreams, we may deceive ourselves by saying it is for the church and the Lord's work. We may even be eagerly pursuing our own success in the name of the Lord's ministry. We have seen that the excessive desire for success can prevent urban believers from being good neighbours. So, what must urban Christians and churches do to become good neighbours?

Urban Believers' Doing: Are You a Good Neighbour?

The Lord wants urban Christians to be good neighbours. As we have seen so far, the first step to being a good neighbour is to not fall into the trap of obsessing over success, as it strips us of the energy required to be good neighbours. We must instead listen to what the Bible says about success.

The success that Christ asks of us is not achieving the A+, becoming the best, and receiving admiration. If so, the lives of Jesus – leaving the crowds who worshipped him as a king – and the Apostle Paul – who waited for death in an underground prison – would get Fs. However, no one considers either of them a failure. Abraham – who left his stable homeland and lived the rest of his life on the move – and Noah – who built an ark on top of a mountain – also lived lives that, although the rest of the world did not understand, God recognises as successful.

For Biblical success in our lives, we must first control the desire to use all of the flow available for our benefit. Without tempering the desire to succeed at all costs, we will attempt to monopolise the surrounding flows. The Apostle Peter told Christians to live wandering lives but those come with "a royal priesthood, a holy nation, a people for [God's] own possession that (you) may proclaim the excellency of Him" (1 Pet. 2:9). Peter also warns that, even if conferred with royal or priestly status, because each of us is vulnerable like aliens and strangers, we must abstain from fleshly lusts (1 Pet. 2:9). Otherwise, we waste precious time solving our problems, instead of serving the people lying on the road to Jericho as a good neighbour.

Second, becoming a trustworthy person in one's network is the first step to becoming a good neighbour. While the Good Samaritan chanced upon a man who had been robbed, our neighbours are mostly those who live close by. Few are willing to show their wounds to those with whom they work and live, as people only show their weaknesses and wounds to those they trust.

"Trustworthy" means worthy of confidence.[14] However, because trust is inherently comprehensive and cultural, its practical meaning is much broader. For example, people trust a medical doctor's expertise or familiarity with people from one's hometown. For Christians in a city today, building trust among their colleagues can happen in multiple ways.

---

14 Merriam Webster Dictionary, "trustworthy", [Available online at: https://www.merriam-webster.com/dictionary/trustworthy], [Last accessed: 28th December 2023].

First, sincerity creates trust. Sincere people are relatively transparent in their words and actions.[15] These people do not change their words easily and back those words up with actions. Their values and standards are somewhat consistent, and their behaviours do not change, whether alone or with a group of people. Sincere people are predictable and do not make others speculate about them unnecessarily.

Second, people trust those who are consistent and stand by what they think is right. Rather than following trends or popularity, they dare to adhere to what they value. People in society always respect those who maintain good moral standards in their minds. These people are interested in justice and may make extraordinary efforts to solve the injustices they see around them. Although their strong principles may make others uncomfortable, people tend to respect and rely on such people rather than treat them rudely. In pain, people are likely to look first toward respected and honest people because they trust them.

Third, people trust those who are kind.[16] Kindness allows people to feel more valued and safer than they expect. When people receive unexpected kindness, they begin to open their hearts. The Bible (Eph. 4:31) mentions this kindness with compassion and forgiveness. Therefore, the concept of kindness includes kind actions rather than just being emotional.

Fourth, people trust those who they think know the truth. Even people who are not interested in the truth seek it once they encounter a dramatic moment. For example, after the death of a close acquaintance, or even after watching a touching movie, people can become more interested in their existence, eternal life, and the existence of God. Likewise, when people groan and suffer in pain (Rom. 8:22), divine desires in their minds make them seek God (Rom. 1:19). This desperation leads people to visit friends or colleagues who they believe know the truth – someone they can trust.

Finally, people trust those who can forgive and reconcile. Such people are respected because these actions go against human nature and are difficult for most people to do. It is almost impossible for our human nature to reconcile. As a result, Jesus' virtue and humility, which broke down the wall between God and humanity, provided Christians with the foundation for forgiveness and reconciliation. As the Bible says, peacemakers "shall be called sons of God" (Mt. 5:9), people respect those who forgive, and this will lead them to respect God.

---

15 Merriam Webster Dictionary defines sincerity as the quality or state of being sincere: honesty of mind: freedom from hypocrisy. [Available at: https://www.merriam-webster.com/dictionary/sincerity], [Last accessed: 28th December 2023].

16 Oxford English Dictionary defines kindness as friendliness and polite behaviour, a friendly character or attitude. *Oxford English Dictionary*, "kindness", [Available (behind paywall) at: https://www.oed.com/view/Entry/103470?redirectedFrom=kindness#eid], [Last accessed: 28th December 2023]. Merriam Webster Dictionary, "kindness", [Available at: https://www.merriam-webster.com/dictionary/kindness], [Last accessed: 28th December 2023].

God has sent out today's believers all over the city because God plans for us to help those who have fallen on the road to Jericho, and the trust we receive from our community becomes the fragrance that attracts those who are robbed (2 Cor. 2:14-16).

Urban Church's Doing: Saints with Gowns and Saints with T-shirts: Leaders in Two Urban Arenas

Mission is always contextual, so as society changes, so must the ways that the church works its mission. No matter in what kind of city, as the water covers the sea, God's missionary plan for all urbanites to know Him remains the same (Hab. 2:14). Simultaneously, since the mission is always contextual, as society changes, the style of the church's mission must also change. No matter how good the past results may have been, if tradition takes us away from our essence and calling, we must develop new approaches.

Typically, the senior pastor is at the centre of church leadership, either as a full-time minister or one who spends much of their time dedicated to the church. In other words, they are the saints who lead the service while wearing the priest's gown. These saints with gowns – the pastors – are good neighbours in the church, equipping the saints for the work of the ministry and protecting them from heresies and worldly affairs. On the other hand, the church members, who are also saints, usually live scattered throughout the city. They wear T-shirts or suits, spending most of the day in their neighbourhoods and workplace. These members, therefore, are saints with T-shirts.

Some examples in the Bible distinguish between the saints with gowns and the saints with T-shirts. While the apostles primarily focused on praying and the Word, the deacons oversaw work of administration and service (Acts 6). Of course, it would be impractical to over-differentiate the types of saints in this way for all places.[17]

The qualifications for deacons, or the office of overseers, seem to emphasise orderly personal management, healthy family life, and good relationships over their religious life or doctrine (1 Tim. 3:1-13). In Titus, the qualifications for elders and bishops are based primarily on being harmonious in their daily lives and setting a good example. Such people should be "holding fast to the faithful word which is in accordance with the teaching" (Titus 1:6-9). This condition also refers to applying the Word learned in the church into their lives rather than just serving in the church.[18] Let us now consider what role these two groups should play for the urban church to realise God's missionary vision today.

---

17 The Bible does not seem to care much about clearly delineating the boundary between the two. Moreover, this dichotomy is not absolute, as the perception, status, and scope of ministry varies greatly according to Christianity in each culture. In the text, however, it is divided into two groups to emphasise the arrival of a new leader and the incidental expectations.

18 This does not mean that the laymen neglected church life or did not prioritise their relationship with God. Rather, they had to endure misunderstandings and damage, just

Saints with Gowns: Good Neighbours of the Church

Unfortunately, urbanisation has widened the discrepancy between church and society. As a result of these two societies developing in different directions, the sense of the gap between pastors – who mainly spend time in church – and saints – who spend time outside of the church – has increased significantly. Sadly, this discrepancy causes the concern of disconnection between the sheep and the shepherd. The solution may not be for the saints with gowns to go to work or join social clubs to understand the lives of the saints with T-shirts. This would be too costly an alternative and the saints with gowns have their own unique roles to fulfil.

Saints with gowns today should still be good neighbours to their surroundings. They are good neighbours because their job is to serve the communities around the church and nurture the saints within the church. The saints with gowns must maintain their church to keep the biblical identity and become a hub of interaction between the community that helps them communicate and be active. They must also participate in community and social organisations as representatives of the church. As a result, saints with gowns act as lighthouses to help the church shine the light of salvation out into a dark world.

Above all, they are leaders who are responsible for the church community. They spend most of their time in the church with other ministers and believers. Therefore, they must be open to the church members to share their stories and concerns. Moreover, these priests perform sacraments and rituals and help the believers to partake in their community from birth until death. This way, the saints with gowns can be good neighbours to every generation of saints with T-shirts.

The saints with gowns are good neighbours who nurture the sheep within the church. This nurturing refers to the entire process of a believer's life from a non-believer to a mature believer stage (Eph. 4:13). For this, the primary responsibility of a pastor is to protect the believers and the church community from non-biblical trends and heresies. They should also nurture the sheep to overcome sin with the Word of God and live daily life as children of the light.

Finally, the saints with gowns should recognise that the saints with T-shirts are the new types of urban leaders, accept them as colleagues of a different type, and develop methods for co-operation.

As such, if saints wear their appropriate clothes and read the city through God's eyes, all church members can be Good Samaritans who, with God's heart, seek out those who have fallen on the road to Jericho.

Saints with T-Shirts: Good Neighbours at Work

The church should encourage saints with T-shirts to be good neighbours in their communities. The community here does not refer to villages, apartments, or

---

for being Christians at the time, and the social persecution clearly proves how noble and strong their spirituality was.

those who live in adjoining buildings. Many people in the city rarely interact with neighbours within walking distance. Especially for people who own their own car, the chances of interaction shrink rapidly. However, urbanites still interact with many neighbours in the workplace, local community activities, and in virtual interactions. This characteristic of urbanites naturally requires their church to teach the believers how to be good neighbours among their urban neighbours.

The saints with T-shirts must first be known for their sincerity and good attitudes by their colleagues and neighbours. They also need to provide family stability (1 Tim. 3:1-13; Tit. 1:6-9). For this, the church should encourage its members to see the biblical meaning and value in their workplaces and communities and the Christian's responsibility to become a good neighbour in those places. Becoming a good neighbour is counted as evangelism and will eventually become good soil for the community to know Jesus. Therefore, the ideal role model for their religious life is not a full-time minister who spends most of their time in the church. In addition, urban churches should remember that the concept of spending more time in the church equals becoming a sincere Christians applies only to a very limited number of persons, such as junior pastors.

The awareness of becoming a good believer in daily life, not just on Sunday, has existed for a long time, but it has not yet become an established movement. The reason is that this relatively new movement did not go beyond the personal level, nor were the believers taught what to do and how to be good neighbours in daily life. Furthermore, for mature believers who are already significantly involved in church work, any new trend or responsibility also becomes a burden. Due to the dualism that overly differentiates the secure and secular works and the lack of human and financial resources, churches intentionally close off from the neighbouring community and emphasise church-centred life.

Saints with T-shirts have grown and have been educated with different backgrounds and daily environments from the full-time ministers. Their environments are places of constant competition and tension, often with no religious values and culture, while maximising profits justifies almost anything. The good neighbours who can help people (those who are robbed in these circumstances) are the saints with T-shirts who have lived there for decades. They may have less theological knowledge and be less balanced than the pastors. Still, they know the organisation's internal dynamics and their colleagues' needs better than anyone else. They also know what kind of people their colleagues in the world respect and rely on. Consequently, urban churches should admit them as good neighbours who, with some coaching and motivation, are ready to help their colleagues in their world as salt and light.[19]

These new leaders, as believers, carry out their basic religious lives through the church on Sundays. However, they do not spend much energy maintaining

---

19 For the organisation and composition of the new leaders, please refer to Chapter 4, Missiological Reflection.

the church's Sunday programmes. The church should be able to provide the training needed to be good neighbours at home, in badminton clubs, in neighbourhood committees, and among colleagues at work, as taught in 1 Timothy and Titus. As a campus mission organisation works for one specific social status, the saints with T-shirts serve as salt and light scattered across the modern city's social, ethnic, and occupational groups. Each subcultural and functional group has its own unique group culture and social norms, and sharing the Gospel must happen in the appropriate context for each. While these group cultures and social rules may be difficult to understand for outsiders, elders and deacons who have lived there as insiders for 30 years find them very natural. Thus, they can be good neighbours with a better contextualised Gospel than anyone else. The Christians within these groups naturally cross the boundaries between social classes created by urban society. They are the good neighbours who can lead urbanites who have become enslaved to the idol of success to rest and healing .

Churches must pray and wait for the emergence of new leaders with T-shirts and must realise that these individuals have massive potential beyond just following the church programmes. Furthermore, we should treat those with T-shirts as partners who make our city a place of glorifying God rather than as rival groups to the church. No matter how devastating the cities become, God still builds stepping stones all over the city and sends missionaries across them.

Closing Reflection to Missional Challenges and Opportunities

This book contains a desire to know what God is doing in our cities. Ever since the fall of Adam, God has been on a mission for the salvation of mankind, and this mission continues to this day. Therefore, knowing what God is doing among us is the first step in walking with God and joining in His work. Otherwise, our ministries easily become irrelevant to God's interests and vision or cater to our own dreams.

To understand God's concerns, we have studied urban society through four social anthropological themes: urban people, urban groups, urban time and space, and urban flows. This book looks at these four urban elements through the lens of social network theory. This social network approach is important because a city is the result of its people and societies. We have found that the cities and urban social networks have a cause-and -effect relationship with each other. A social network is the interconnectedness of the people that provides cities with the culture and resources to make places become cities. Cities are also characterised by the behaviours and values of the people.

As Edward Glaser shows in his book "The Triumph of the City," cities have demonstrated their greatness with such creativity and collaboration that they can declare victory over human history.[1] These victorious cities are only possible because they have urban people and societies behind them, and urbanity is the result of people thinking and connecting in urban ways. Advances in science and communication technology have revolutionised people's mobility and allowed those who used to live in small communities to be part of an infinite network of connections. In addition, the power of globalisation has enabled people to connect and collaborate with people they never knew existed. As a result, people mobilise vast quantities of goods and services to satisfy their ever-growing creativity and desires. These new flows break down barriers to information that was once reserved for a select few, open people's eyes to justice and equality, and enable collaboration across social class and race with a renewed sense of self and dignity for others (Chapter 7). These changes in connectivity, a function of the social networks, have transformed our lives and societies from the ground up.

---

1 Glaeser, *Triumph of the City*.

On the other hand, ironically, this connectivity has given urbanites a new taste of disconnection. This environment of endless competition and the successism created by the new demands have instilled in everyone's mind a sense of compulsion that they must keep running or fail. Because of this obsession, people leave behind the blessings of today, forget their own dignity, and forget their loved ones to pursue the idol of success. This obsessive successism and fear of failure naturally prevents people from taking the time to read the pain of their fellow colleague as he groans from the attack of robbers (Chapter 8).

Although we see many people in this connected society, we largely live disconnected lives. Mass production and automation allow us to have meals delivered to our doorsteps without ever seeing a human face, and we can sit in front of a monitor all day and still get work done. The irony of this connected, urban society is that we are also disconnected from what we value. Not only are families less likely to share meals together, but even when they do, there is a lack of common ground and too much disparity between them. It is not unusual for people to merely greet their relatives who live in the same city on the phone once a year during the holidays and have little contact with neighbours (Chapter 3).

On the other hand, some people actively use the disconnectedness and connectivity of cities to maximise their opportunities and benefits. Urbanites actively use these disconnections and connections to maximise personal opportunities and benefits. While in the past, people were often assigned to pre-determined identities and groups, modern people have more freedom to choose their own groups, whether they are for hobbies, work, or religion. Not only can people pick and choose which groups to join, but they can also easily switch to new groups. This type of group activity allows people to own I-centred group packets that organise the groups around the self. This I-centred group packet is a tremendous source of power and opportunity that allows people to choose their own lives and futures (Chapter 4). People use this power and opportunity to pursue greater success and benefits. A structure in which a person is the centre of their life, and can use the world around them as stepping stones and resources for success, eventually leads to a life where they are the king of their lives. People can be kings in their own lives because they can open up their lives as much as possible to connect with more resources and better people, or they can be closed off and not allow anyone to enter their territory in order to protect themselves.

These "be your own kings" have no king above them, nor do they know from whom come the power and opportunities they possess. With no master to fear, and no idea of what the opportunities and abilities they have been given are for, it is natural for them to use them to manifest their sinfulness.

The selfishness, sinfulness, and destructiveness of these self-appointed kings confirms, more than ever, who we are as sinners before God. No matter how much a city may be filled with myths of abundance and success, the kings of the city are now exposing their sinfulness more than ever before. Cities are able to publicly, structurally, and unabashedly practice human sinfulness and selfishness that were previously practiced primitively on a smaller scale. Certainly, as

Edward Glaser says, the city of today has given humanity a victory never before achieved, but it does not eliminate our selfishness and sinfulness. Rather, cities give people power beyond their control, and people have normalised using that power to have more fun, gain promotion, fill their own bellies, and take what belongs to others and use it to be kings on Earth, because kings have no one to fear and can use their power for themselves. Thus, the city becomes a more accurate and clearer reflection of the fact that "all have sinned and fall short of the glory of God" (Rom. 3:23-24).

Christians and churches in the city are no exception to this temptation. We too must be careful not to take for granted the opportunities and blessings of connectivity and disconnection and hoard them for ourselves. Those who become the king find it easy to use up the power and opportunities they have been given for themselves, missing out on opportunities to care for loved ones and participate in the work of God's kingdom. We must take seriously the blessings entrusted to us as stewards and partners in building the kingdom of the God who shows that "much is given, much is required" (Lk. 12:48). The urban social networks can give Christians tremendous opportunities to come down from our thrones and connect with others, rescue the mugged, and make the good and joyful news flow to those who need it. That opportunity is the privilege that the God who is determined to save humanity has granted us: to partner with him in this amazing and glorious mission.

Missional Challenges and Opportunities for Urban Churches

The last part of every chapter in this book tries to answer the questions, "What is the church in this context?" and "What should the church do?" By combining the reflections of each chapter, the final challenges and opportunities for the church are summarised below.

First and foremost, the church in the city must engage in a missional endeavour to transform themselves into a truly urban church for urban people (Chapter 4). The church in the city here means that a church is located in the city area, but it lacks the consciousness to change the nature of its ministry to be urban, and it has no idea how to do urban ministry. These churches in the city do not give much weight to cultural and social factors in their ministry. The churches in the city do not even understand the urban people and ministry to the urbanites: they are not urban churches but merely churches in the city. A church in the city refers to a church whose address belongs to the city and which has urbanite members, but the actual ministry is still the old wineskin. This old wineskin church does not understand the characteristics and circumstances of urbanites and engages in traditional thinking and ministry instead of ministry for urbanites. Such old wineskin churches consist of an excessively church-centred paradigm and an overly content-oriented nurturing philosophy and leadership. As a result, church leaders have poor understanding of context and are unable to proactively help their sheep.[2] Instead, they believe that their traditions and heritage become the essentials of the church. As a result, when they plant a new church, they often follow the same methods of ministry that they have learned from past churches.

In contrast, an urban church takes it seriously that it is a church of urban people. Because they are ministering to urban people, they feel a great responsibility to understand them. This understanding of the urbanite is the key to urban ministry. When planting a new church, knowing what God is doing in our city is the starting point rather than replicating the pastoral patterns from past churches. Where God's heart is, our church's heart should go too, and we should partake in his work.

To transform from being a church in the city to being an urban church, having a contextualised posture and receptor-oriented approach to the community is necessary because both of these missiological postures seek to make the gospel effectively understood so that it never loses its dynamism in the context of everlastingly changing receptors. To do this, the church must first pay attention to the growing disconnect between the changing environment inside and outside the church and the operating systems of our churches. This is because the church's ways of operating and ministering that have been normalised for us were not created in the context of the current urban environment. For hundreds of years in Europe and North America, the church was a place where people who lived in the same village and were culturally homogeneous could find spiritual care and religious practice. The leader of the church was usually an intelligent spiritual leader from the same cultural background as the villagers, but with a high level of education and the ability to connect with the outside world. Ministers usually worked within the church and spent their time studying the truths of the Bible and teaching the congregation rather than engaging in worldly affairs. Since members of the congregation attended church within walking distance and kinship groups attended the same church, the pastor easily encountered members on the street. The same contexts and overlapping social networks provided by traditional society were good soil for the church's ministry to become holistic and their relationships more multi-faceted. However, churches need to realise that the operating systems developed in traditional social networks are actually hindering the ministry of the church today. This is because the social networking system of society has changed, but the ministry system of the church still uses the old village model. For example, members of urban churches rarely interact with other members throughout the week outside of Sunday services. It's also difficult for ministers to meet with members unless they intentionally make an appointment. When a new person comes to church, most of the people in the church are new to them. This situation, where the church's network has become increasingly distant from its neighbors, and the

---

2 Phillip Berryman, *Religion in the Megacity: Catholic and Protestant Portraits from Latin America* (Maryknoll, NY: Orbis, 1996): 15; Peter Kaldor, *Who Goes Where?: Who Doesn't Care?* (Homebush West, N.S.W.: Lancer, 1987): 97.

advantages of being part of a village have almost disappeared, shows that the church in the city urgently need to transform into urban church.

Second, the groupings of the city have created so much division, competition, and resentment. It also provides missional opportunities for the urban church to be at the forefront of reconciliation and forgiveness. Cities are forced to divide people into categories for the sake of efficiency, and each group creates their norms. As McGavran notes, these homogeneous groups have many missional advantages because they have a powerful internal unifying force.[3] On the other hand, such groupings can easily divide people and create competition and stratification (chapters 3 and 4). As in many societies, the haves, the learned, and the powerful seek to marginalise the have-nots and monopolise the gains. As a result, the enemy, who holds power in the air and spirit, causes people to divide and hate one another. God is still at work to tear down the high walls that people have built and reconnect the divided, which is why the urban church must pay attention to God's zeal to break down barriers and invite us to cross over to the other side and shake hands of reconciliation and forgiveness. In an urban culture that does not believe in being the underdog and values success, the church must believe that connecting with the other side of the divide and shaking hands of reconciliation is what makes a strong church. The urban church is an important agent that says "stop!" to the divisions in the city that cause people to be evil.

Third, the modern trend of people feeling uncomfortable about gathering is a crisis for the urban church. Urban churches must use these crises as opportunities to shift structure. These crises challenge the assumption that the act of worship and the time and space of worship are one and the same. These theological and practical questions have opened our eyes to the fact that worship is not just about being in a place of worship at a certain time, but that any space and time in which God's sovereignty is at work is a holy place where we must take off our shoes. Conventional worship involves many people doing several activities in a small space in a short amount of time, and as a result, leaders thoroughly prepare the day before to make those few hours of worship a success. On Sunday, they conduct worship as if it were a performance on a stage. It is as if the church must be run like a conveyor belt for mass production. But now, the separation of time and space from the act of worship actually allows the church to focus on the happiness and maturity of its members in the places they live, rather than the growth of the church itself.

If the ministry of the church can cross the limits of space and time, then the church can disperse and reach out to believers and non-Christians in the space-time zones that are natural to them (Chapter 6, Missiological Reflection). If the time and space that is familiar to non-believers is unfamiliar to church workers, can it really be called incarnational ministry to bring non-believers to church? If the church that is in one place on Sunday can be found at different times of the day in a restaurant in front of a member's workplace, in a coffee shop where

3 Wagner and McGavran, *Understanding Church Growth.*

mothers are pushing strollers at 10am on a Tuesday morning, at a badminton club on a Saturday afternoon, in an infinite online space, in the radio communication between taxi drivers, in a small prayer room on the side of a financial street, and so on, then the church becomes connected and dispersed among the citizens.

Fourth, the emergence of new unreached urban groups becomes a huge threat for urban evangelism, but the church must use this challenge as an opportunity to keep its eyes open to where God is at work, and to expect and actively prepare for the rise of new leaders (chapter 4). Economic, professional, or interest groups have very distinct identities that make it uncomfortable to engage in faith-based activities within them. It is even more difficult for ministers to approach the daily lives and workplaces of believers, so it is no wonder that the religious influence of Christians in urban social spaces is diminishing. Nevertheless, God has already placed countless Christians amid new unreached groups in these cities.

The church must recognise that these saints with T-shirts will emerge as the new Christian leadership and take a proactive stance (Chapter 8, Missiological Reflection). Thus, urban Christians must prepare for the emergence of this new leadership and position the traditional church's role accordingly. This involves two theological considerations. One is the church's stance towards mission organisations. Churches and mission organisations must be able to recognise each other as partners in teamwork for the Kingdom of God, not as competitors. This partnership is not easy in practice because both organisations can quickly harden in the face of limited human and material resources. To solve this problem, both organisations must be able to understand each other's roles and positions. Collaboration is also possible when both organisations have a theological framework and vision of the mission of God (*Missio Dei*), and when they seek together to discover what God is doing in our cities.

Next, both churches and mission organisations must realistically redefine their understanding to the membership. In a society where everything is connected, it is practically impossible for a person to belong to only one organisation and be spiritually influenced by only one leader. The fence of the church is now very low, and urbanites who have become accustomed to the I-centred group packet are free to choose different places and belong to multiple organisations. They do not want to be loyal to one organisation, they want leaders to follow, opportunities to participate, and activities in different places that have meaning and value. This is not to say that a local church is unnecessary, but rather concerns an individual believer's spontaneity, given that self-motivation is diminished when it is restricted (Chapter 4, Missiological Reflection).

Missional Challenges and Opportunities for Urban Christians

Changes in social networks have transformed the lives of urbanites and the Christians who are a part of them. What are some of the missionary challenges and opportunities that these changes present for Christians? Over the course of eight chapters, this book has outlined who Christians are and what they are to do. Now we will synthesise all of this and summarise how Christians should think and live.

First, instead of selfishly using the power of multiple identities, Christians should see it as a missional opportunity to connect the disconnected with the good news. Multiplicity has vastly increased the connections and opportunities for people to meet (Chapter 2). Moreover, globalisation, urbanisation, and advances in media and technology have enabled people to transcend time and space. This capability immediately stimulates people's selfishness and desire to achieve greater success. Christians are no exceptions to this. These challenges can only be transformed into opportunities through God's missionary vision. Only by knowing themselves as missional beings can they be brought to overcome the temptations of selfishness and successism and find the vision of themselves as a channel of blessing. Therefore, Urban Christians must take the infinite possibilities offered by their multiple identities seriously. This multiplicity is a pathway to reconnecting relationships between classes, ethnicities, and genders that have been severed for centuries. Because of this ability to connect people from different backgrounds, their missional potential is enormous. For Christians who have lost sight of their God-given mission, these multiple identities are nothing more than a lowly way to fulfil their greed, fill their bellies, and becoming kings on Earth. In contrast, the missional vision made the Apostle Paul, a man of multiple identities, into an in-between person for sharing the blessings.

Second, every Christian should realise that they are in a real game with non-Christians.

Traditionally, the church has introduced the truth in the form of apologetics and messages. Worship services include a well-rehearsed sermon and a series of carefully prepared sequences that are presented as if they are performances on stage. The congregation sits in a large audience and listens to the prepared ministry. Unfortunately, this stage and audience composition has little impact, at least on today's unbelievers. No matter how successful the church's programme is, most of the people in the pews are already believers. Fewer non-believers come to the church because they have less need to go into urban societies, and if they do, the cultural differences in worship style, terminology, and atmosphere are so great that it is very difficult for them to adapt. In the past, when churches were located in villages, newcomers often had friends and relatives from the village at the church, so they were already connected. However, the unbelievers who find a church in the city faces an entirely different situation. It is very rare for an unbeliever to visit a church, and the journey of cultural adjustment in a place full of strangers and unfamiliar languages and worship patterns often proves too much for them. This cultural distance and lack of social network increase the barriers to church.

Ironically, non-Christians in cities today are exposed to Christianity much more so than in the past. They are constantly exposed to Christianity in their social lives and through mass media. Collaboration between non-Christians and Christians is more common in urban life than ever before. Non-believers form their own opinions of Christianity by watching the real lives of the Christians they sit next to and work with all day every day. Christians also observe the lives of their non-Christian and unbelieving coworkers in their daily lives. Contrasting with a well-rehearsed sermon or staged worship programme, this real life is literally about life as it happens spontaneously. As a result, comparing these lives is, in some ways, a real spiritual game of who is the true God. The spiritual battles that were once seen on the mission field and in the Holy Spirit ministries are now being fought quietly in offices, in front of apartments, and in parks, throughout the city.

While in the past, the real game was played primarily by pitting religious doctrines against each other, now it has expanded to include a much more practical look at our lives holistically. Whereas in the past, non-believers were the audience for the gospel presented on the stage of the church, they now look over their shoulders into our lives and interpret the gospel in their own way. In this way, the field of urban evangelism has expanded from church services into our daily lives, and the areas of interaction between Christians and unbelievers is wider than ever before.

Third, the gospel should be good news in the context of non-Christians and Christians together. The impact of secularism has caused modern people to be less interested in religion and religious doctrines. Instead, interest has shifted to the emotional, relative, and personal areas. On the other hand, Christianity has traditionally evangelised others through apologetics and sought spiritual growth mainly through knowledge. This familiarity with apologetic evangelism among unbelievers, for whom emotion and the individual are important, is often a significant weakness for Christianity today. This does not mean the gospel itself has lost power. In fact, the gospel is so great that it is the good news that has an answer to any problem in any area of our lives, an answer so fundamental that it is superior to any alternative. Therefore, finding and practicing the gospel in everyday life in a way that non-believers and people of other religions can understand becomes the good news for the city.

Modern people's emphasis on personal issues and emotions means that the good news they need is not just about religion or a worship service, but about everyday life. That is, Christians, unbelievers, and people of other faiths alike are stirred by the issues that concern their lives, and they want to hear a message that is radical and superior to any other answer. The real game that modern Christians play in life is not about winning by overwhelming the others with apologetics and logic. This real game is less about explaining the exclusive or uncommon area in the Christian faith and more about whose life testifies to the truth. Whereas apologetics in the past highlighted the Christianity's differences, the focus is now on common issues in life that non-Christians are also familiar with and consider their own.

Fourth, Christians must have the courage to walk slowly in order to be the good neighbour that Jesus described. In a time when people shout, "everybody run!" to achieve success, Christians must dare to walk slowly (Chapter 7). In a society that believes that one cannot afford to be left behind, it is only by intentionally walking slowly that one can gain something more valuable. A person who is busy running around all day, using up all their energy, naturally cannot afford to take care of their fellow neighbour who has been robbed. We can only help our hurt neighbour by deliberately removing ourselves from the hustle and bustle of the city, the overflow, and the desire to succeed. To do this, we must have the courage to realise that in many areas of our lives, a B+ isn't so bad (Chapter 8). Unlike the priest and teacher of the law who walked past the robbed man, the Good Samaritan was not so immersed in his schedule, money, and opportunities so that he chose to care for the man and courageously chose the B+.

This book examines the missional challenges and opportunities that urban churches and Christians need to be aware of as social networks change. No matter how much society changes, God's missional vision remains the same: for every city to be full of the knowledge of the Lord, as the waters cover the sea (Is. 11:9). Therefore, we must seek to know what God is doing in our cities and become partners in that work. Only then can we return to the mission of God (*Missio Dei*), rather than the mission of the church.

Bibliography

Abercrombie, Nicholas, Stephen Hill, and S. Bryan Turner. "Dictionary of Sociology." In *Dictionary of Sociology*. London: Penguin Reference, 2006.

Achor, Shirley. *Mexican Americans in a Dallas Barrio*. Tucson, AZ: University of Arizona Press, 1978.

"Affordable Housing and Social Protection Systems for All to Address Homelessness." *Commission for Social Development*. United Nations Economic and Social Council, 2019.

Alan, Smart, and Josephine Smart. "Urbanization and the Global Perspective." *Annual Review of Anthropology*, 32 (2003): 263-285.

Alexandra, Maryanski. *The Social Cage: Human Nature and the Evolution of Society*. Stanford, CA: Stanford University Press, 1992.

Alford, R.R. "Critical Evaluation of the Principles of City Classification," In Brian J.L. Berry, Ed. *City Classification Handbook: Methods and Applications* New York: John Wiley, 1972: 331–59.

Allan, G.A. *A Sociology of Friendship and Kinship*. London: Allen and Unwin, 1979.

Archer, John. "Colonial Suburbs in South Asia 1700-1850, and the Spaces of Modernity," In R. Silverston, Ed. *Visions of Suburbia*. London: Routledge, 1996: 26–54.

Arjun, Appadurai. "Disjuncture and Difference in the Global Cultural Economy," *Theory, Culture and Economy* 7(2), (1986): 295–310.

Bakhtin, M.M. "Forms of Time and of the Chronotope in the Novel: Notes towards a Historical Poetic," In M.M. Bakhtin and Michael Holquist, Eds. *The Dialogic Imagination: Four Essays.* Austin, TX: University of Texas Press, 1981: 84–258.

Barth, Karl. *Letters, 1961-1968*. Grand Rapids, MI: Eerdmans, 1981.

Barth, Karl, and Edwyn Clement Hoskyns. *The Epistle to the Romans*. London: Oxford University Press, 1968.

Baskauskas, Liucija. "Multiple Identities: Adjusted Lithuanian Refugees in Los Angeles," *Urban Anthropology* 6(2), (1977): 141–54.

Beavans, Stephen B. *Models of Contextual Theology*. Maryknoll, NY: Orbis, 2000.

Beavans, Stephen B., and Roger Schroeder. *Prophetic Dialogue: Reflections on Christian Mission Today*. Maryknoll, NY: Orbis, 2011.

Becci, Irene, Marian Burchardt, and José Casanova. *Topographies of Faith: Religion in Urban Spaces*. Leiden: Brill, 2013.

Beck, Ulrich and Ciaran Cronin. *The Cosmopolitan Vision*. Cambridge: Polity, 2006.

Bell, David R., and Mary Douglas. "Natural Symbols: Explorations in Cosmology", *The Philosophical Quarterly* 22(88), (1972): 280.

Bennett, Andy, and Richard A. Peterson, Eds. *Music Scenes: Local, Translocal and Virtual*. Nashville, TN: Vanderbilt University Press, 2004.

Berkhof, Handrikus. *Christian Faith: An Introduction to the Study of the Faith*. Grand Rapids: MI: Eerdmans, 1979.

Berry, Brian J.L., and Adam Okulicz-Kozaryn. "An Urban-Rural Happiness Gradient," *Urban Geography* 32(6), (2011): 871–83.

Berryman, Phillip. *Religion in the Megacity: Catholic and Protestant Portraits from Latin America*. Maryknoll, NY: Orbis, 1996.

Bestor, Theodore C. "Supply-Side Sushi: Commodity, Market, and the Global City," *American Anthropologist* 103(1), (2001): 76–95.

Bicchieri, Cristina. *Norms in the Wild: How to Diagnose, Measure, and Change Social Norms*. New York, NY: Oxford University Press, 2017.

Bicchieri, Cristina, Ryan Muldoon, and Alessandro Sontuoso. "Social Norm," *Standard Encyclopedia of Philosophy*, 1st March 2011. [Available at: https://plato.stanford.edu/entries/social-norms/], [Last accessed: 24th December 2023]

Bicchieri, Cristina, and Erte Xiao. "Do the Right Thing: But Only If Others Do So," *Journal of Behavioral Decision Making* 22(2), (2009): 191–208.

Boissevain, Jeremy. *Friends of Friends: Networks, Manipulators and Coalitions*. Pavilion Series Social Anthropology. Oxford: Blackwell, 1974.

Bonhoeffer, Dietrich, Christian Gremmels, Eberhard Bethge, Renate Bethge, Ilse Tödt, and John W. De Gruchy. *Letters and Papers from Prison*. 1st English edn. v. 8. Minneapolis, MI: Fortress, 2010.

Bourdieu, Pierre. "Distinction: A Social Critique of the Judgment of Taste," In *Handbook of Theory and Research for the Sociology of Education*, translated by Richard Nice. New York: Greenwood Press, 1986: 241–58.

Brueggemann, Walter. *The Land: Place as Gift, Promise, and Challenge in Biblical Faith*. Overtures to Biblical Theology. Philadelphia, PA: Fortress, 1977.

Burgess, Ernest W. "The Growth of the City: An Introduction to a Research Project," In Robert Ezra Park, E.W. Burgess, and Roderick Duncan McKenzie, Eds. *The City*. Chicago, IL: University of Chicago Press, 1925: 47–62.

Burnett, David. *Clash of Worlds*. Eastbourne: Monarch, 1990.

Calhoun, John B. "Population Density and Social Pathology," *Scientific American* 206(2), (1962): 139–49.

Caplow, Theodore, Howard M. Bahr, Bruce A. Chadwick, Reuben Hill, and Margaret Holms Williamson. *Middletown Families: Fifty Years of Change and Continuity*. New York: Bantam, 1982.

Capra, C. Mónica, Rachel T.A. Croson, Mary L. Rigdon, and Tanya S. Rosenblat, Eds. "Game-Theoretic Accounts of Social Norms." In *Handbook of Experimental Game Theory*. Cheltenham: Edward Elgar, 2020: 241–55.

Castells, Manuel. *The Rise of the Network Society*. 2nd edn. Vol. 1: Information Age. Malden, MA: Blackwell, 2010.

Castells, Manuel. *The Informational City: Information Technology, Economic Restructuring, and the Urban-Regional Process*. Oxford, UK: Blackwell, 1989.

Chung, Byung Gwan. *Urban Church Growth (도시교회 성장학)*. Seoul: Chongshin DaehakGyo, 2009.

Clinard, M.B. "Deviation Behavior: Urban-Rural Contrasts," In C.E. Elias, J. Gillies, and S. Reimer, Eds. *Metropolis: Values in Conflict.* Belmont, CA: Wadsworth, 1964: 237–44.

Cohen, S.D. "Environmental Load and the Allocation of Attention," In Andrew Baum and Jerome E. Singer, Eds. *Advances in Environmental Psychology.* Volume 1, The Urban Environment. 3rd edn. Hillsdale, NJ: Erlbaum, 1978: 1–30.

Colombo, Enzo, and Paola Rebughini. "The Children of Immigrants in Italy: A New Generation of Italians?" In Paul Spickard, Ed. *Multiple Identities: Migrants, Ethnicity, and Membership*. Bloomington, IN: Indiana University Press, 2013: 188–212.

Conn, Harvie M. *Eternal Word and Changing Worlds: Theology, Anthropology, and Mission in Trialogue.* Phillipsburg, NJ: P&R, 1984.

Conn, Harvie M., and Manuel Ortiz. *Urban Ministry: The Kingdom, the City & the People of God*. Downers Grove, IL: InterVarsity, 2001.

Connerton, Paul. *How Societies Remember*. Cambridge: Cambridge University Press, 1989.

Conrad, Phillip Kottak. *Cultural Anthropology*. 13th edn. Boston, MA: McGraw-Hill Humanities, 2009.

Cooley, Charles Horton. *Human Nature and the Social Order*. New York: Charles Scribner's Sons, 1902.

Cornell, Stephen. "Discovered Identities and American Indian Supratribalism," In Paul Spickard and Jeffrey W. Burroughs, Eds. *We Are a People: Narrative and Multiplicity in Constructing Ethnic Identity*. Philadelphia, PA: Temple University Press, 2000: 98–123.

Cox, Harvey Gallagher. *The Secular City: Secularization and Urbanization in Theological Perspective*. Princeton, NJ: Princeton University Press, 2013.

Crang, Mike. "Rhythms of the City: Temporalised Space and Motion," In Jon May and N.J. Thrift, Eds. *TimeSpace: Geographies of Temporality.* Critical Geographies 13. London: Routledge, Taylor & Francis, 2001: 187–207.

———. "Time: Space," In Paul J. Cloke and Ron Johnston, Eds. *Spaces of Geographical Thought: Deconstructing Human Geography's Binaries*. London: SAGE, 2005: 199–220.

Crenshaw, Kimberlé. "Demarginalizing the Intersection of Race and Sex: A Black Feminist Critique of Antidiscrimination Doctrine, Feminist Theory and Antiracist Politics," *University of Chicago Legal Forum* 1(8), (1989): 139–67.

Cresswell, Tim. *Place: A Short Introduction*. Hoboken, NJ: Wiley, 2013.

Crowe, P. "Social Networks in an Urban Context," In M.C. Romanos, Ed. *Western European Cities in Crisis*. Lexington, MA: Lexington Press, 1979: 67–80.

Day, Christopher. *Places of the Soul: Architecture and Environmental Design as a Healing Art*. London: Aquarian, 1990.

Devos, T., and M.R. Banaji. "American = White?" *Journal of Personality and Social Psychology* 88(3), (2005): 447–66.

Diel, Kathi, Sonja Grelle, and Wilhelm Hofmann. "A Motivational Framework of Social Comparison," *Journal of Personality and Social Psychology* 120 (2021): 1415–30. [Available at: https://doi.org/10.1037/pspa0000204], [Last accessed: 29th December 2023].

Douglas, Mary. *Cultural Bias*. Royal Anthropological Institute Occasional Paper. London: Royal Anthropological Institute, 1978.

Dublin, L. *Suicide*. New York: Roland, 1963.

Eames, Edwin, and Judith Goode. *Anthropology of the City: An Introduction to Urban Anthropology*. Prentice-Hall Series in Anthropology. Englewood Cliffs, NJ: Prentice-Hall, 1977.

Ellul, Jacques. *The Meaning of the City*. Grand Rapids, MI: Eerdmans, 1970.

Ferraro, Gary P. *Cultural Anthropology: An Applied Perspective*. Minneapolis/St. Paul, MN: West, 1995.

Fischer, Claude S. *The Urban Experience*. 2nd ed. San Diego, CA: Harcourt Brace Jovanovich, 1984.

———. *To Dwell Among Friends: Personal Networks in Town and City*. Chicago, IL: University of Chicago Press, 1982.

Flanagan, William G. *Contemporary Urban Sociology*. Cambridge; New York: Cambridge University Press, 1993.

———. *Urban Sociology: Images and Structure*. 5th edn. Rowman & Littlefield, 2010.

Foucault, Michel. *Power/Knowledge: Selected Interviews & Other Writings 1972-1977*. Edited by Colin Gordon. Translated by Colin Gordon, Leo Marshall, John Mepham, and Kate Soper. New York: Pantheon, 1980.

Frankenberg, Ronald. *Communities in Britain: Social Life in Town and Country*. Modern Revivals in Sociology. Aldershot: Gregg Revivals, 1994.

Fraser, Matthew, and Soumitra Dutta. *Throwing Sheep in the Boardroom: How Online Social Networking Will Transform Your Life, Work and World*. Chichester, England; Hoboken, NJ: Wiley, 2008.

Geoffrey, Brennan, Lina Eriksson, Robert E. Goodin, and Nicholas Southwood. *Explaining Norms*. New York: Oxford University Press, 2013.

Gergen, Kenneth. "Multiple Identity: The Healthy, Happy Human Being Wears Many Masks," *Psychology Today* 12 (May 1972): 31–35.

Gibbs, J.P. "Suicide," In R.K. Merton and R. Nisbet, Eds. *Contemporary Social Problems*. New York: Harcourt Brace Jovanovich, 1971: 271–312.

Gibson, William. *Neuromancer*. Reprint. New York: Ace, 1987.

Giedion, Sigfried. *Space, Time and Architecture: The Growth of a New Tradition*. Cambridge, MA: Harvard University Press, 1974.

Gillette, Maris Boyd. *Between Mecca and Beijing: Modernization and Consumption among Urban Chinese Muslims*. Stanford ,CA: Stanford University Press, 2000.

Gilliland, Dean S. *Pauline Theology & Mission Practice*. Jos Plateau State, Nigeria: Albishir, 1983.

———. *The World Among Us: Contextualizing Theology for Mission Today*. Dallas, TX: Word, 1989.

Glaeser, Edward. *Triumph of the City: How Our Greatest Invention Makes Us Richer, Smarter, Greener, Healthier, and Happier*. Reprint edition. New York: Penguin, 2012.

Goffman, Erving. *Relations in Public*. New York: Basic Books, 1972.

Gordon, Milton M. "Toward a General Theory of Racial and Ethnic Group Relations," In Nathan Glazer and Daniel Moynihan, Eds. *Ethnicity*. Cambridge, MA: Harvard University Press, 1975: 84–110.

Gorringe, Timothy. *A Theology of the Built Environment: Justice, Empowerment, Redemption*. Cambridge: Cambridge University Press, 2002.

Gottdiener, Mark, and Leslie Budd. *Key Concepts in Urban Studies*. London; Thousand Oaks, CA: SAGE, 2005.

Gottdiener, Mark, Randolph Hohle, and Colby King. *The New Urban Sociology*. 6th edn. New York: Routledge, Taylor & Francis, 2019.

Gottdiener, Mark, and Ray Hutchison. *The New Urban Sociology*. 4th edn. Boulder, CO: Westview, 2011.

Gould, Harold. "Lucknow Rickshawallas: The Social Organization of an Occupational Category," *International Journal of Comparative Sociology* 6 (1965): 27–47.

Greeley, Andrew M. *Ethnicity in the United States: A Preliminary Reconnaissance*. New York: Wiley, 1974.

Greenway, Roger S., and Timothy M. Monsma. *Cities: Missions' New Frontier*. 2nd edn. Grand Rapids, MI: Baker, 2000.

Gregory, Steven. *Black Corona: Race and the Politics of Place in an Urban Community*. Princeton, NJ: Princeton University Press, 1998.

Grenz, Stanley James. *Theology for the Community of God*. Grand Rapids, MI: Eerdmans, 2000.

Gruebner, Oliver, Michael A Rapp, Mazda Adli, Ulrike Kluge, Sandro Galea, and Andreas Heinz. "Cities and Mental Health," *Deutsches Arzteblatt International* 114(8), (2017): 121–27.

Gulick, John. *The Humanity of Cities: An Introduction to Urban Societies*. Granby, MA: Bergin & Garvey, 1989.

———. "Urban Anthropology," In J.J. Honigman, Ed. *Handbook of Social and Cultural Anthropology*. Chicago, IL: Rand-McNally College, 1973: 979–1029.

Gunnarsson, Serine. "Doing Belonging: Young Women of Middle Eastern Backgrounds in Sweden," In Paul Spickard, Ed. *Multiple Identities: Migrants, Ethnicity, and Membership*. Bloomington, IN: Indiana University Press, 2013: 88–113.

Habermas, Jürgen. *The Structural Transformation of the Public Sphere: An Inquiry into a Category of Bourgeois Society*. Cambridge, MA: The MIT Press, 1991.

Halbwachs, Maurice, Francis J. Ditter, and Vida Yazdi Ditter. *The Collective Memory*. 1st edn. New York: Harper & Row, 1980.

Hamman, Robin. "Introduction to Virtual Communities," *Cybersociology: Magazine for Social-Scientific Researches of Cyberspace*, 20th November 1997, Issue 2. [Available at: http://www.cybersociology.com/files/2_1_hamman.html], [Last accessed: 24th December 2023].

Han, Wansang and Gyunja Han. *People and Society*. Seoul: Korean Broad-communication, College Depart Press, 2011.

Han, Wansang, and Gyunja Han. *Human and Society*. Seoul: Korea National Open University Press, 2011.

Hancock, Mary, and Smriti Srinivas. "Spaces of Modernity: Religion and the Urban in Asia and Africa," *International Journal of Urban and Regional Research* 32 (2008): 617–30.

Hannerz, Ulf. *Exploring the City: Inquiries toward an Urban Anthropology*. New York: Columbia University Press, 1980.

———. *Soulside: Inquiries into Ghetto Culture and Community*. New York: Columbia University Press, 1969.

Hansen, Drew D. *The Dream: Martin Luther King, Jr., and the Speech That Inspired a Nation*. 1st edn. New York: Ecco, 2003.

Harvey, David. *The Urban Experience*. Baltimore, MD: Johns Hopkins University Press, 1989.

Havens, Betty, Madelyn Hall, Gina Sylvestre, and Tyler Jivan. "Social Isolation and Loneliness: Differences between Older Rural and Urban Manitobans," *Canadian Journal on Aging* 23(2), (Summer 2004): 129–40.

Hays, K. Michael. *Architecture Theory Since 1968*. Cambridge, MA: The MIT Press, 2015.

Hechter, Michael, and Karl-Dieter Opp. *Social Norms*. New York: Russell Sage Foundation, 2001.

Helliwell, John F., Hugh Shiplett, Christopher P. Barrington-Leigh, and National Bureau of Economic Research. *How Happy Are Your Neighbours? Variation in Life Satisfaction among 1200 Canadian Neighbourhoods and Communities*. NBER Working Paper Series; No. 24592. Cambridge, MA: National Bureau of Economic Research, 2018.

Hiebert, Paul G. "Cultural Differences and the Communication of the Gospel," In Ralph D. Winter and Steven C. Hawthorne, Eds. *Perspectives on the World Christian Movement: A Reader*. Pasadena, CA: William Carey Library, 1999: 373–83.

———. *Anthropological Insights for Missionaries*. Grand Rapids, MI: Baker, 1985.

Hiebert, Paul G., and Eloise Hiebert Meneses. *Incarnational Ministry: Planting Churches in Band, Tribal, Peasant, and Urban Societies*. Grand Rapids, MI: Baker, 1995.

Hill Collins, Patricia. *Toward a New Vision: Race, Class and Gender as Categories of Analysis and Connection*. Memphis, TN: Research Clearinghouse and Curriculum Integration Project, Center for Research on Women, 1989.

Hitching, Bob. *McDonalds, Minarets and Modernity: The Anatomy of the Emerging Secular Muslim World*. Sevenoaks, Kent: Spear, 1996.

Hollander, Jocelyn A. "Vulnerability and Dangerousness: The Construction of Gender through Conversation about Violence", *Gender and Society* 15(1), (2001): 83–109.

Hollingsworth, Roger, and Robert Boyer. *Contemporary Capitalism: The Embeddedness of Institutions*. Cambridge: Cambridge University Press, 1997.

Horowitz, Donald L. "Ethnic Identity," In Nathan Glazer and Daniel Moynihan, Eds. *Ethnicity*. Cambridge, MA: Harvard University Press, 1975: 111–40.

House, James S., and Sharon Wolf. "Effects of Urban Residence on Interpersonal Trust and Helping Behavior," *Journal of Personality and Social Psychology* 36(9), (1978): 1029–43.

Ingold, Tim. "Toward an Ecology of Materials," *Annual Review of Anthropology* 41 (2012): 427–42. [Available at: https://www.annualreviews.org/doi/abs/10.1146/annurev-anthro-081309-145920], [Last accessed: 6th December 2023].

Iorizzo, Luciano J., and Salvatore Mondello. *The Italian Americans*. Revised. Boston, MA: Twayne, 1980.

Jacobsen, Eric O. *Sidewalks in the Kingdom: New Urbanism and the Christian Faith*. The Christian Practice of Everyday Life. Grand Rapids, MI: Brazos, 2003.

Jacobson, David. *Itinerant Townsmen*. Menlo Park, CA: Cummings, 1973.

Jacqueline, Mithum. "Cooperation and Solidarity as Survival Necessities in a Black Urban Community," *Urban Anthropology* 2 (1973): 25–34.

Jaffe, Rivke, and Anouk de Koning. *Introducing Urban Anthropology*. London: Routledge, 2015.

Kaldor, Peter. *Who Goes Where? Who Doesn't Care?* Homebush West, N.S.W.: Lancer, 1987.

Kang, Myungsoo. *Dijitel Sidae Community Hualyong Junliak. (Strategy for Community Building in the Digital Age)*. Kyung Gee, Korea: Korea Academic Information, 2006.

Kim, Enoch J. "A New Entrance Gate in Urban Minorities: Chinese Muslim Minority, the Hui People Case," *Missiology: An International Review* 39(3), (2011): 353–71.

———. "Receptor-Oriented Communication for Hui Muslims in China: With Special Reference to Church Planting," Pasadena, CA: Fuller Theological Seminary, 2009.

Kim, Enoch Jinsik. *Mission Strategy in the City: Cultivation of Inter-Ethnic Common Grounds*. Eugene, OR: Pickwick, 2017.

———. *Receptor-Oriented Communication for Hui Muslims in China: With Special Reference to Church Planting*. Vol. 34. American Society of Missiology Monograph Series. Eugene, OR: Pickwick, 2018.

———. "'Us' or 'Me'? Modernization and Social Networks among China's Urban Hui," In David Greenlee, Ed. *Longing for Community: Church, Ummah, or Somewhere In Between?* Pasadena, CA: William Carey Library, 2013: 93–103.

Knight, John, and Ramani Gunatilaka. "Rural-Urban Migration and Happiness in China," In Richard Lavard, John F. Helliwell, and Jeffrey Sachs, Eds. *World Happiness Report 2018*. New York: Sustainable Development Solutions Network, 2018: Chapter 4.

Koyama, T. "Rural-Urban Comparisons of Kinship Relations in Japan," In R. Hill and R. Konig, Eds. *Families in East and West*. Paris: Mouton, 1970: 318–37.

Kraft, Charles H. *Anthropology for Christian Witness*. Maryknoll, NY: Orbis, 1996.

———. *Christianity in Culture: A Study in Dynamic Biblical Theologizing in Cross-Cultural Perspective*. Maryknoll, NY: Orbis, 1979.

———. *Communication Theory for Christian Witness*. Maryknoll, NY: Orbis, 1997.

Kricheldorf, Hans Rytger. *Getting It Right in Science and Medicine: Can Science Progress through Errors? Fallacies and Facts*. Cham, Switzerland: Springer, 2016.

Kuyper, Abraham. "Sphere Sovereignty," In James D. Bratt, Ed. *Abraham Kuyper: A Centennial Reader*. Grand Rapids, MI: Eerdmans, 1998.

Bunnell, Lafayette H. *Discovery of the Yosemite, and the Indian War of 1851*. New York; Chicago: F.H. Revell, 1892.

Lapinski, M.K., and R.N. Rimal. "An Explication of Social Norms," *Communication Theory* 15(2), (2005): 127–47.

Latane, B., and J.M. Darley. "Bystander 'apathy'," *American Scientist* 58 (1969): 244–68.

Lefebvre, Henri. *The Production of Space*. Translated by Donald Nicholson-Smith. Cambridge, MA: Balil Blackwell, 1991.

LeMasters, E.E. *Blue Collar Aristocrats: Life-Styles at a Working-Class at a Tavern*. Madison, WI: University of Wisconsin Press, 1976.

Leong, David P., and Soong-Chan Rah. *Race and Place: How Urban Geography Shapes the Journey to Reconciliation*. Downers Grove, IL: InterVarsity, 2017.

Levitt, P., and Schiller Gulick. "Transnational Perspectives on Migration: Conceptualizing Simultaneity," *International Migration Review* 38(3), (2004): 1002–39.

Lindberg, Leon. "Economic Governance and the Analysis of Structural Change in the American Economy," In John L. Campbell, J.R. Hollingsworth, and L.N. Lindberg, Eds. *Governance of American Economy: Structural Analysis in the Social Sciences*. Cambridge: Cambridge University Press, 1991: 3–34.

Lingenfelter, Sherwood. *Transforming Culture: A Challenge for Christian Mission*. Grand Rapids, MI: Baker, 1998.

Litwak, Eugene. "Occupational Mobility and Extended Family Cohesion," *American Sociological Review* 25 (1960): 9–21.

Litwak, Eugene, and Ivan Szelenyi. "Primary Group Structures and Their Functions: Kin, Neighbors and Friends," *American Sociological Review* 34 (1969): 465–81.

Lod, S.M. *Theorizing the City: The New Urban Anthropology Reader*. New Brunswick, NJ: Rutgers University Press, 1999.

Low, Setha M. *On the Plaza: The Politics of Public Space and Culture*. 1st edn. Austin, TX: University of Texas Press, 2000.

———. "Spatiality: The Rebirth of Urban Anthropology through Studies of Urban Space," In Donald Macon Nonini, Ed. *A Companion to Urban Anthropology*. Chichester, West Sussex: Wiley-Blackwell, 2014: 15–27.

Lynch, Owen. *The Politics of Untouchability*. New York: Columbia University Press, 1969.

Mahler, Sarah J. and Patricia R. Pessar. "Gender Matters: Ethnographers Bring Gender from the Periphery toward the Core of Migration Studies," *IMRE International Migration Review* 40(1), (2006): 27–63.

Mangalam, J.J. and Harry K. Schwarzweller. "Some Theoretical Guidelines toward a Sociology of Migration," *International Migration Review* 4(2), (1970): 5–21.

Mangin, William. "Squatter Settlements," *Scientific American* 217(4), (1967): 21–29.

Mangin, William. "Sociological, Cultural, and Political Characteristics of Some Urban Migrants in Peru," In Aidan Southall, Ed. *Urban Anthropology: Cross-Cultural Studies of Urbanization*. Oxford: Oxford University Press, 1973: 315–50.

Marcus, George E. "Ethnography in/of the World System: The Emergence of Multi-Sited Ethnography," *Annual Review of Anthropology* 24 (1995): 95.

Massey, Douglas S. and Nancy A. Denton. *American Apartheid: Segregation and the Making of the Underclass*. Cambridge, MA: Harvard University Press, 1993.

McDonogh, Gary W. "Flow," In Donald Macon Nonini, Ed. *A Companion to Urban Anthropology*. Chichester, West Sussex: Wiley-Blackwell, 2014: 28–45.

McKenzie, Roderick Duncan. *The Metropolitan Community*. New York; London: McGraw-Hill, 1933.

McLuhan, Herbert Marshall. *Understanding Media: The Extensions of Man*. London: The MIT Press, 1964.

Merton, R.K. "Social Structure and Anomie." In *Social Theory and Social Structure*. New York: Free Press, 1980: 185–214.

Michaelson, William M. *Man and His Urban Environment: A Sociological Approach*. Reading, MA: Addison-Wesley, 1976.

Mitchell, Don. *The Right to the City: Social Justice and the Fight for Public Space*. New York: Guilford Press, 2003.

Mulíček, Ondřej, Robert Osman, and Daniel Seidenglanz. "Urban Rhythms: A Chronotopic Approach to Urban Timespace," *Time & Society* 24(3), (January 2014): 304–25.
Mumford, Lewis. *The City in History: Its Origins, Its Transformations, and Its Prospects*. New York: Harcourt, Brace & World, 1961.
Munger, Robert Boyd. *My Heart: Christ's Home*. Rev. ed. Downers Grove, IL: InterVarsity, 1986.
Munn, Nancy D. "Excluded Spaces: The Figure in the Australian Aboriginal Landscape," 22(3), (1996): 446–65.
Myers, Bryant L. *Engaging Globalization: The Poor, Christian Mission, and Our Hyperconnected World*. Mission in Global Community. Grand Rapids, MI: Baker Academic, 2017.
Nelson, Joan M. *Access to Power: Politics and the Urban Poor in Developing Nations*. Princeton, NJ: Princeton University Press, 2017.
Newberry, Jan. "Women's Ways of Walking: Gender and Urban Space in Java," In Judith N. DeSena, Ed. *Gender in an Urban World*. Research in Urban Sociology. Leeds: Emerald, 2008.
Newman, Peter. *Cities as Sustainable Ecosystems: Principles and Practices*. Washington DC: Island, 2008.
Nida, Eugene Albert. *Message and Mission: the Communication of the Christian Faith*. New York: Harper, 1960.
Niebuhr, H. Richard. *Radical Monotheism and Western Culture: With Supplementary Essays*. Library of Theological Ethics. Louisville, KY: Westminster/John Knox Press, 1993.
Noh Choonhee and Kim Iltae (노춘희, 김일태). *DosihakGaeron (도시학 개론)*. Revised. Seoul, Korea: Hyungsul, 2004.
Oishi, Nana. *Women in Motion: Globalization, State Policies, and Labor Migration in Asia*. Stanford, CA: Stanford University Press, 2005.
Oldenburg, Ray. *The Great Good Place: Cafés, Coffee Shops, Bookstores, Bars, Hair Salons, and Other Hangouts at the Heart of a Community*. Cambridge, MA: Da Capo, 1999.
Olson, D.H. "Circulplex Model of Marital and Family Systems: Assessing Family Functioning," In F. Walsh, Ed. *Normal Family Processes*. New York: Guilford, 1993: 104–37.
Orun, A.M. and Xiangming Chen. *The World of Cities: Places in Comparative and Historical Perspective*. Malden, MA: Wiley-Blackwell, 2003.
Palen, J. John. *The Urban World*. New York: McGraw-Hill, 1992.
Park, Robert Ezra and E.W. Burgess. *Introduction to the Science of Sociology, Including the Original Index to Basic Sociological Concepts*. Chicago, IL: University of Chicago Press, 1969.
Park, Sangpil. *NGO Hak(Korean)*. Seoul, Korea: Arke, 2011.
Parratt, John. *A Guide to Doing Theology*. Vol. 35. London: SPCK, 2000.
Pellow, Deborah. *Setting Boundaries: The Anthropology of Spatial and Social Organization*. Westport, CT: Bergin & Garvey, 1996.

Pellow, Deborah, and Denise Lawrence-Zuniga. "Built Structures and Planning," In Donald Macon Nonini, Ed. *A Companion to Urban Anthropology*. Chichester, West Sussex: Wiley-Blackwell, 2014: 85–102.

Pescosolido, Bernice A., and Beth A. Rubin. "The Web of Group Affiliations Revisited: Social Life, Postmodernism, and Sociology," *American Sociological Review* 65 (February 2000): 52–76.

Peters, Ronald Edward. *Urban Ministry: An Introduction*. Nashville, TN: Abingdon Press, 2007.

Pierre, J. "Models of Urban Governance: The Institutional Dimension of Urban Politics," *Urban Affairs Review* 34(3), (1999): 372–96.

Piper, Nicola and Mina Roces. *Wife or Worker? Asian Women and Migration*. Lanham, MD: Rowman & Littlefield, 2003.

Pollock, Griselda. *Vision and Difference: Femininity, Feminism and Histories of Art*. London: Routledge, 1988.

Rastas, Anna. "Ethnic Identities and Transnational Subjectivities," In Paul Spickard, Ed. *Multiple Identities: Migrants, Ethnicity, and Membership.* Bloomington, IN: Indiana University Press, 2013: 41–60.

Read, Cressida Jervis. "Urban Pollution: Cultural Meanings, Social Practices - Edited by Eveline Dürr & Rivke Jaffe," *Journal of the Royal Anthropological Institute* 18(2), (2012): 508-509.

Sapp, Rebecca. "Family Conflict and Family Cohesion: Their Relationship to Youths' Problem Behaviors," PhD diss., University of Tennessee. Knoxville, TN: University of Tennessee, 2003.

Reginald, Bibby. *Fragmented Gods*. Toronto: Irwin, 1987.

Robson, William Alexander. *Great Cities of the World: Their Government, Politics and Planning*. London: Allen and Unwin, 1954.

Rockefeller, Stuart Alexander. *Starting from Quirpini: The Travels and Places of a Bolivian People*. Bloomington, IN: Indiana University Press, 2010.

Rogers, Everett M. *Diffusion of Innovations*. 5th ed. New York: Free Press, 2003.

Rufenacht, Christina. "2000 Technology Strengthens Family Bonds," *Women in Business* 52(1), (2000): 46.

Safa, Helen. "The Social Isolation of the Urban Poor: Life in a Puerto Rican Shanty Town," In Isaac Deutscher and E. Thompson, Eds. *Among the People: Encounters with the Poor*. New York: Basic Books, 1968.

Schultz, Emily A. and Robert H. Lavenda. *Cultural Anthropology: A Perspective on the Human Condition*. St Paul, MN: West, 1987.

Schwarzweller, Harry K., James S. Brown, and J.J. Mangalam. *Mountain Families in Transition: A Case Study of Appalachian Migration*. University Park: Pennsylvania State University Press, 1971.

Sennett, Richard. *Classic Essays on the Culture of Cities*. New York: Appleton-Century-Crofts, 1969.

———. "The Public Realm," In Gary Bridge and Sophie Watson, Eds. *The Blackwell City Reader*, 2nd edn. Chichester, West Sussex: Wiley-Blackwell, 2010: 267–72.

———. *The Uses of Disorder: Personal Identity & City Life*. New York: W.W. Norton, 1992.

Shaw, Daniel R. *Transculturation: The Cultural Factor in Translation and Other Communication Tasks*. Pasadena, CA: William Carey Library, 1988.

Shulman, N. *Urban Social Networks*. Toronto: University of Toronto, 1972.

Silver, Laura. "Smartphone Ownership Is Growing Rapidly Around the World, But Not Always Equally," Pew Research Center, 5th February 2019, [Available at: https://www.pewresearch.org/global/2019/02/05/smartphone-ownership-is-growing-rapidly-around-the-world-but-not-always-equally/], [Last accessed: 5th August 2023].

Simmel, Georg. "The Metropolis and Mental Life," In Richard Sennett, Ed. *Classic Essays of the Culture of Cities*. New York: Appleton-Century-Crofts, 1965: 47–60.

Smart, Alan, and Filippo M. Zerilli. "Extralegality," In Donald Macon Nonini, Ed. *A Companion to Urban Anthropology*. Chichester, West Sussex: Wiley-Blackwell, 2014: 222–38.

Smith, Donald K. *Creating Understanding: A Handbook for Christian Communication Across Cultural Landscapes*. Grand Rapids, MI: Zondervan, 1992.

Spain, Daphne. "Gendered Spaces and the Public Realm," In Judith N. DeSena, Ed. *Gender in an Urban World*. Research in Urban Sociology. Leeds: Emerald, 2008: 9-28.

Spradley, James P. and David W. McCurdy. *Anthropology, the Cultural Perspective*. New York: Wiley, 1980.

Stokols, Daniel. "The Experience of Crowding in Primary and Secondary Environments," *Environment and Behavior* 8(1), (1976): 49–86.

Streeck, Wolfgang and Philippe Schmitter. "Market, State, Community, and Association? The Prospective Contribution of Interest Governance to Social Order," In Wolfgang Streeck and Philippe Schmitter, Eds. *Private Interest Government: Beyond Market and the State*. London: SAGE, 1985.

Suh, Yijong. *Internet Community Wa Hangook Sahue (Internet Community and Korean Society)*. Seoul, Korea: Hanwool, 2002.

Sundstorm, E. "Crowding as a Sequential Process: Review of Research on the Effects of Population Density on Humans," In A. Baum and Y.M. Epstein, Eds. *Human Responses to Crowding*. Hillsdale, NJ: Lawrence Erlbaum, 1978: 32–116.

Suttles, Gerald D. *The Man-Made City: The Land-Use Confidence Game in Chicago*. Chicago, IL: University of Chicago Press, 1990.

Swyngedouw, Erik. *Social Power and the Urbanization of Water: Flows of Power*. Oxford Geographical and Environmental Studies. Oxford: Oxford University Press, 2004.

Thomas, William Isaac and Morris Janowitz. *On Social Organization and Social Personality: Selected Papers*. Chicago, IL: University of Chicago Press, 1966.

Tillich, Paul. *On Art and Architecture*. New York: Crossroad, 1987.

Timms, Duncan. *The Urban Mosaic: Towards a Theory of Residential Differentiation*. Cambridge: Cambridge University Press, 1971.

Todaro, Michael P. "Urbanization in Developing Nations: Trends, Prospects, and Policies," In Pradip K. Ghosh, Ed. *Urban Development in the Third World*. Westport, CT: Greenwood, 1979: 7–26.

Torsello, D. *The New Environmentalism? Civil Society and Corruption in the Enlarged EU.* Farnham: Ashgate, 2012.

Travis, J. Grosser, Virginie Lopez-Kidwell and Giuseppe Labianca. "A Social Network Analysis of Positive and Negative Gossip in Organizational Life," *Group & Organization Management* 35(2), (2010): 177–212.

Truong, Thanh-Dam, and Des Gasper. "Trans-Local Livelihoods and Connections," *Gender, Technology and Development* 12(3), (2008): 285–302.

United Nations. "The Millennium Development Goals Report 2015." New York: United Nations, 2015.

"Urban and Rural Victimization." *2017 National Crime Victims' Rights Week Resource Guide: Crime and Victimization Fact Sheets*. Washington, DC: Office for Victims of Crime, the Office of Justice Programs, U.S. Department of Justice, 2017. [Available at: https://www.ncjrs.gov/ovc_archives/ncvrw/2017/index.html], [Last accessed: 5th August 2023].

U.S. Department of Commerce. "America's Families and Living Arrangements: 2010." *United States Census Bureau* (blog), 2010. https://www.census.gov/data/tables/2010/demo/families/cps-2010.html.

Useem, J. and R. Useem. "The Interfaces of a Binational Third Culture: A Study of the American Community in India," *Journal of Social Issues* 23(1), (1967): 130–43.

Van Engen, Charles. *God's Missionary People: Rethinking the Purpose of the Local Church*. 6th ed. Grand Rapids, MI: Baker Books, 2001.

Ven, Cornelis van de. *Space in Architecture: The Evolution of a New Idea in the Theory and History of the Modern Movements*. Assen: Van Gorcum, 1980.

Voss, Barbara L. "Domesticating Imperialism: Sexual Politics and the Archaeology of Empire," *American Anthropologist* 110(2), (2008): 191–203.

Wagner, C. Peter and Donald A. McGavran. *Understanding Church Growth.* 3rd edn. Grand Rapids, MI: Eerdmans, 1991.

Wallace, Anthony F.C. *Revitalizations and Mazeway: Essays on Culture Change*. Edited by Robert S. Grumet. Lincoln, NE: University of Nebraska Press, 2003.

Wallach, Joel and Gale Metcalf. *Working with Americans: A Practical Guide to Business Success for Asian Managers*. New York: McGraw-Hill, 1995.

Wallman, S. "Identity Options," In C. Fried, Ed. *Minorities: Community and Identity.* Berlin; Heidelberg; New York; Tokyo: Springer-Verlag: Dahlem Konferenzen, 1983: 69–78.

Ward, Janet. "Mayors Want Homelessness Back on National Agenda," *The American City & County* 115(2), (2000).

Warner, W. Lloyd and Paul S. Lunt. *The Status System of a Modern Community*. New Haven; London: Yale University Press; H. Milford; Oxford University Press, 1942.

Watson, James. "Restaurants and Remittances; Chinese Emigrant Workers in London," In G. Foster and R. Kemper, Eds. *Anthropologist in Cities.* Boston, MA: Little Brown, 1974: 201–11.

Wellman, Barry. *Networks in the Global Village: Life in Contemporary Communities*. Boulder, CO: Westview, 1999.

Whyte, Martin King. *China's Revolutions and Intergenerational Relations*. Michigan Monographs in Chinese Studies. Ann Arbor, MI: Center for Chinese Studies University of Michigan, 2003.

Wilson, Ara. "Sexuality," In Donald Macon Nonini, Ed. *A Companion to Urban Anthropology.* Chichester, West Sussex: Wiley-Blackwell, 2014: 193–209.

———. *The Intimate Economies of Bangkok: Tomboys, Tycoons, and Avon Ladies in the Global City*. Berkeley, CA: University of California Press, 2004.

Winders, J. "Seeing Immigrants: Institutional Visibility and Immigrant Incorporation in New Immigrant Destinations," *Annals of the American Academy of Political and Social Science* 641(1), (2012): 58–78.

Wirth, Louis. *The Ghetto*. Chicago, IL: The University of Chicago Press, 1928.

———. "Urbanism as a Way of Life," *American Journal of Sociology* 44(1), (1938): 1–24.

Wolterstorff, Nicholas P. *Art in Action: Towards a Christian Aesthetic*. Grand Rapids, MI: Paternoster, 1997.

Wylie, Laurence. *Village in the Vaucluse*. 2nd edn. Cambridge, MA: Harvard University Press, 1964.

Yang, Philip Q. *Ethnic Studies: Issues and Approaches*. Albany, NY: State University of New York Press, 2000.

Youmans, E.G. "The Rural Aged," *Annals* 429 (1977): 81–90.

Young, Iris Marion. *City Life and Difference*. Princeton, NJ: Princeton University Press, 1990.

Young, Michael Dunlop and Peter Willmott. *Family and Kinship in East London*. Reports of the Institute of Community Studies, 1. Glencoe, IL: Free Press, 1957.

Yu, Hyunjoon. *What the city live with? (Korean)*. Ch'op'an. Sŏul: Ŭlyu Munhwasa, 2019.

Zang, Xiaowei, Jonathan N. Lipman and Matthew McKeever. "Ethnicity and Urban Life in China: A Comparative Study of Hui Muslims and Han Chinese," *The China Journal* 60 (2008): 205.

Zubrinsky, Camille Charles. "The Dynamics of Racial Residential Segregation," *Annual Review of Sociology* 29 (2003): 167–207.

Index